A History of the
American Sociological Association
1981–2004

AMERICAN SOCIOLOGICAL ASSOCIATION
Washington, DC

Copyright © 2005 by the American Sociological Association.

All rights reserved. No part of this book may be reproduced or utilized in any form or by any means, electronic or mechanical, including photocopying, recording, or by any information storage or retrieval system, without permission in writing from the publisher.

Cite as:

Rosich, Katherine J. 2005. *A History of the American Sociological Association, 1981–2004*. Washington, DC: American Sociological Association.

For information:

American Sociological Association
1307 New York Avenue NW
Suite 700
Washington, DC 20005-4701
(202) 383-9005
E-mail: publications@asanet.org
Website: www.asanet.org

Library of Congress Catalog Card Number: 2005931388

ISBN 0-912764-43-0

Officers of the Association (2005)

President
Troy Duster

Vice-President
Caroline Hodges Persell

Secretary
Franklin D. Wilson

Executive Officer
Sally T. Hillsman

Contents

Preface vii

Acknowledgments x

Abbreviations xii

Introduction: Scope and Nature of Presentation xv

Chapter 1: The 1980s: Critical Challenges and New Resolve 1

1. Introduction 1
   Background and Context 1
   ASA Priorities in the 1980s 2

2. ASA Membership Trends and Fiscal Status 3
   Membership 3
   Budgets and Fiscal Policies 5

3. The Executive Office (EO) 6
   Transitions and Reorganization 6
   Application of New Information Technologies (IT) 8

4. Governance: Constitution/Bylaws Changes and Council Policymaking 9
   The ASA Constitution and Bylaws 9
   Code of Ethics 10
   Amicus Briefs 11
   Awards Policy 12
   Member Resolutions 12

5. Governance: Structural Changes 13
   ASA Sections 13
   Committee on Freedom of Research and Teaching (COFRAT) 14
   The American Sociological Foundation (ASF) 14

6. ASA Programs and Activities 15
   Research and Publications 15
   Publications 19
   Teaching Services Program (TSP) 22
   Professional Development Program (PDP) 24
   Certification Program 26
   Public Information Program 26
   Minority Fellowship Programs 27

7. Other ASA Programs and Activities 29
   ASA Honors Program 29
   Fund for the Advancement of the Discipline (FAD) 29
   International Issues and Human Rights 30

8. Annual Meeting 33

Chapter 2: The 1991–2002 Period: Transformations and Innovations 35

1. Introduction 35
   Background and Context 35
   Revisiting Strategic Planning in 1998 37

2. Membership and Fiscal Status 37
   ASA Membership in the 1990s 37
   Profile of ASA Members and Minority Participation in ASA 38
   Budgets and Finances.. 40
   Development Campaign 41

3. Executive Office... 41
   Executive Office Staffing.. 41
   Information Technology (IT) 43
   Sale of the 1722 N Street NW Building 46

4. Governance: Bylaws, Ethical Standards, and Policy Changes 47
   ASA Bylaws Changes 47
   ASA Code of Ethics 48
   Amicus Briefs... 48
   ASA Policy Statements 49

5. Governance Structural Changes 51
   Awards Policy.. 51
   Restructuring of ASA Committees... 52
   ASA Sections during the 1990s... 55
   Certification... 56
   Committee on Freedom of Research and Teaching (COFRAT)...................... 57
   Dues Restructuring... 58
   American Sociological Foundation (ASF) 59

6. Publications Program of the ASA 59
   Publication Guidelines.. 59
   Scope of Publication 60
   Other Publications.. 61
   ASA's Association with Boyd Printing Company 62
   Electronic Publishing and Access 62
   Controversy over *ASR*... 63

7. Core Programs of the ASA 65
   Academic and Professional Affairs Program (APAP) 65
   Minority Affairs Program (MAP) 68
   The Sydney S. Spivack Program in Applied Social Research and Social Policy 70
   The Research Program on the Discipline and Profession............................ 72
   Public Affairs Program 73
   Public Information Program 77

8. Other Programs and Activities 78
   Fund for the Advancement of the Discipline (FAD).................................. 78
   International Activities 78
   Human Rights 80
   The ASA Archiving Project 81

9. Annual Meeting... 82

Chapter 3: Moving Forward at Century's End: ASA at 2002–2004 85

1. Background and Context 85
   Context and Issues 85
   Leadership Changes 86

2. Highlights from Council Actions: 2002–4 87
   Data on Race and Ethnicity 87
   Defense of Scientific Integrity 88
   Amicus Briefs 89
   Member Resolutions 90
   Other Council Actions/Policy Issues 91
   Governance: ASA Council Bylaws Changes 93

3. Governance: Structural Changes 93
   Sections 93
   Task Forces and Committees 94
   Status Committees 94

4. Executive Office Initiatives 94
   ASA Departmental Activity: 2002–4 95
   Highlights from Programs of the ASA: 2002–4 97
   Other Programs and Activities 99

5. Centennial Planning 100
   Centennial Events and Projects 100
   The Focus of the 100th Annual Meeting 101

Epilogue: The American Sociological Association at its Centenary 103
   Mission 103
   Key Components of Success 103

Appendix 105

Appendix 1: Chronology of ASA Events 106

Appendix 2: ASA Presidents by Year of Term 118

Appendix 3: Vice Presidents of the ASA 120

Appendix 4: Secretaries of the ASA 122

Appendix 5: Executive Officers of the ASA 123

Appendix 6: Editors of ASA Publications 124

Appendix 7: Administrative Officers of the Association 128

Appendix 8: Executive Associates, Specialists,
            and Deputy Executive Officers of the Association 129

Appendix 9: Directors of the ASA Minority Fellowship Program 130

Appendix 10: Governing Bodies of the ASA 131

Appendix 11: Recipients of ASA Awards 133

Appendix 12: Membership by Year 140

Appendix 13: Characteristics of Membership and
    Membership Participation in ASA: 1982, 1992, 2001 141
Appendix 14: ASA Section Membership: Selected Years 1975–2004. 145
Appendix 15: Changes in the ASA Constitution and Bylaws 146
Appendix 16: ASA Committees and Task Forces 150
Appendix 17: ASA Section Formation History. 154
Appendix 18: Major Publications of the ASA 156
Appendix 19: The Presidential Series 159
Appendix 20: Teaching Services Program (TSP). 160
Appendix 21: Professional Development Program (PDP) 166
Appendix 22: Academic and Professional Affairs Program (APAP) 167
Appendix 23: Minority Fellowship Program Awards 173
Appendix 24: Other ASA Publications 174
Appendix 25: The Spivack Program: Policy Briefings, Issue Series, and Special Initiatives 176
Appendix 26: The Spivack Program: Congressional Fellows 179
Appendix 27: The Spivack Program: AAAS/ASA Mass Media Science Fellowship 180
Appendix 28: ASA's Organizational Affiliations and Collaborations: January 1, 2005 181
Appendix 29: ASA Departments and Programs: January 1, 2005. 184
Appendix 30: ASA Executive Office Staff: January 1, 2005 186

References 190

Name Index 191

Subject Index 195

Preface

This year 2005 marks the centenary of the founding of the American Sociological Society, the professional society for sociologists that became known as the American Sociological Association in 1959. Established in 1905 by a small group led by Lester Ward, William Graham Sumner, Franklin Giddings, and Albion Small at meetings of the American Economic Association, the Society held its first meeting the following year in Providence, Rhode Island. The membership in 1906 stood at 115. For the first several decades, the activities of the Society were centered on publishing a journal, holding an annual meeting, and performing various secretariat functions such as record keeping, sending out communications and so forth. In 1949, the first Executive Officer was appointed on a part-time basis, and in 1963 the Association established its permanent headquarters in Washington, DC. By the end of the 20th century, the American Sociological Association evolved into a complex organization with a roster of journals, other publications, meetings, workshops, and programs serving over 13,000 members.

There has been a keen interest expressed by members, leaders, and professional staff of the ASA in preserving the history of the Association. In 1983, ASA donated its records to the Library of Congress, where some 57,900 ASA administrative records and documents from 1931 to 1986 became part of the Library's Manuscript Division Materials. When the ASA was informed by the Library of Congress in 1992 that it would no longer accept additional materials in the ASA archives, the ASA Council approved exploration of other options for archiving its records. In September 1997, ASA signed a contract with Pennsylvania State University for this purpose. Since then, the ASA has been actively involved with Penn State in creating a complete ASA archive at its library in University Park, Pennsylvania, including all materials from the Library of Congress transferred in 2005.

Over the years, sociologists have also examined the history and development of the American Sociological Association from a range of perspectives in articles and books published on this topic. In 1980, Lawrence J. Rhoades, then Executive Associate for Program and Teaching in the ASA Executive Office, wrote a series of articles on the history of ASA from its founding in 1905 through 1980 to mark ASA's 75th anniversary. Originally published in the ASA newsletter *Footnotes* during 1980, these articles were subsequently edited and published by ASA in 1981 as *A History of the American Sociological Association, 1905–1980*, with Rhoades as author.

The Rhoades volume has been used widely and serves as a valuable resource on historical events during the first 75 years of ASA. In 2003, ASA Council approved a project to update the 1981 publication by documenting the major issues and events in the Association since 1980 as part of a collection of historical materials to mark the ASA Centennial. This new publication, *A History of the American Sociological Association, 1981–2004*, authored by Katherine J. Rosich, picks up in 1981 where Rhoades left off, and reports on ASA's history over the past quarter century.

Because the *ASA History, 1981-2004* is an update of the 1981 volume, it seeks generally to follow the first volume's structure and orientation. Thus, the basic outline of the current volume captures highlights following a chronological rather than functional or structural analysis. It is divided into three chapters which report on the ASA organizational history covering the periods 1981–91 (Chapter 1), 1991–2002 (Chapter 2), and 2002–4 (Chapter 3). An Epilogue provides a closing commentary, and detailed Appendices contain extensive historical documentation and information about the Association over its 100 years. The general orientation and style of this new volume—like the earlier one—is to present an analysis on each topic with "broad brush strokes" to feature the important events in each area, particularly focusing on institutional development and change. It does not, therefore, present an in-depth analysis of functional areas during this time.

We also emphasize that this volume is not a history of the discipline of sociology in the United States since 1980. That is the task of others, including Craig J. Calhoun who is editing an independent volume on the history of sociology in the United States supported by the ASA Council. Written by sociologists, that book will focus on the development of the discipline of sociology in the United States, and on institutional patterns shaping the field. An outstanding group of sociologists, with diverse backgrounds, subdisciplines, and intellectual orientations has been invited to contribute articles to that volume.

Finally, on the occasion of this historic event, it is worthwhile to reflect briefly on the question: What is the "state of the American Sociological Association" in 2005 as it marks its 100th anniversary?

In 1981, at the beginning of the period covered by this volume, retiring Executive Officer Russell R. Dynes summed up the complexity of the Association's goals, and described some of the issues that had been at the center of debates within the ASA for decades. He described the challenges of implementing a publishing program that meets the highest standards of excellence, providing an annual meeting that is an opportunity for stimulating exchange of ideas and research findings, and creating programs that serve the changing needs of the membership. Not all of these goals, Dynes noted, are complementary. Tensions arise from differences in priorities focusing on research over teaching, in perspectives that advocate the goals of the discipline over those of the profession, and in advancing the traditionally academic base of the membership with the increasingly non-academic impulses in the profession. Dynes went on to say that the Association values diversity, but hopes for unity and integration; it seeks acceptance in the wider scientific community, while emphasizing the uniqueness of sociology. The Association promotes inclusiveness in the Association (particularly increasing the participation of women and minorities), and strives to foster democracy while electing excellence (*Footnotes*, August 1982:9).

These challenges echo those discussed earlier by Talcott Parsons in his 1966 Editor's Column in what was then the Association's publication *The American Sociologist*. Parsons described new functions undertaken by the Association with regard to the role of sociology in secondary and graduate education, the organizational problems posed by the multiplication of sections, and the issues arising with new journals and publications. He also emphasized that ASA is a democratically elected body, and thus is challenged by "preserving and extending this democratic base of the Association and at the same time providing institutions which could focus effective responsibility, on behalf of the membership in their special position as members of a learned, primarily academic, group, for the formulation of coherent policies and *both* the support *and* the control of the Executive Office."

Many of these challenges still remain although with different shapes and new dimensions. Like the other social sciences, sociology must continuously redefine its role and relationships with wider publics. The challenge for "public sociologies," for example, is to engage an ever-wider audience including the media, policy makers, think tanks, social movement, and others, both at a national and international level. A new world of publishing is also emerging, posing important challenges and opportunities for the ASA as a major publisher of scholarly journals. The legal implications of electronic publishing, access to scholarly research on the Internet and other electronic formats, and how to reach audiences of teachers and learners as well as the general public and policy leaders are just a few of the exciting challenges for the ASA. Sociology, along with other social science associations, must also find creative, innovative, and persuasive ways to advocate for scientific funding and to develop research agendas that embrace and expand sociology's leadership within the scientific community.

As the American Sociological Association moves into the 21st century, there is a larger emphasis on the need for cooperation and collaboration across the social and behavioral sciences in order to respond to the increasingly complex problems of a global society. The war on terror, interethnic conflicts, wars, inequality, social disparities, forced migrations, and poverty are just a few of the critical challenges confronting an interdependent world. Fortunately, there is also growing recognition of the contributions that knowledge from the social and behavioral sciences can make to enhance understanding of effective responses to these challenges. The pages of this *History, 1981-2004* show continued growth and professionalization of the ASA, including the formation of well-established collaborations with other professional and scientific societies, the Consortium of Social Science Associations (COSSA), the National Humanities Alliance (NHA), the American Council of Learned Societies (ACLS), the American Association for the Advancement of Science (AAAS), and other organized efforts to address issues of importance to the social and behavioral sciences. In 2005, as it celebrates its 100th anniversary and looks toward the future, the American Sociological Association is well-situated to meet the challenges that need the profession and discipline of sociology.

Sally T. Hillsman
Katherine J. Rosich

Acknowledgments

A work such as this could not have been accomplished without the engagement and support of individuals who know the records, key events, and issues of the Association, especially over the past several decades. The Introduction, which includes a summary of the sources and methodology used to conduct the analysis, emphasizes the use of published ASA sources (Council minutes, articles in *Footnotes*, and so forth) as the primary records for this analysis. Yet the insights and diligent pursuit of facts and verification of data by past and present ASA members and staff helped to clarify inconsistencies and identify gaps in the data.

The reflections of the Executive Officers who served since 1981—Russell R. Dynes (1977–1982), William V. D'Antonio (1982–1991), and Felice J. Levine (1991–2002)—were invaluable to this publication. In addition to thoughtful reviews of an early draft of the manuscript, they were always available to comment on or corroborate information, raise questions, and clarify sequences of events and outcomes discussed in the text. They searched through their personal records and files and provided additional detail and precision where information in published records was limited. Although any interpretations in the text are those of the author, the three Executive Officers were essential partners in the effort to ensure complete documentary data. We greatly appreciate their contributions and the spirit in which they gave of their time and recollections to this effort.

The commitment and support of the current ASA Executive Office staff was also key to the success of this project. It especially benefited from the extraordinary circumstance of having three senior level staff members in the Executive Office whose tenure at ASA spans the entire period of this history. In 2005, Janet L. Astner marks her 30th year in the ASA Executive Office, Karen Gray Edwards celebrates her 25th year, and Carla B. Howery her 24th. In addition to their commitment and contributions to the ASA over the years, these staff members provide an invaluable institutional memory for ASA staff, officers and members—one that was essential in preparing the history of ASA in this period. The information they provided on documentary sources, issues, people, and events as well as their insights and recollections of the last quarter century added significantly to the writing of this history. We are grateful to them for their contributions that enriched this "story" of ASA at the end of the 20th Century.

It is important to note that these three staff members were involved in key areas of Executive Office and Association programmatic activities at a time of significant change and growth. In 2004, Janet Astner concluded the 25th ASA Annual Meeting for which she has been responsible, an unprecedented success in what is undoubtedly the singular most important event in the ASA annual calendar and, indeed, in the calendar of many sociologists in the U.S. For more than two decades, Karen Gray Edwards has been the mainstay of ASA's publishing program with a command of the scholarly publishing business that has enabled the ASA Committee on Publications, editorial offices and Council to meet the complex demands of ASA as a major publisher in the print and now in the newly emerging electronic world of scholarly publishing. Carla Howery has been the face of the ASA in both its outreach and its commitment to higher education for more than two decades, 13 of which she has served as Deputy Executive Officer. Since 1995, as Director of the Association's Academic and Professional Affairs Program (and prior to that the Teaching Services Program), her work at ASA has helped the profession face the challenges of the 21st century through testing new forms of pedagogy, new interdisciplinary partnerships in teaching and research, and new technologies for learning and communicating.

Other staff members at ASA also provided essential assistance to this effort. ASA Archivist Michael Murphy was a key source of information, records, and critical support throughout the entire project.

The breadth of his knowledge about both documentary sources and events and his skill in navigating ASA materials in storage, at the Library of Congress, or archived at Pennsylvania State University were very helpful. Michael and Dan Sackett jointly undertook the important task of reading and copy-editing the entire manuscript with dedication and extraordinary professional skill. This project also greatly benefited from the systematization and digitizing of ASA governance information which Michael has undertaken in his capacity as ASA Director of Governance and Sections.

Because the records used for this analysis are on site at the ASA headquarters, at its off-site storage location in Maryland, and in the archive at Pennsylvania State University, the author relied on staff cooperation for access to relevant documents. Roberta Spalter-Roth, Mercedes Rubio, Lee Herring, and Johanna Ebner not only made this process seamless, but also provided data and information for the appendices as well as valuable interpretation of some materials. Les Briggs reviewed the budgetary and financial data referenced in the text, and verified facts and figures by searching old financial and personnel records. Kevin Darrow Brown gave information on technical specifications for the information technology descriptions and also provided essential support on the computer systems. This was particularly important since all the documents extracted for the analysis were scanned and are now stored on the ASA computer network. Much of this document preparation took place in the ASA Executive Office where David Matthews has managed production services for more than 18 years, ensuring the smooth and efficient operation of ASA "backstage."

We also thank Theresa A. Bicanic, a digital production specialist for her creativity, care, and professionalism in producing the cover and manuscript for final publication. In addition, we want to express our appreciation to Jane Carey and her staff at Boyd Printing Company who, as always, provide the extra measures of support to produce ASA publications.

Finally, we want to acknowledge the initiative and leadership of Troy Duster, Michael Buroway and William T. Bielby, the three most recent Presidents of ASA, and the ASA Council for their support and encouragement of this work. At the suggestion of President Duster, Arne Kalleberg and Eduardo Bonilla-Silva read the manuscript and provided thoughtful scrutiny of the substance and style of the text. They helped to clarify information, and made suggestions that significantly added to material covered in the history. We are deeply indebted to them for the considerable energy they devoted to this effort.

Because some of the period under consideration is relatively recent, the research process itself highlighted the value of preserving the Association's historical records. In addition to a description of key events over the past several decades, this volume has resulted in a compilation of a great many facts and documents about the Association's recent history. We hope this publication will not only become a useful resource, but that it will also serve as a stimulus for other investigations and more in-depth organizational analysis of the ASA and its place in the profession.

Sally T. Hillsman
Katherine J. Rosich

Abbreviations

AAAS	American Association for the Advancement of Science
AAASHRAN	AAAS Human Rights Action Network
AAC&U	Association of American Colleges and Universities (formerly the AAC, the Association of American Colleges)
AAP	Association of American Publishers
ABS	Association of Black Sociologists
ACLS	American Council of Learned Societies
AKD	Alpha Kappa Delta
AM	ASA Annual Meeting
AP	Advanced Placement
APA	American Psychological Association
APAP	Academic and Professional Affairs Program
APSA	American Political Science Association
ASA	American Sociological Association
ASF	American Sociological Foundation
ASR	*American Sociological Review*
BSSR-CC	Behavioral and Social Science Coordinating Committee (NIH)
CAFLIS	Coalition of Associations for Foreign Language and International Studies
CAHT-BSSR	Coalition for the Advancement of Health through Behavioral and Social Science Research
CARI	Community Action Research Initiative
CASTL	Carnegie Academy for the Scholarship of Teaching and Learning
CCS	Certified Clinical Sociologist
CGS	Council of Graduate Schools
CNSF	Coalition for National Science Funding
COC	Committee on Committees
COFRAT	Committee on Freedom of Research and Teaching
CON	Committee on Nominations
COP	Committee on Publications
COPAFS	Council of Professional Associations for Federal Statistics
COPE	Committee on Professional Ethics
COS	Committee on Sections
COSSA	Consortium of Social Science Associations
CPST	Commission on Professions in Science and Technology
CRECNO	Classification by Race, Ethnicity, Color and National Origin (California Proposition 54)
CSGLBT	Committee on the Status of Gay, Lesbian, Bisexual, and Transgender Persons in Sociology
CSREMS	Committee on the Status of Racial and Ethnic Minorities in Sociology

CS	*Contemporary Sociology*
CSWS	Committee on the Status of Women in Sociology
CUPA-HR	College and University Professional Association for Human Resources
CUR	Council for Undergraduate Research
CUSS	Community and Urban Sociology Section
DBASSE	Division of Behavioral and Social Sciences and Education
DFA	Dimensional Fund Advisors
DHHS	Department of Health and Human Services
DOJ	Department of Justice
DRG	Departmental Resources Group
EB	*Employment Bulletin*
EO	Executive Office of ASA
EOB	Committee on the Executive Office and Budget
FAD	Fund for the Advancement of the Discipline
FIPSE	Fund for the Improvement of Postsecondary Education
FOIA	Freedom of Information Act
GSS	General Social Survey
ICPSR	Inter-university Consortium for Political and Social Research
IDA	Integrating Data Analysis Project
ISA	International Sociological Association
IIS	International Institute of Sociology
IT	Information Technology
IRBs	Institutional Review Boards
IREX	International Research & Exchanges Board
JHSB	*Journal of Health and Social Behavior*
JSTOR	The Scholarly Journal Archive
MAP	Minority Affairs Program
MFP	Minority Fellowship Program
MLA	Modern Language Association of America
MOST I	Minority Opportunity Summer Training
MOST	Minority Opportunities Through School Transformation
NAS	National Academy of Sciences
NCES	National Center for Education Statistics
NCSS	National Council on Social Studies
NCOVR	National Consortium on Violence Research
NEH	National Endowment for the Humanities
NHA	National Humanities Alliance
NIA	National Institute on Aging

NICHD	National Institute of Child Health and Human Development
NIE	National Institute of Education
NIH	National Institutes of Health
NIMH	National Institute of Mental Health
NHRPAC	National Human Research Protections Advisory Committee
NSF	National Science Foundation
NOAH	Name of specialized associations software and office automation system developed by JL Systems installed at ASA in 1993
NORC	National Opinion Research Center
OBSSR	Office of Behavioral and Social Science Research
OFAC	Office of Foreign Assets Control
OSTP	Office of Science Technology and Policy
PAA	Population Association of American
PFF	Preparing Future Faculty
PDP	Professional Development Program
POD	Problems of the Discipline
SBE	Social, Behavioral, and Economic Sciences
SES	Social and Economic Sciences
SM	*Sociological Methodology*
SOE	*Sociology of Education*
SPA	Sociological Practice Association
SPSSI	Society for the Psychological Study of Social Issues
SPQ	*Social Psychology Quarterly*
SPR	*Sociological Practice Review*
SSDAN	Social Science Data Analysis Network
SSRC	Social Science Research Council
ST	*Sociological Theory*
SWS	Sociologists for Women in Society
TAGGE	Task Group On Graduate Education
TAS	*The American Sociologist*
TRC	Teaching Resources Center
TRG	Teaching Resources Group
TS	*Teaching Sociology*
TSP	Teaching Services Program

Introduction:
Scope and Nature of Presentation

This volume captures highlights in the history of the American Sociological Association (ASA) from 1981 through 2004. The objective of this work is to describe and report on the major events in the life of ASA during the last two decades of the 20th century—leading up to a new century and millennium, and also to ASA's commemoration of its 100th anniversary in 2005. This introduction provides a brief overview of the structure and organization of this volume; describes the methodology used to compile, analyze, and conceptualize the topics for discussion; and explains the publication format in both its printed (pdf) and electronic (html) formats.

As noted in the preface, this volume is a companion volume to the 1981 ASA publication, *A History of the American Sociological Association, 1905–1980*, by Lawrence J. Rhoades. The 1981 Rhoades volume shaped the basic ideas for topics and the general approach used in this second volume. As in the 1981 publication, descriptive text is presented on key events within a specified time frame—for the decade of the 1980s, the 1990s (through the 2002 Council), and for key events in 2002 through 2004. Like the preceding volume, the descriptive analysis of each topic in this volume is reported using a style that features the important events, particularly focusing on institutional development and change. On occasion, evaluative comments by ASA leadership or others are included to lend perspective in the reporting.

There are several important differences between the two volumes. The subject matter and content of this history of ASA since 1980 were considerably expanded because source material for events of the past quarter century was generally more accessible than for earlier decades of ASA history. This also meant that a more rigorous and systematic review could be conducted for each topical area. Current technologies also permitted compilation of source material in electronic formats, which facilitated both analysis and the preparation of text (and also resulted in a digitized archive of basic sources, which can be used for other organizational or research purposes). Finally, the text is annotated with references.

Structure of this Volume and its Contents

Organization of Volume

The major events of the Association over the past quarter century are described in three chapters and detailed appendices (a list of common abbreviations is also included). The contents of the volume include:

- **History of the 1980s:** Covers events beginning with the 1981 Council and ending with the 1991 August Council; coincides with the tenure of Executive Officers Russell R. Dynes and William V. D'Antonio, and the year of transition with Felice J. Levine;

- **History of the 1990s:** Covers the period beginning with the August 1991 meeting of the 1992 Council to the end of the 2001 Council in August 2002; coincides with the tenure of Executive Officer Felice J. Levine;

- **ASA in 2002 to 2004:** Includes a brief overview of major events in 2002 through 2004 leading up to the Centennial year 2005 (coincides with the arrival of Executive Officer Sally T. Hillsman); and
- **Appendices:** Include (1) a timeline of major events from 1905, (2) lists of Association leaders over time, (3) data on membership and participation in ASA, (4) summaries of key information on governance, (5) information on ASA programs, and (6) a summary of Executive Office organizational affiliations, departments, programs, and staff in 2005.

Conceptual Framework

For each of Chapters 1 and 2, the text includes a discussion of the following issues:

- **Background:** Provides contextual setting and key goals of ASA;
- **Profile of ASA:** Includes summary of key facts about the ASA (e.g., data on membership, participation, budget, and finances);
- **Executive Office:** Describes staffing, operations, application of new technologies, and so forth;
- **ASA governance/policy changes:** Provides description of changes relating to ASA's authority to govern and conduct its work (i.e., amend its Constitution and Bylaws, change its Code of Ethics; modify policies on ASA awards, define guidelines for signing on to amicus briefs, or issue policy statements on behalf of ASA);
- **ASA governance/structural changes:** Includes summary of institutional changes in ASA structures and governance systems, such as its committees or sections, dues restructuring, and so forth;
- **Core programmatic activities:** Describes the growth and evolution of major ASA Programs (e.g., Publications, Certification, Teaching, Professional Development, Applied Sociology, Academic Affairs, the Sydney Spivack Program in Applied Social Research and Social Policy, Minority Affairs, Research on the Discipline and the Profession, Public Affairs, and Public Information);
- **Other programs and activities:** Describes other programs such as the Honors Program and the Fund for the Advancement of the Discipline (FAD), and activities focused on international events and issues; and
- **The Annual Meeting:** Includes highlights of key changes relating to the Annual Meeting.

The report on the history concludes in Chapter 3 with highlights of ASA activities from 2002 through 2004—leading up to the 2005 Centennial. An Epilogue provides a closing commentary.

Methodology

The primary sources of information are those published in *Footnotes* (particularly minutes of Council meetings, reports of the Secretaries and Executive Officers, "Reflections of the Presidents," feature articles by Executive Officers ("Inter Nos" by Russell Dynes, "Observing" by William D'Antonio, "Open Window" by Felice Levine, and "Vantage Point" by Sally Hillsman), and other official records. Other sources included minutes of the meetings of the Committee on the Executive Office and Budget (EOB), Council and EOB Agenda books, program file records, Annual Meeting Programs, committee and other reports to Council, and other records in the ASA files. The Executive Officers who served (or are serving) during this period, and ASA staff in 2003–5 provided valuable information and insights. Finally, extant literature on relevant topics was also reviewed.

Council and EOB minutes were systematically reviewed to obtain a comprehensive list of topics for consideration (starting with those topics used in the 1981 volume). Special attention was placed on examining milestone events, major structural changes, constitutional changes, major programmatic innovations, and the development of Council policies and resolutions that had major impacts on the Association and the profession. The objective was to describe as succinctly and factually as possible the "what," "who," "when," "why" (to the extent recorded) and "how" of these major events and issues over this time period, with a particular focus on outcomes ("what finally happened?"). An extensive set of notes was prepared (both in electronic and scanned form) during this analytic process that formed the basis for the final text. The review of materials and preparation of the text was accomplished between October 2003 and April 2004. Final text was reviewed by the three Executive Officers who served during this period (Russell R. Dynes, William V. D'Antonio, and Felice J. Levine), and by the current Executive Officer, Sally T. Hillsman. ASA President Troy Duster also appointed an ad hoc committee to review the manuscript in early 2005.

Publication Formats

This *History of the American Sociological Association, 1981–2004* is published electronically in .pdf and .html form on the ASA homepage at www.asanet.org. A limited run of printed volumes is also published primarily for archival purposes.

Chapter 1

The 1980s: Critical Challenges and New Resolve

1. INTRODUCTION

Background and Context

The 1980s opened to critical challenges for the discipline and the Association. The period of "decline and retrenchment" which began in the mid-1970s continued well into the 1980s: The recession of 1978 to 1982 severely reduced employment opportunities for sociologists, the pool of research funds contracted, and the number of sociology majors dropped dramatically between 1974 and 1985. To many, these conditions created a generally pessimistic picture for the future of sociology.

These crises affected the Association as well. In 1982, William Form observed that, "ASA has gone into debt even as members call for more and more expensive services. . . . Some Sections of the Association think that they are being done in by the Program Committee. Traditionalists insist that the Association should focus exclusively on academic concerns while others think that more emphasis should be given to teaching. Attendance at the annual meetings is down and the costs of meetings are rising." (*Footnotes*, August 1982:1) President Alice Rossi wrote in 1983 that the profession "may have 'crested' in terms of numerical size" resulting in potentially new complexities in balancing goals and providing services to ASA membership in the future (*Footnotes*, December 1983:3). ASA priorities were also shifting as graduate enrollments in sociology declined, and an increasing number of people holding sociology degrees found employment in non-academic settings.

The Association responded to these challenges with determination and focus. The changing needs of sociologists were addressed by enhancing existing programs and designing and implementing new initiatives. Organizational and governance structures of the Association were improved to better serve the membership. A major change occurred in 1984 when the Executive Office was restructured, leading to more effective and efficient operations. Council and the Executive Office also worked aggressively to achieve fiscal stability for the ASA—even as they sought to improve and expand services for the membership. The Executive Office operations were greatly enhanced in this respect by new information technologies and systems, which facilitated the continuing professionalization of services provided by ASA.

Special attention during the 1980s was focused on the needs of sociologists who were facing hardships as a result of the economic downturn. The ASA sponsored a major workshop on applied sociology in late 1981 that signaled its new interest and commitment to sociologists working in non-academic settings. In January 1982, Edna Bonacich presented a statement to Council on the "Crisis in the Occupation of Sociology," with recommendations on how to respond to this serious challenge. A high priority on professional opportunities for un- and underemployed and the "independent scholar" was also expressed through initiatives advancing sociological practice, and through various committees with mandates on related issues (e.g., the Committee on Employment, which was established to deal specifically with problems of unemployment and underemployment of sociologists).

To a considerable extent, shifts in public policies and societal and global changes of the 1980s exacerbated the difficulties which sociology was experiencing. Under the Reagan administration, federal agencies reduced levels of support for research and scholarship in the social sciences, and the National Institute of Mental Health (NIMH) proposed eliminating social research altogether. Some agencies, like the National Institute of Education (NIE) were heavily shaped by political agendas, and others, such as the National Endowment for the Humanities (NEH) had their very existence threatened. Budget cuts in social programs, increasing social inequality, homelessness, racism, discrimination, and policies on education and the environment posed serious challenges. Public support for dealing with AIDS and its consequences was slow in coming. Human rights violations, which continued to threaten the lives of many around the world, resulted in the persecution or death of sociologists in several countries, most notably in El Salvador.

By the mid-1980s, prospects for employment opportunities for sociologists had improved somewhat, membership in the Association was climbing again, attendance was up at the Annual Meetings, and, by 1990, the ASA had four straight years of budget surplus. ASA worked closely with the Consortium of Social Science Associations (COSSA), the National Humanities Alliance (NHA), and the Council of Professional Associations for Federal Statistics (COPAFS), which contributed substantially to reversing or reducing the effects of cutbacks in federal funding programs. New relationships were forged with sociologists in China and other places around the world and old ties were strengthened through various initiatives. The fall of the Berlin Wall in 1989 made possible new collaborations with colleagues in Eastern Europe.

By the end of the decade, new challenges appeared in the form of movements to downsize or eliminate departments of sociology. As experienced in other disciplines as well, some sociology departments confronted challenges from external factors (e.g., the faltering economy affecting academic institutions); others experienced internal challenges (e.g., faculty conflicts, insufficient planning for retirements) that made them targets of opportunity at their institutions. The issue emerged earlier in 1981 with the public inquiry that threatened to lead to the closing of the sociology department at Duke University. In 1990, the Department of Sociology at Washington University in St. Louis was closed over protests and considerable efforts by ASA, sociologists nationwide, and other social science organizations to encourage a reversal of the decision.

ASA Priorities in the 1980s

The major focus of the Association during the 1980s was to accomplish its major objectives by (1) supporting basic research and publications, (2) advancing programs to support sociological practice, and (3) enhancing the teaching of sociology. These goals were achieved through committees and initiatives of ASA Council as well as a variety of programs carried out by the Executive Office, such as the Professional Development Program (PDP), the Certification Program, the Public Information Program, and the Teaching Services Program (TSP).

Promoting Diversity and Inclusivity

ASA also continued its strong commitment to promoting diversity in the discipline and the profession through support of the Minority Fellowship Program (MFP) and other policies and initiatives aimed at greater representation and inclusivity. The Status Committees of ASA Council—the Committee on the Status of Racial and Ethnic Minorities in Sociology (CSREMS), and the Committee on the Status of Women in Sociology (CSWS) worked to promote awareness of and improve the situation for minorities and women in the ASA and in sociology. Both CSREMS and CSWS, for example, strongly urged that minorities and women have a larger role in the activities and programs of the ASA, that data be collected on such activities, and that analytic reports be published periodically about these issues.

Discrimination against homosexuals was also a recurring theme in Council meetings since the mid-1970s, and Council consistently showed support for rights of homosexuals. In 1979, Council created a Task Group to examine the situation of homosexuals in academia, and in 1982, ASA published the Report of the ASA's Task Group on Homosexuality in *The American Sociologist* (*TAS*). In accepting the Report, Council also appointed a new task force to make recommendations on how to combat discrimination against homosexuals. The Committee on Society and Persons with Disabilities also became a standing committee in February 1985 and contributed to ASA policies and practices for improvements with respect to persons with disabilities in the Association, in the profession, and in the discipline.

Committees of Council also urged that a greater effort should be made to include in ASA activities members who are affiliated with smaller colleges and universities, private and governmental agencies, and foundations. In sum, throughout the 1980s, there were intentional efforts to work toward greater inclusiveness at all levels of ASA with respect to race, ethnicity, gender, sexual orientation, disability, and employment status and context.

2. ASA MEMBERSHIP TRENDS AND FISCAL STATUS

During the 1980s, significant progress was made toward routine collection of data on the ASA membership as part of the process of compiling information for the *Directory of Members*. Also, through ASA Council resolutions, an emphasis was placed on collecting systematic data on minority participation in the ASA and in the discipline of sociology in general. The application of computer technologies, as well as the focused efforts of the Committee for Research on the Profession after 1988 advanced the opportunities in this area.

Membership

Change in Definition of Membership

The 1982 Council made two important changes to membership practices, by changing (a) the definition of Association membership, and (b) the dues structure. The objective of the membership change was to "shift the focus of membership qualifications away from the 'status' or 'credentials' criteria to commitment to the purposes of the Association" (*Footnotes*, March 1982:1). Prior to 1982, eligibility for membership was based on individuals having a PhD in sociology or in closely-related fields, or evidence of near attainment of that status. An Associates Membership was open to "any person interested in the field of sociology." In addition, sociology students in degree-granting institutions were eligible for Student Associate, and persons who were both non-citizens and non-residents of the U.S. could become International Members.

According to the 1982 summary of Council actions in *Footnotes*, membership in the Association was defined as follows: "Persons subscribing to the objectives of the Association may become Members. Those subscribing to the objectives of the Association, but desiring fewer membership services may become Associate Members. Students enrolled in undergraduate or graduate institutions can become Student Members." Also, Council, as the elected representatives of the members, voted to place authority with Council to set dues for the membership up to cost of living adjustments, with only increases above cost of living requiring approval of members through a mail ballot. These Council changes were implemented after amendments to the Constitution and Bylaws were approved by voting members (see below).

The shift in membership classification eliminated the need for the Committee on Classification and greatly reduced the work of the Membership Services Department of the Executive Office, necessary to verify the credentials of prospective members.

The Membership Committee

The Association pursued innovative campaigns to increase ASA membership (with particular emphasis on recruiting graduate students), and library subscriptions for its journals. Through an active Membership Committee, chaired by John Schnabel, and initiatives directed by Carla Howery at the Executive Office, ASA sought to make the renewal process more efficient by introducing use of credit cards for payment of dues, special discounts for early renewal, user-friendly approach to those slow to renew, and special brochures and other materials to better acquaint members and prospective new members about the ASA. The Committee explored options such as a dues structure based on a fee-for-services principle, alliances with regional associations, dues breaks for multiple association membership, and an introductory ASA membership fee. The Membership Committee articulated goals of "recruitment, retention, and research" in its strategy to stabilize and increase membership in ASA.

Membership Trends During the 1980s

Membership declined each year from 1980 when it was 12,868 to 1984 when it reached a low point at 11,223. From 1985 to 1990 membership again climbed steadily so that by the end of 1990, the membership stood at 12,841 (Appendix 12).

In an analysis of membership trends from 1984 to 1990, Executive Officer D'Antonio noted that: (1) most of the growth in membership was in the student membership category, (2) regular membership increased by only about 600, and (3) numbers in the emeriti category increased significantly. This analysis also revealed shifts in membership among income categories. In 1983, due to the dire effects of the recession, more than two-thirds of the ASA regular members were in the two lowest income categories (Less than or equal to $20,000). By 1990, there were significant increases in membership in the two highest categories ($40,000–$49,999 and $50,000+), and a dramatic decrease in the number reporting incomes in the ranges from $15,000 through $29,000. The number in the low dues category (under $15,000) remained steady at about 1,000 (*Footnotes*, February 1991:2).

Profile of ASA Members and Minority Participation in ASA in 1981

In the summer of 1981, ASA for the first time collected certain demographic information on its membership as part of the process of compiling information for the 1982 *Directory of Members*. Also, data were collected on characteristics of faculty and students through "audits" of 238 departments of sociology (audits had also been conducted from 1972–74). A report on the analysis of these data was presented by Paul R. Williams in the December 1982 issue of *Footnotes*. Williams emphasized that the results from the membership survey should be viewed as estimates because of several methodological issues—most notably the substantial nonresponse rates on certain key questions (16 percent of the members, for example, did not provide information on race/ethnicity). Nevertheless, Williams wrote that some general statements on the sex and racial/ethnic composition of ASA's membership were possible from these analyses.

These data indicate that in 1981, ASA membership was largely male (67 percent male and 33 percent female) and predominately white: Of those members who reported on race/ethnicity, 91 percent were white, 5 percent Asian, 3 percent black, 1 percent Hispanic, and less than 1 percent Native American (see Appendix 13). In 1981, more than half of ASA members in the student category were women; and except for the international category, which had large numbers of Asians, students were more likely to be minorities. Audits of graduate departments of sociology also show that numbers of minorities and women increased substantially from 1970 to 1981.

In terms of employment, the data show that ASA members were overwhelmingly employed full-time in the academy. Both white males and minority males were more likely to work in universities and have a higher income. Women were more likely to be employed in the federal government and in non-profit organizations, and minority women were more likely to work in two- and four-year colleges. Minority women were also more disadvantaged both in terms of income and educational attainment.

Williams also examined trends in the participation of minorities and women in ASA leadership activities from 1970 to 1981. Comparisons of the 1981 data with those from an earlier study (published by Joan R. Harris in *Footnotes* in January 1975) show that women ASA members made substantial gains in ASA positions (i.e., as elected officers, on Council, on elected committees, via Council/Presidential appointments, as elected section officers and on section councils) during this time—to reach levels representative of their proportions in the Associations (the exception being on editorial boards). Minorities gained in some areas, but lost ground overall from the mid-1970s: There was one black member of Council on the 1982 Council, and minority representation in other governance areas had generally declined. Minority representation on committees of Council was considerably higher than their levels in the Association, but minorities were concentrated in committees such as the Committee on the Minority Fellowship Program, the Dubois-Johnson-Frazier Award Committee, and the Committee on Racial and Ethnic Minorities.

Budgets and Fiscal Policies

The budget of the ASA grew dramatically during the 1980s. At the end of 1980, the income of ASA was $1,161,886, with expenditures totaling $1,175,124; by the end of 1990, the income of ASA more than doubled to $2,632,649, with expenditures at $2,523,222. The total operating budget at the end of 1990 was $2,915,897, and reserves stood at $649,662 or about 25 percent of expenditures. In 1990, the value of ASA's equity was $1,371,071, and real estate taxes at the time suggest that the Association's property (its headquarters building) was worth about $1.4 million (*Footnotes*, May 1981 and August 1991).

In 1980, the equity of ASA was reported at $740,082, and the general reserves stood at $395,345 or about 34 percent of that year's expenditure. During 1980, 1981, and 1982, the Association sustained deficits of $15,067, $49,275, and $83,253, respectively. Several factors, including inflation, loss of membership, and the recession of the early 1980s reduced the reserves from a high of $410,000 in 1980 to $262,817 in 1982.

By 1990, ASA had balanced its budget for four straight years in a row, permitting it to rebuild the reserves of the Association, which had been greatly depleted in the early 1980s. The goal was to have reserves equal to at least one half of the size of the annual budget—generally considered prudent fiscal policy for a non-profit association like the ASA.

ASA also established an investment policy that took into account prudent finances as well as social policies and concerns. As articulated by Secretary Michael Aiken and recorded in the August 22, 1987 minutes of Council, EOB "endorsed a flexible program according to the formula of at least 20–25 percent in money markets, 30 percent in diversified equities, and 45–50 percent in bonds, utilities and preferred stocks. Investments would be made with the following restrictions: no investments in (1) South African companies, (2) companies that are notoriously anti-labor, (3) that are primarily defense related, and (4) that discriminate against women and minorities."

In 1989, Secretary Aiken described "the ASA as having reached certain limits or plateaus—in assets, in membership size, and in Executive Office capability. Although the current budget provides some flexibility, he said that an annual surplus is needed just to account for normal growth." (Council Minutes, January 1989)

3. THE EXECUTIVE OFFICE (EO)

The Executive Office of ASA evolved through several important transitions during the 1980s, including changes in leadership and a major reorganization of functions and operations. After the reorganization of the Executive Office in 1984, the functions and role of the professional staff grew significantly. The introduction of computer technologies also enhanced the operations of the Executive Office, and laid the foundation for a more streamlined delivery of services to the membership.

Transitions and Reorganization

Transitions

In August 1982, Executive Officer Russell R. Dynes left the ASA to become Chair of the Department of Sociology at the University of Delaware, and at present he remains professor emeritus on the faculty of the University. William V. D'Antonio, then Professor of Sociology at the University of Connecticut became Executive Officer in August 1982 and served until his retirement from ASA in August 1991. In 1993, D'Antonio joined the faculty of the Catholic University of America as an Adjunct Research Professor (his current position). Felice J. Levine who succeeded D'Antonio, also served as Executive Officer-designate from her appointment in May 1990 until she joined the ASA staff on August 1, 1991. Levine was Director of the Law and Social Science Program at the National Science Foundation before becoming Executive Director of the ASA.

Executive Office staffing changed in other ways during the early 1980s as well. In February 1981, long-time staff member Marjorie E. (Midge) Miles left her position as Administrative Officer and was succeeded by Jo Ann Ruckel. Also, Lawrence J. Rhoades, who had served as Executive Associate of the Association in 1974 and 1975 and from 1977 to 1981 left the Executive Office in 1981 for a position at the National Institute of Mental Health. Three sociologists joined the professional staff during 1981, including Bettina J. Huber, as Assistant Executive Officer, Carla B. Howery as Professional Associate with a focus on teaching, and Paul R. Williams, as Director of the Minority Fellowship Program.

Reorganization

A variety of staffing issues emerged in the Executive Office over the years. In his 1981 Report to the membership, Secretary Herbert L. Costner noted that, depending on how and when counting was done, the Executive Office had a professional staff of three to five people and an administrative/clerical staff of 12. He also reported that the EOB conducted a review of the Executive Office in 1979 and 1980 in response to the concerns raised by women and minority sociologists on how to better integrate them into the Executive Office. Concerns were also raised about the demand on Executive Office staff time by several of the interest groups within the Association. Costner wrote that one professional person was added to the staff at this time.

The complexities and tensions existing in Executive Office operations were described by outgoing ASA President James F. Short, who said that, "[the] [o]rganization of both sociologists and the staff, authority relations and the division of labor among them, were often ad hoc, with little rationale save personal preference or equally ad hoc precedent . . . . Over the years conflicts had arisen and remained unresolved, however, to the detriment of both interpersonal relationships within the office and of service to the Association." (*Footnotes*, December 1984:1–2)

In October 1983, The Committee on the Executive Office and Budget (EOB) retained management consultants Robert Atwell and Madeleine Green to conduct a study of the Executive Office. In January 1984, Council approved an EOB recommendation to give broad authorities to the Executive Officer to "reorganize the Executive Office in order to improve efficiency and effectiveness" of operations. Secretary Theodore Caplow noted that recommendations were communicated to the Executive Office staff by the Executive Officer. The position of Administrative Officer was eliminated and new managerial positions were created.

The reorganization of the Executive Office included five new managerial positions: Convention and Meetings Manager, Governance Manager, Publications Manager, Business Manager, and Office Manager. At the time of the reorganization, the staff also consisted of a Membership Secretary, three staff sociologists, and a support staff of seven. The only other professional staff position added during the 1980s was that of Director for the Professional Development Program, which was established in 1986.

The reorganization of 1984 significantly affected the operations of the Executive Office. Key functional authorities were shifted from the Administrative Officer to the Executive Officer, thus laying the foundations for an administrative structure that could build professional services in the five managerial areas. The ASA staff (both professional and administrative) was thereafter able to focus attention in their respective functional areas, resulting in an enhancement in the quality and level of services to the membership. Programmatic activities were also realigned and institutionalized around the key areas established in the restructuring.

Other changes took place with respect to staffing in the early 1980s. Professional staff sociologists were appointed to positions for specific tasks, rather than for fixed two-year periods as had been the practice up to that time. The Executive Officer's position also was extended to a second term. In 1988, an Ad Hoc EOB/Council Committee on Professional Staff Appointments formulated a detailed professional staff hiring and evaluation policy, which was adopted by Council with slight modifications in January 1990.

In February 1985, Council created the position of Ombudsperson for the Executive Office, and in August 1985, Joseph Scimecca of George Mason University became the first Ombudsman. The Ombudsman was charged with hearing staff grievances within the Executive Office not satisfied by the Executive Officer. Scimecca served from 1986 to 1988; no one was appointed for 1989, and William Anderson was Ombudsman from 1990 to 1992. (It appears that no staff person contacted Scimecca or Anderson, and the position was eliminated after 1992.)

In 1991, D'Antonio noted that during his nine-year tenure at ASA the staff grew from 17 to 19 full-time persons, and from two to six part-timers. However, while the staff increased by only a few people, the workload of the Executive Office increased substantially during that period through the addition of several new journals and programmatic services. (The issue of whether the ASA Executive Office was "overstaffed" was raised a number of times during Council meetings during the 1980s.)

ASA's Headquarters

The housing situation at 1722 N Street NW in Washington, the headquarters of the Executive Office, was also assessed from time to time. During the early 1980s, ASA engaged in discussions to relocate to one building with two other social science associations in the Washington area, but, in January 1982, Executive Officer Dynes informed Council that this was deemed not feasible. The outdated condition of the 1722 N Street headquarters was observed by Council in January 1982, when the boiler blew out (fortunately without injuries). Council instructed the Executive Office in 1986 to explore alternatives for its housing. In 1989, Secretary Aiken noted that the ASA building was close to staffing capacity, in effect placing some limits on Association activities, and he encouraged EOB "to remain open and to continue to review options for moving ASA to new quarters." (Council Minutes, August 12, 1989)

Despite these constraints, in 1990, ASA entered into a five-year agreement to house the Population Association of America (PAA) at the ASA Executive Office at 1722 N Street when PAA's office sharing arrangement with the American Statistical Association was discontinued. The PAA, with a membership of about 2,800 at the time, had close ties to the ASA through an overlapping membership, and collaborative arrangements of many of its members. Part-time administrative services to PAA were provided by two ASA staff members, and there was one full-time PAA staff member. In 1995, the PAA moved to a new location in the Washington, DC area when its lease and services agreement with ASA expired.

Application of New Information Technologies (IT)

Executive Office operations also gained in efficiency as a result of implementing new technologies and systems. The 1980s saw the rapid development of office computer systems, and ASA struggled to keep up with the opportunities they presented. Computer systems at the time however, required specially designed software programs, which took time and money, and the search for proper expertise.

In 1982, Council approved a special capital expenditure for the purchase of computer equipment for the Executive Office, and a Burroughs Convergent Technologies system was purchased and installed that year. This system, however, could accommodate a limited number of users and required considerable reprogramming to adapt to Association needs. Janet Astner of the Executive Office worked closely with the systems programmers to augment the software applications for membership records, subscriptions, accounting, and other ASA requirements. In 1986, ASA increased the capacity of its information system by adding ten computers for staff workstations.

Council also addressed the opportunities for adapting the new technologies to enhance communication among sociologists more generally. In 1985, Hans Mauksch, James Campbell, and Edward Brent wrote a proposal to establish an electronic bulletin board to link sociologists through a communications system at ASA, which Council approved in 1986. The Committee advocated moving slowly by developing a network for communications among research scholars in sociology, and between ASA committees and members of ASA sections.

Electronic enhancements to the ASA were also introduced during the late 1980s. The ASA Executive Office established Bitnet communications through a terminal linked to the George Washington University mainframe computer, with Karen Gray Edwards, Manager of Publications, monitoring traffic for staff. Edwards, working in close collaboration with Boyd Printing Company, ASA's primary publisher, introduced innovations such as use of electronic media and formats into the publishing program of the ASA. Other innovations during the 1980s included publication of electronic addresses in the *Directory of Members* for the first time in 1988.

In January 1989, Executive Officer D'Antonio reported to Council that equipment problems "plagued the office," and requested upgrades in some areas, noting that the main computer system would need to be updated. Later in 1989, D'Antonio reported that some equipment had been purchased, including a FAX machine, a personal computer for access to Bitnet, and a more advanced Xerox copier. In 1990, a more advanced phone system was also installed.

By the end of 1990, the ASA Executive Office had a computer system consisting of ten personal computer work stations with word processing and other office applications (Lotus, Harvard Graphics), networked to the Burroughs Convergent Technologies System (including its database system with basic accounting, subscription, and membership record information), several printers, and a network connection to Bitnet through George Washington University.

4. GOVERNANCE: CONSTITUTION/BYLAWS CHANGES AND COUNCIL POLICYMAKING

Changes to the Association Constitution or Bylaws require the approval of the voting members. While members have the official capacity to petition for such changes, during the 1980s, as throughout the history of the Association, members voted on such changes based on amendments proposed by ASA Council. As the primary elected body of the Association, ASA Council considers issues that may require changes to the Constitution and Bylaws, including alternations to the dues that exceed cost of living and revisions of the ASA Code of Ethics.

Only ASA Council has the authority to set the policies of the Association and issue policy statements on behalf of the Association. Such initiatives could originate with committees, sections or other groups established by Council; member resolutions, or from Council itself. During the 1980s, ASA Council clarified ASA policies and practices in several areas that do not require membership approval, including the Association's participation in amicus briefs, and awards bestowed by ASA. Council also adopted a number of member resolutions, thus signaling ASA support for these policies and issues.

The Bylaws also allow members to take actions otherwise within the powers of the Council. The process for doing so is specified in Article II, Section 8 and requires voting members' adopting a resolution advanced by at least three percent of the voting members of the Association. No such resolutions were advanced by the members during the 1980s.

The ASA Constitution and Bylaws

From 1980 through 1990, ASA Council approved the following changes to the Constitution and Bylaws (for a more complete statement of each change, see Appendix 15):

- The 1981 Council approved an amendment to the Bylaws increasing the minimum number of members required to establish a new section from 200 to 250, and keeping the existing limit to retain section status at 200 members.

- The 1982 Council made two important changes to membership practices, by changing (a) the definition of Association membership, and (b) the process for increasing the dues structure (see preceding section on Membership).

- The 1983 Council approved emeritus membership for persons 70 years of age or older, who would be entitled to all rights of active membership except journals, without further payment of annual dues, provided that at the time of application, they were dues paying members of the Association for the preceding 10 years.

- The 1985 Council approved changes in the structure of the Program Committee to increase its membership from 9 to 11 members.

- The 1988 Council amended the ASA Constitution by adding the current President and Past President as voting members of the Committee on the Executive Office and Budget (EOB).

- The 1989 Council voted to adopt an eight-district proposal for revising the ASA election system. A five-district system for nominating procedures for ASA elections had been instituted in 1965, but demographic shifts and the decision of Canadian sociologists to form their own national association had made the districts uneven in size. In January 1987, Council appointed a subcommittee to "examine ASA redistricting, with the objective of creating a more equitable system based on geography and the distribution of the ASA membership." A December 1988 *Footnotes* article summarized the pros and cons of a five- versus eight-district system.

- The 1990 Council adjusted the qualifications for the emeritus category, by removing the existing restrictions of age 70 and consecutive ten-year membership prior to that age.

- The 1991 Council passed a resolution giving students the right to vote and hold office, noting that students choosing the low-income category (at the same dues rates) already enjoyed full membership privileges.

Code of Ethics

On several occasions throughout the 1980s, Council stated that the ASA Code of Ethics should be viewed as a "living" document and revised periodically.

The Code was revised in 1980 and approved by Council and the membership in 1982. At the time, Council upheld the recommendation of the Committee on Professional Ethics (COPE) that the document be voted on by the membership in its entirety rather than section by section. In addition, a request was approved from the Ad Hoc Group of Sociology Editors to incorporate a statement on multiple submissions to journals, which had been deleted from an earlier version of the Code.

In 1983, Council accepted a recommendation by COPE for an implementation section to be included as part of the ASA Code of Ethics. Council also voted to clarify the extent of COPE's enforcement jurisdiction, indicating that allegations of ethical violations of the Code could only be adjudicated against members of the Association.

A report by COPE in 1988 recommended updating the Code of Ethics to improve the form of the Code and to address ethical standards of those employed in sociological practice. New sections were also added on ethical standards on fair employment practices and on the rights of human subjects of research. After extensive discussion and feedback, Council approved the revised Code of Ethics in January 1989.

In August 1989, COPE reported that ethical standards for teaching responsibilities and ethnographic research were still problems, and approved changes relating to Item III of the Code on these issues.

Brajuha Case

A landmark case with wide implications for ASA as well as the ethics of conducting research in general was decided in 1984 in the federal courts. The case involved a graduate student in sociology at SUNY-Stony Brook, Mario Brajuha, who was ordered to turn over data he had been collecting for his dissertation while employed at a local restaurant. Brajuha's research notes were subpoenaed after a suspicious fire at the restaurant.

On September 5, 1983, Council approved a motion upholding the applicability of the Association's Code of Ethics in a situation where research notes are under subpoena. The ASA Council notified Brajuha's lawyer that if research documents prepared under promise of confidentiality were provided by the sociologist, it would place him in violation of the ASA's Code of Ethics. A decision by federal Judge Jack B. Weinstein of the Eastern District of New York on April 5, 1984 ruled that, "[s]erious scholars cannot be required to turn over their fieldnotes in a grand jury investigation when the government fails to establish 'substantial need' for them to do so." *(Footnotes,* August 1984:11; *Footnotes,* December 1985:1,13)

On September 1, 1984, the prosecution appealed the Brajuha ruling, and ASA filed an amicus brief in support of the decision. Kai Erikson, the President of ASA in 1985, and William Foote Whyte, Past President of the ASA, appeared in court as witnesses on Brajuha's behalf on February 13, 1985. Council appropriated $2,500 in behalf of Brajuha's defense, and ASA worked vigorously to raise awareness of the case and support on his behalf.

Judge Weinstein's decision was reversed on appeal and the case was remanded back to the lower courts for additional evidence. At the same time, the Federal District Attorney's Office went through an organizational change, and after several continuances, it accepted Brajuha's redacted notes as fulfilling the subpoena (as did the county District Attorney). While the case in general resulted in a positive solution, questions remained about what constituted "scholars privilege" and the types of research that may be protected (Hallowell, *Footnotes*, December 1985:1,13).

Husch Case

In 1988, Jerri Husch of Tufts University filed a complaint to the ASA Executive Office alleging that her dissertation had been plagiarized by Steven Barnes, who was then Dean of Fine Arts at Eastern New Mexico University. An Ad Hoc Committee of ASA Council investigated the matter and rendered a unanimous opinion that plagiarism had indeed occurred. In February 1989, Executive Officer D'Antonio wrote to the Edwin Mellen Press, the publisher of the Barnes book, requesting that certain actions be taken. Since he received no reply from the publisher, D'Antonio wrote to the University, asking that the University take action, and indicating that ASA would report the case to the *Chronicle of Higher Education* if no action were taken by May 1st. An article on the case appeared in the *Chronicle* on May 10, 1989.

The Eastern New Mexico University took up the case, and Barnes left the university in August 1989 following an internal faculty review. Edwin Mellen Press, however, refused to take action and published a second edition of the Barnes book with certain changes in attribution. With the strong support of the Committee on Publications, Council adopted a resolution In January 1990 urging the publisher to take appropriate actions, and outlined specific measures that would be taken against the Press, should it not comply. In March 1990, Herbert Richardson, publisher of the Mellen Press met with the Association, and worked out an agreement to withdraw the Barnes book from print, notify libraries and those known to have purchased the book that its contents were plagiarized, and refund money to those who returned the book. Richardson also agreed to write a letter of apology to Husch for the adverse publicity caused by the incident, and to write a letter to the ASA Council detailing the action taken by the Press, thus bringing the case to a close.

Amicus Briefs

ASA was involved in a legal case in 1989, which led Council to examine procedures for the Association signing on to future amicus briefs. In 1989, ASA became involved in the case of the Unification Church vs. Molko/Leal (No.88–1600), which involved two young adults who alleged that they were unwittingly coerced to join the Unification Church (often known as the "Moonies"). At issue for the ASA was whether or not the Association should remain as a signatory on the amicus briefs submitted to the U.S. Supreme Court. At a hearing at Council on August 12, 1989, Richard Ofshe, presented the argument against the ASA's position on the case and John Lofland and Richard Anthony spoke in support of the ASA's position. Council also raised questions about precedents for ASA actions in legal cases. Council voted to appoint a subcommittee to review the procedures by which the ASA should sign on to legal briefs, and also passed a motion that the ASA withdraw from the amicus brief in the Unification Church case. (Lawsuits brought by Ofshe and Margaret Singer in 1992 against the American Psychological Association, the American Sociological Association, principal officers of these organizations and others in 1989, were dismissed in 1994. Executive Officer Felice J. Levine and President William A. Gamson—in consultation with past officers—worked with the ASA legal counsel on settlement of the case.)

The Subcommittee on Legal Briefs reported back to Council on August 14, 1990. Wendy H. Baldwin reported for the Subcommittee and Council minutes note that, "[I]n the past ASA relied on the Executive Office to handle such matters, but an alternative structure with specific procedures would be preferable. Ideally, all decisions on legal briefs should be brought before Council. However, in between regular meetings of Council when action cannot wait, Baldwin proposed that a subcommittee should act on its behalf." Council then offered some guidelines on how the Subcommittee would operate in deliberating on whether to join in legal cases.

At the request of Council, Executive Officer (William D'Antonio) and Executive Officer-designate (Felice Levine) jointly filed a report in January 1991 "affirming the adequacy of existing procedures as outlined in the Bylaws: Specifically, the Executive Officer, as chief administrative officer of the ASA, 'shall consult with the President and Secretary as questions of policy arise,' and may choose jointly to act on behalf of the Association, poll Council members by mail ballot, or defer action to the next regular meeting of Council." Council took no further action on this issue at that time (Council Minutes, January 1991).

Awards Policy

The ASA has made honorific awards to individuals since the 1950s. Concerned about the proliferation of new named awards, Council approved a new policy in March 1979, resulting in four categories of awards: General, Traditional, Section, and Special Awards and Monetary Prizes. According to the new policy, the General Awards were renamed (to the ASA Award for a Distinguished Contribution to Scholarship, and the ASA Career of Distinguished Scholarship Award), and the practice of naming ASA awards for individuals was eliminated. The policy also authorized sections to make awards within guidelines established by Council. Over the past quarter century, Council has looked to the Committee on Awards Policy for oversight of and guidance on policies and procedures for all awards. The Committee on Awards Policy (which has had various names) was first established in 1954.

Awards policy issues during the 1980s centered on the nature and timing of awards announcements, the presentation of awards (i.e., at what point during the Annual Meeting should the awards ceremony take place), and the proliferation of new awards. Two new awards were established: In 1985, Council approved the ASA Distinguished Career Award for the Practice of Sociology with Conrad Taeuber as its first recipient in 1986, and the Dissertation Award, first presented in 1989 to Richard Biernacki. Council also approved a recommendation by the Committee on Awards Policy that Award Committees name award recipients early enough for publication prior to the Annual Meeting. By the end of the 1980s, the Awards Ceremony was held at the same event as the Presidential Address.

Concerned about the proliferation of awards, and how to respond to the requests for special award nominations, Council approved a Committee in January 1991 consisting of the Past-President, President, President-Elect, and Executive Officer to handle such requests. At the same meeting, Council approved a Committee consisting of Barbara Reskin (Chair), Joan Aldous, Myra Marx Ferree, Jill Quadagno, and Executive Officer D'Antonio to develop guidelines for handling gifts and grants to the ASA and to assess the structure of and mandate to the Committee on Awards Policy (see Chapter 2).

Member Resolutions

ASA Council approved a number of resolutions passed by members at the Association's Business Meetings, which take place at each Annual Meeting. These include resolutions on human rights and international issues (see the discussion on International Activities), federal government policies and domestic issues, and issues relating to ASA policies and practices. For example, Council passed resolutions (1) urging the U.S. Government to direct all agencies to ban discrimination on the basis of sexual orientation, (2) condemning violence against gays, (3) supporting rights for nonmarried domestic partners, (4) opposing any attempt to overturn *Roe v. Wade*, (4) supporting the Civil Rights Act of 1984, (5) encouraging support for research on AIDS, (6) urging the free flow of government information (which was to be submitted for vote by mail ballot), and (7) opposing the death penalty.

Member resolutions approved by Council relating to Association activities, included: (1) banning the Central Intelligence Agency from access to ASA employment services at Annual Meetings, (2) urging ASA to undertake a survey of departments of sociology, (3) urging action to ensure equity for minorities and women at all levels of ASA, (4) calling on ASA to only use airlines that have collective bargaining arrangements, and (5) urging ASA and its membership to take action regarding the closing of departments of sociology.

5. GOVERNANCE: STRUCTURAL CHANGES

The Association accomplished its objectives through Council meetings, sections, committees, subcommittees of Council, commissions, task groups, and other ad hoc groups with specific charges and assignments. ASA also appointed official representatives to other professional and scientific societies. Major ASA committee work is considered elsewhere in this chapter under relevant functional or programmatic areas (e.g., Ethics, Publications, Certification, and Membership). Changes in key organizational entities (i.e., Sections) and other committees such as the Committee on Freedom of Research and Teaching (COFRAT), and the American Sociological Foundation (ASF) are discussed below. (See Appendix 16 for a detailed list of the ASA Committees and organizations to which ASA had official representation in August, 1990.)

ASA Sections

Sections, defined by specific areas of institutional interest, have consistently been affirmed by Council as a vital aspect of the Association, and an important part of membership in the ASA. Debates have surfaced occasionally, however, regarding various aspects of the Association's section structure, including sections': (1) proliferation, (2) viability, (3) role (and share of program sessions) at the Annual Meeting, and (4) internal governance structure (i.e., awards, dues, and so forth).

Section Growth in the 1980s

In 1980, ASA members held 9,006 memberships in 20 sections (ASA membership as a whole was 12,868). Section memberships declined from 1981 to 1985, reflecting the general trends in membership in the ASA during this period. Section memberships began climbing again in 1985 (with a slight dip in 1989) to a new high of 13,263 in 27 sections at the end of the 1990 membership year when ASA membership overall was 12,841 (see Appendix 14 for section membership counts for selected years).

At the January 1991 Council meeting, Executive Officer D'Antonio reported stability in the size of the ASA's 27 sections, with about one-half of the ASA membership belonging to at least one section, and more than 25 percent belonging to more than two sections. During the 1980s, about one-third of the sections showed growth in membership although two-thirds experienced declines, leading some Council members to request better data on section membership trends—especially for those members who drop and those who hold multiple memberships. Appendix 17 contains a table with years that sections attained full section status.

Significant Events Relating to Sections in the 1980s

An important change took place relating to section formation on January 23, 1981, when Council passed a resolution raising the minimum number of members required to establish a new section from 200 to 250, but kept the limit to retain section status at 200 members. The Committee on Sections also undertook a revision of the *Section Manual* to reflect changes in the Bylaws for the new procedures.

In January 1988, ASA Council voted to establish a committee to assess "the future course of relations between sections and the ASA, with Council liaison but composed of non-Council members familiar with other organizations and relevant fields of specialization." An Ad Hoc Committee on

ASA Future Organizational Trends was created, consisting of Randall Collins (Chair), John McCarthy, Marshall Meyer, Pamela Oliver, and Jonathan Turner. At the request of ASA President Herbert J. Gans, the Committee examined "relevant data from sociology and other social sciences to develop some scenarios about what the increasing number of sections and the rapid growth of membership in sections, will mean for ASA and sociology in the coming decade." *(Footnotes,* October 1988:8)

The Committee delivered a Report to Council in January 1989, which addressed the nature and implications of section growth for the future of ASA and its governance structure. The Report reviewed the history of sections since the early 1970s, cited factors that might explain their popularity, and described their impact on the governance structure, as compared with other associations. In presenting the Report, Collins said that, "the ASA could be viewed as a 'peak' association with a number of options as to how it might relate to its sections, including curtailing sections, encouraging interlocking memberships, or becoming little more than a collection of sections. Extensive discussion ensued on topics such as who sections are serving, the characteristics of section members, the relationship to ASA voting patterns and such things as the demand for academic productivity, and how to interpret the growth and decline in sections." (Council Minutes, January 1989) The 1989 Report was published in full in the September 1989 issue of *Footnotes.*

Committee on Freedom of Research and Teaching (COFRAT)

During the 1980s, the Committee on Freedom of Research and Teaching (COFRAT) continued to handle complaints by individual members against alleged infringement of academic freedoms and rights by institutions. For example, COFRAT heard the case of Nancy Stoller Shaw in her complaint against the University of California-Santa Cruz that her tenure review had procedural irregularities. When the University administration refused to reopen the case, Council censured UC-Santa Cruz in February 1985 on COFRAT's recommendation for denying Shaw due process during her tenure and promotion review.

In the 1970s, COFRAT began to deal with and prepare reports on systemic issues underlying the cases brought before it, such as the *Guidelines for Initial Appointments in Sociology* (1978), which were widely circulated. COFRAT also prepared the *Guidelines for Employment of Part-Time Faculty in Departments of Sociology* (approved by Council in 1986). In 1989, COFRAT was asked by Council to examine the closing of the sociology departments at the University of Rochester and Washington University. COFRAT, however, reported back to Council in January 1990 that, as then constituted, "it was ill-suited to respond to institutional, as compared to individual cases."

Throughout the 1980s, COFRAT increasingly became involved in complicated situations involving acrimonious interactions, including actions between ASA legal counsel and the institutions against which complaints were directed. One COFRAT chair reported intimidation. COFRAT was therefore finding itself in cases that raised questions about the appropriate role of the Association, how effective it could be, and what situations potentially placed it at legal risk. (1993 COFRAT Report). Council continued to discuss these issues during the 1990s (see Chapter 2).

The American Sociological Foundation (ASF)

In January 1983, Council approved in principle a resolution presented by Secretary-Elect Theodore Caplow for establishing a "Memorial Fund" (as the Endowment was initially called) for the ASA, with the goal of achieving an endowment of $1 million. The purpose was to broaden the reserves of the Association, and use only the interest money from the fund to sponsor sociological initiatives in new directions. The Endowment, eventually structured as the American Sociological Foundation (ASF) in 1985, was incorporated as a separate, autonomous 501(c)(3) organization within the ASA, with decision-making authority entrusted to a Board of Trustees consisting of the five most recent past presidents of the ASA.

Council established the ASF to raise and provide funds for the long-range needs of sociology as a discipline and profession. When the fundraising campaign was launched in 1986, these needs were defined as follows: "The Foundation and its Endowment are responding to three particular crises of need and opportunity: first, increasing our minority fellowships and professional development at a time when outside support is plummeting; second, enhancing sociology's public image and policy pertinence during a period when we have more to say but too few may be listening; and third, continuing to enrich our teaching, so that quality is not sacrificed to quantity during a period of increased enrollment competitions." *(Footnotes*, February 1986:1)

The hard work of William Sewell and Jay Demerath especially did much to move the ASF forward. As Chair of the Endowment Campaign Committee, Demerath led the efforts from 1984 to 1986 to establish the Endowment and plan the fundraising campaigns. Other members of the Committee included Jack Riley, Beth Hess, Charles Willie, David Sills, and William Sewell.

In 1986, the ASF began an intensive three-year campaign to raise an endowment fund. By 1988, the Endowment Campaign had raised $200,000 in gifts and pledges from more than 900 donors. A significant contribution of $50,000 from Rev. Andrew Greeley was matched in a two-year (1987–88) Challenge Grant campaign directed at members. The Trustees of the ASF accepted the offer of a second challenge grant for a Congressional Fellowship program in 1990. In the early 1990s, however, a moratorium was placed on ASA's acceptance of further challenge grants. The ASF made its first grant of $10,000 (from interest earnings of the Endowment) to the Minority Fellowship Program summer institutes (later known as MOST I).

6. ASA PROGRAMS AND ACTIVITIES

ASA programmatic activity grew dramatically during the 1980s. In the early 1980s, ASA had strong publications and Minority Fellowship (MFP) programs, and also developed a process for an institutional response in support of research. Programs on Teaching Services (TSP), Professional Development (PDP), Certification, Research on the Profession, and Public Information evolved over the course of the decade. The following section describes these core ASA programs and activities during the 1980s.

Research and Publications

A primary objective of ASA is to support basic research and to promote a program of publication that reports on and disseminates those research findings. Thus, the major part of ASA activities in this area during the 1980s was focused on activities such as:

- Monitoring federal funding agencies and providing information about their activities through articles in *Footnotes*, sessions at meetings, workshops and so forth;
- Responding to actions of federal agencies and Congress, both by advocating on behalf of social research programs and educating officials about the value and importance of social science research in the policy-making process;
- Taking initiatives in many areas affecting research, such as protection of human subjects of research, ethics, and regulation of research;
- Providing direct assistance through small grants, such as the Fund for the Advancement of the Discipline (FAD) which provides seed money for groundbreaking research projects. FAD was designed to support projects of direct relevance to the discipline, rather than the profession and Council approved use of the Fund to be restricted "for workshops, seminars or mini-courses whose aim is to upgrade the scholarly and research skills of ASA members as appropriate uses of the Fund." (Council Minutes, September 9, 1982);

- Establishing a program of research on the profession;
- Undertaking modest data gathering and analytic projects by Executive Office Staff, ASA committees, task forces, and through other special initiatives of ASA Council; and
- Emphasizing a publications program that aims for excellence and wide dissemination of sociological research, but also recognizes the need for specific priorities and prudent management.

Collaborations with Other Associations

The major challenge for ASA during the 1980s was defending federal social science research programs from attacks by the Reagan Administration. At the NSF, budget cuts severely reduced the pool of funds for social research (the first Reagan budget threatened to cut the NSF budget by 75 percent). At the National Institute of Mental Health (NIMH) the Administration proposed to phase out social research altogether. These cuts had severe impacts on federal funding for social science research generally (sociology proposals for NIMH funding were down in the early 1980s), and directly threatened the Minority Fellowship Program, a core ASA program funded primarily by NIMH.

Some agencies, however, were supportive of social science research: The National Institute on Aging (NIA) was a consistent advocate of sociological research, and ASA was fortunate in this respect to have had Matilda White Riley as the Associate Director for Behavioral and Social Research at NIA from 1979 to 1991. Riley, the first Executive Officer of ASA (1949–60) and ASA President in 1986, was the founding NIA Associate Director, Senior Social Scientist from 1991 through 1997, and Scientist Emeritus, from 1998 until her death in 2004.

CONSORTIUM OF SOCIAL SCIENCE ASSOCIATIONS (COSSA)

ASA worked in close collaboration with other social science associations in support of the lobbying and education efforts for social science research, especially with the Consortium of Social Science Associations (COSSA), the Council of Professional Associations for Federal Statistics (COPAFS), and the National Humanities Alliance (NHA). Actions taken included making personal calls upon members of Congress and their staffs, providing testimony, holding seminars for Congressional staff, conducting letter writing campaigns, and generally raising awareness among associations' memberships and urging them to join in various campaigns.

COSSA played a major role in monitoring social research funding and in galvanizing the response to the federal budgetary policies. COSSA established its Washington Office with a two-person staff in May 1981. Under the direction of Roberta B. Miller, COSSA emerged as a significant force both in lobbying on behalf of the social sciences, as well as in educating policy makers on the relevance and significance of social scientific research. Executive Officer D'Antonio noted that there was a general consensus that the willingness of Congress "to add more dollars to Reagan Administration budget proposals for the social sciences . . . is in no small measure the result of the increasingly effective lobbying efforts of COSSA, COPAFS and NHA." *(Footnotes,* August 1984:13) The Association was an active member of COSSA, COPAFS, and NHA.

ASA and COSSA also cosponsored a series of Breakfast Seminars for Congressional leaders and their staffs around the general theme of "The Long Term Consequences of Unemployment"—with the support of Reps. Paul Simon (D-IL), Augustus Hawkins (D-CA), and James Jeffords (R-VT). In the summer of 1983, William Kornblum, Graduate Center of the City University of New York, and Paula Rayman, Brandeis University, were speakers at two such Congressional Seminars.

ASA was a major supporter of COSSA, and worked closely with it in its mission to advance the social sciences. Executive Officer Russell Dynes played a leading role in "activating COSSA," chaired the Executive Committee of COSSA in 1982, and represented COSSA and the NHA on the Executive Committee of the American Council of Learned Societies (ACLS). In 1984, Executive

Officer D'Antonio was chair of the Search Committee of COSSA to find a successor to Roberta Miller, and ASA President-Elect Kai Erikson was on COSSA's Executive Board. In 1990, D'Antonio completed four years as chair of COSSA's Executive Committee.

AMERICAN ASSOCIATION FOR THE ADVANCEMENT OF SCIENCE (AAAS)

The Association also worked through the Social Science Research Council (SSRC) and the American Association for the Advancement of Science (AAAS) in support of research and professional activities—although there were tensions in the relationships with these organizations. With respect to the AAAS, there was a general feeling among social scientists that *Science* magazine did not give sufficient attention to the work of social scientists, that the social science presence at AAAS annual meetings was very limited, that social science involvement in the Section K (Section on Social, Economic, and Political Science) should be enhanced, and that, in general, the involvement of ASA in the AAAS needed to be expanded.

David Sills of the SSRC, who was Secretary of Section K in 1983, informed D'Antonio that the editor of *Science* had assured him that if "appropriate sociological topics were proposed to him, he would proceed to commission articles on them." D'Antonio reported that "Sills urges that sociologists inform him of ideas for articles that they think appropriate." *(Footnotes,* August 1983:9) In 1984, Council appointed a special Ad Hoc Committee (chaired by Matilda Riley, with members JoAnne Miller and James Zuiches), to work with the ASA representatives to Sections K and U (Statistics) to increase ASA participation in the annual meetings of the AAAS.

SOCIAL SCIENCE RESEARCH COUNCIL (SSRC)

ASA's relationship with the SSRC was also complex. In August 1990, Executive Officer D'Antonio summed up for Council the existing tensions in the relationship between COSSA and the SSRC. A growing dissatisfaction with existing arrangements had prompted COSSA members to ask for reorganization of SSRC's Board to acknowledge all the social sciences, not just founding members. Since the SSRC Board had not acted on the proposed change, D'Antonio reported that the situation was at a standstill. D'Antonio added that the ASA representative to SSRC was not appointed by the ASA (it could only recommend candidates) and, as such, was under no obligation to report to Council.

Discussion in Council focused on four specific issues—the ASA relationship to SSRC, ASA Council relationship to its representative to SSRC, how this representative is appointed, and how ASA should support "sister associations" in their quest for more formal recognition within SSRC. Council also directed its attention, however, to the broader issue of assessing ASA's ties to all external organizations, and appointed a subcommittee to assess "the whole 'map' of organizational ties so that individual cases could be more clearly understood." (Council Minutes, August 15, 1990)

In January 1991, the Committee on ASA's Organizational Ties reported to Council, indicating that categories of ties may be summed up as lobbying, interprofessional, international, and interdisciplinary. In speaking for the Committee, W. Richard Scott noted that, while "there are difficulties in attempting to maintain the range of ties involved, Scott deemed it an appropriate effort and recommended no changes. Four Recommendations were offered, however, to improve the reporting, exchange and use of information," including through annual reports to ASA of representatives to such organizations and periodic meetings of such representatives with ASA officers (Council Minutes, January 1991). Scott and incoming Executive Officer Felice Levine hosted the first of such meetings at the Annual Meeting in August 1991.

The Research on the Profession

Herbert J. Gans, ASA President in 1988, initiated efforts to establish a capacity for ASA to do "some practical sociological research about itself." *(Footnotes,* October 1988:2) On August 28, 1988,

Council passed a resolution creating an Ad Hoc Committee for Research on the Profession the mandate of which was to prepare a plan of action "toward developing a coherent research capacity for the ASA." By 1989, under the guidance of the Committee, preparations were under way for a survey of graduate departments and an RFP had been issued for data collection and analysis services. Discussion at the first 1990 Council focused on the importance of having a research capacity and the need for an advisory committee to establish priorities. The Research Program on the Discipline and the Profession was instituted as one of the core ASA Programs in 1992 (see Chapter 2).

Human Subjects of Research

ASA also contributed to the process of refining the federal regulations relating to the protection of human subjects in research. In January 1981, Council minutes note that, "the final version of the regulations amending basic HHS [Department of Health and Human Services] policy for the protection of human subjects of research has been completed and is to appear in the Federal Register on January 26, 1981. The chair of ASA's Standing Committee on Regulation of Research indicated that the final regulations are responsive to the concerns expressed by the Association in that the regulations apply only to federally funded research, and certain types of social science research will no longer require review of human subjects to meet Federal requirements." (Council Minutes; *Footnotes*, November 1981:1,7)

Research-Related Social Policy Issues

Following a "spirited discussion" led by Amitai Etzioni at the January 1984 meeting of the ASA Council, the Association created a special Commission on Sociology and Society with the general mandate "to examine the interrelationship of sociological analysis and the public policy process and to investigate how each might have a more beneficial impact on the other." (Council Minutes, August 30, 1984) Discussion of the Commission's report on August 30, 1984 led Council to conclude, "that a committee of Council was not the appropriate vehicle for pursuing the intellectual direction charted by the Commission. Council cannot effectively define directions the discipline should take." As a result, the Commission on Sociology and Society was dissolved at that meeting.

In 1990, Edna Bonacich presented a preliminary report of the Subcommittee on the ASA and the Needs of the Poor and Dispossessed showing how ASA could demonstrate leadership in setting policy agendas on major social issues relating to inequality (class, race, gender) based on social science research. The ASA President appointed a Blue Ribbon Committee (consisting of Ivar Berg, Edna Bonacich, Troy Duster, and Jill Quadagno) to act on issues raised by the Subcommittee. Council, however, deferred action in this area on August 15, 1990 pending a decision on the Cornerhouse Fund proposal (which was being prepared at the time).

Cornerhouse Fund

Informed by the Cornerhouse Board of Trustees in 1989 that Fund operations would cease, ASA and The Center for Advanced Study at Stanford were invited to write proposals to receive all remaining monies held by the Fund. The Cornerhouse Fund awarded a variety of grants, primarily in the form of support of dissertation research for minority students (See Minority Fellowship Program). It was established in 1969 as a provision of the will of sociologist Sydney S. Spivack, faculty member at Princeton University. (For further background on the Cornerhouse Fund and Spivack's career, see *Footnotes*, September 1991.)

In 1989, the Cornerhouse Board of Trustees consisted of Charles Glock (President), Spivack's widow Dorothy Eweson, Marvin Bressler, Melvin Tumin, Clara Shapiro, and Joan Waldron. In 1990, ASA was awarded a planning grant of $25,000 for the purpose of preparing a full proposal on how the ASA would manage and disperse such a gift. A Committee, chaired by Cora Marrett, and including Wendy Baldwin, Ivar Berg, Robert Dentler, Reynolds Farley, Marvin Olsen, Jill Quadagno, Matilda White Riley, Joan Waring, and William Julius Wilson was formed to prepare the proposal. Executive Officer D'Antonio (joined in 1990 by Felice Levine, the incoming Executive Officer), participated in writing the proposal. The initial set of proposals were directed to identifying projects that might be attractive to the Cornerhouse Board; Levine and D'Antonio shifted the orientation in 1990 to propose the establishment of a fund to create a lasting program connecting sociological research and social policy to honor Sydney S. Spivack. The ASA Council closely monitored this process throughout.

ASA proposed to create a program in applied social research and social policy, which would have two interdependent goals: to advance applied social policy, and to foster the use of sociological knowledge in social policy. It would have the broadest definition of institutions of modern society—including government, law, business, family, religion, health, welfare, and education. Building on existing research and various programs in applied sociology that had been developed over the prior decade, ASA outlined a range of possible initiatives on topics covering issues such as homelessness, poverty, health care, crime prevention, gender inequality, aging, discrimination, and environmental degradation. A point of emphasis in ASA's proposal was that sound policies should be based on sound research and knowledge, that sociology has a long tradition of substantial contribution in this area, and that ASA has in place mechanisms to pursue program goals effectively.

The proposal was accepted by the Cornerhouse Trustees, and the funds were awarded to ASA in February 1991 to establish the Sydney S. Spivack Program in Applied Social Research and Social Policy. The award, valued at $750,000 at the time, was formally presented by Eweson at the Awards Ceremony and Presidential session at the August Annual Meeting in Cincinnati. (See Chapter 2 on Spivack Program.)

Publications

The Association placed a high priority during the 1980s on supporting a publications program focused on excellence and enhancement of the discipline of sociology, while being attentive to prudent decisions on managing such a program. The publications program accounted for the largest expenditure and revenue stream in the Association budget and, therefore, was consistently a priority on the Council's agenda.

From 1984 to the present, the Publications Program has been directed at the Executive Office by Karen Gray Edwards, who has managed and coordinated its activities (including representation of ASA with journal editors, Committee on Publications, and Boyd Printing Company) through a complex period of enormous change in technologies related to publication processes. Edwards also produced the Association newsletter, *Footnotes*, the *Employment Bulletin*, and handled most other aspects of ASA's publishing needs—such as those relating to the Annual Meeting.

Scope of Publications

At the end of 1990, ASA was publishing nine journals: the *American Sociological Review* (*ASR*), *Contemporary Sociology* (*CS*), *Journal of Health and Social Behavior* (*JHSB*), *Social Psychology Quarterly* (*SPQ*), *Sociology of Education* (*SOE*), *Teaching Sociology* (*TS*), *Sociological Theory* (*ST*), and *Sociological Practice Review* (*SPR*), *Sociological Methodology* (*SM*), several guides and directories, as well as the *Employment Bulletin* (*EB*), and the Association newsletter, *Footnotes*. The ASA added 24 volumes to the *Rose Monograph Series* from 1980 through 1990, published by the Cambridge University Press (see Appendix 18).

In January 1986, Council formalized a *Presidential Series* for publications of ASA presidents with the provision "that no president be required to publish in the Series and that editorial control by publishers not be permitted." (see Appendix 19) The *Series* consisted of volumes produced by presidents drawn primarily from the Thematic and Plenary Sessions of their Annual Meetings. Council terminated the Executive Office's involvement in the *Presidential Series* at the conclusion of the Sage Publication Inc. contract in 1991 because of low publisher interest in the project.

Changes in the Publication Program During the 1980s

During the 1980s, several important changes took place in the ASA publications program. In 1982, after a lapse of eight years, the Executive Office again published the *Biographical Directory of Members* (the *Directory of Members* was published for each of these eight years, but not with biographical entries). *The American Sociologist (TAS)* was phased out in 1982 (the last issue was published in November 1982) after considerable debate, including discussion on possibly incorporating *TAS* into *ASR*.

In 1986, three ASA journals evolved through major transitions: (1) After almost two years of negotiations with Sage Publications, ASA purchased *Teaching Sociology* in 1985, and began publication of *TS* in 1986. The *Teaching Newsletter* was also incorporated into *TS* at this time. (2) The journal *Sociological Theory*, previously published as an annual review by Jossey-Bass, became a semi-annual journal published by the ASA. (3) The 1986 volume of the annual *Sociological Methodology* was published by the ASA after it was purchased from Jossey-Bass. In addition, the 15-year *Cumulative Index* for *ASR, CS, JHSB, SPQ, SOE, TAS, SM*, and *ST* (and including the *American Journal of Sociology* and *Social Forces*) was also published in 1986. In 1989, ASA Council approved a recommendation from the Committee on Publications for a contract with Basil Blackwell for the publication of *SM* and *ST*.

One new journal, *Sociological Practice Review* (*SPR*), was added to the ASA's family of journals on a three-year experimental basis. In January 1987, Council approved a resolution to establish *SPR* and directed that a campaign be undertaken to raise funds to help launch it. In 1989, Robert Dentler was chosen as the first editor. After publication of two issues in 1990, *SPR* was published quarterly in 1991 and 1992, and discontinued at the end of 1992 because of low subscriptions (see Chapter 2).

Attention was also focused on the production quality and appearance of ASA journals. In 1985, Council approved a Committee on Publication's request that the quality of paper used for journals be upgraded, because libraries were complaining "that bound volumes of ASA journals are falling apart due to the use of low quality paper." (Council Minutes, August 31, 1985) Journal covers were also upgraded, type size increased, page numbers added to journals, and shrink-wrapping introduced for mailings.

Council also took action to formalize certain legal aspects of its publishing program. In 1982, Council accepted a copyright statement for inclusion in ASA journals. In 1985, Council approved trademarking its journals, and passed a resolution that ASA not lend its logo to outsiders but that it publish its own journals. Council also issued a policy statement that ASA regard all publications as experimental and conduct periodic reviews of them. In addition, Council passed a resolution giving Irving Horowitz (on behalf of Transaction Publishers) the right to use the name *The American Sociologist* for a new publication, with the stipulation that the name reverts to ASA if publication does not move forward or ceases to exist.

By the end of the 1980s, electronic and desktop publishing emerged as an option for producing publications, although in January 1990, "Council expressed concern for any shifting of the burden for editorial cost to individual authors, many of whom have fewer office resources available for manuscript preparation. There was sentiment that electronically submitted manuscript should be optional."

General Policies and Priorities

Over the years, especially through its Publications Committee, ASA dealt with a wide range of policy issues affecting the publishing program. A comprehensive review of ASA's publishing program took place in 1980 and 1981 resulting in a 145-page report of analysis, alternative publication models, and recommendations. At the end of the decade, Secretary Michael Aiken "praised the action of the Publication[s] Committee in establishing a five year plan to define other goals and targets." (Council Minutes, August 12, 1989)

Some of the recurring themes emerging from these policy reviews include determining appropriate responses to: (1) members' enthusiasm for publications (especially the startup of new ones)—while dealing with the scarce resources of ASA, (2) Association responsibility and support for specialty journals, (3) the need to conduct periodic reviews of all ASA journals, (4) procedures for evaluating submissions to publications, (5) procedures for setting editorial policies, (6) sound governance structures, (7) circulation growth and the viability of journals, and (7) questions about relevance of journals, especially of *ASR* and its content.

A few other examples of issues and debates pertaining to publications from the 1980s include the following: In February 1986, Council resolved that, at this time, it would not publish a social issues journal; that the voting members of the Committee on Publications should continue the practice of meeting separately; and that the position of "editor-designate" be created to deal with problems in transitions between editors on ASA journals. In January 1991, Council rejected a request from the Committee on Publications for jurisdiction over *Footnotes*. Council also appointed a subcommittee of Council to conduct a review of *Footnotes*, including the identification of appropriate criteria for evaluating the newsletter.

Also, several times during the 1980s criticism was raised in Council about the relevance and representativeness of *ASR*. In January 1982, some Council members noted that, over the years, *ASR* "has not changed much." Council members were encouraged to conduct a "minisurvey" on why authors do or do not choose to publish articles in *ASR* (Council Minutes, January 1982, and September 9,1982). A Report of the Committee to Evaluate the *ASR* was also produced in 1984. Again, on August 28, 1988, Council member Edna Bonacich asked for formation of a committee to review *ASR* in response to "continuing indications of dissatisfaction." A resolution was passed authorizing President Joan Huber, in consultation with the chair of the Committee on Publications, to jointly develop a mechanism for review of *ASR*.

A Subcommittee of the Committee on Publications (COP) consisting of Maureen T. Hallinan (Chair), Jeylan T. Mortimer, Teresa A. Sullivan, and Douglas W. Maynard was appointed in 1989 to evaluate *ASR*. The Subcommittee produced a report in the fall of 1989, which was circulated to Council (along with a packet of 23 letters compiled by Bonacich from section officers who responded to a call for input on the issue) in December 1989. The Report was presented to Council at the January 1990 meeting: "At issue was whether or not the *ASR* did or should represent the diversity of topical interests in the discipline, as well as theoretical and methodological orientations." After considerable discussion, (and defeat of a motion that the next editor "be strongly sympathetic to qualitative work"), a consensus emerged that publication of special issues of *ASR* which would reflect diversity of the discipline should be further explored by the Committee on Publications.

Political Science Review of Journals

ASA journals received high ratings in a 1986 survey of political scientists, who were asked to evaluate journal quality. The survey undertaken by three political scientists was published in the American Political Science Association's *PS: Political Science and Politics* and reported in the December 1989 edition of *Footnotes*. Out of some 78 journals, the two leading general sociological journals received very high scores: *ASR* was tied in second place with the American Political Science Association's flagship journal, the *American Political Science Review;* the *American Journal of Sociology* was tied in fourth place with the *American Journal of Political Science*. This strong showing of sociological journals in another social science field with its own journals and specialized content was significant in another respect: The 1986 evaluation was a replication of a 1975 study which produced similar high ratings for sociological journals.

Teaching Services Program (TSP)

A key component of the Association's activities during the 1980s was promoting excellence in teaching. ASA initiatives in these areas were complemented by joint efforts with regional associations, the critical support of ASA committees and past officers and, in some areas, collaborations with other social science organizations.

Core TSP Activities

The cornerstone of ASA's activity in this area was the Teaching Services Program (TSP), a multifaceted effort dedicated to improving and supporting teaching quality and effectiveness. Established in 1975 with grants from the Lilly Foundation and the Fund for the Improvement of Postsecondary Education (FIPSE), TSP was launched under the leadership of Hans Mauksch, Executive Officer during 1975 and 1976, who provided the vision and impetus for the Program. Lawrence J. Rhoades handled most project activities from 1978 to 1981; and Carla Howery, Assistant Executive Director and Director for TSP from 1981 to 1993, brought the program to fruition and provided it with continuing energy, guidance, and direction.

Originally located at Oberlin College, TSP became a part of ASA operations in the 1978 budget year. Hans Mauksch, who had coordinated the fieldwork of the Teaching Resources Group (TRG) from its inception, retired from the project in 1983. In 1985, Council moved the TRG to a campus location with a Field Coordinator appointed for three-year terms, with rotations among colleges and universities similar to that of journal editors. William Ewens of Michigan State University was named the first Field Coordinator (1985–88); he was succeeded by J. Michael Brooks, Texas Christian University (1988–91), and Jeanne H. Ballantine, Wright State University (1991–94).

The purchase by the ASA of the journal *Teaching Sociology* from Sage Publications in 1985 also marked a "culmination of a fifteen year period of activity designed to make teaching a central part of Association activities." (D'Antonio in *Footnotes*, August 1991:2) Theodore Wagenaar of Miami University was the first editor. The TSP had its own *Teaching Newsletter*, which was published bimonthly under the editorship (1982–85) of Carla Howery, who also managed all aspects of the publication. The *Teaching Newsletter* was merged with *Teaching Sociology* (*TS*) when ASA began publication of *TS* in 1986. The Section on Undergraduate Education also published a newsletter.

In the 1980s, the TSP consisted of three components:

- The Teaching Resources Center (TRC) distributed products written by and for sociologists to help them as teachers. By 1990, the TRC had produced more than 75 titles and in 1990 sold more than $35,000 worth of teaching materials. Individual members of the Association and sections of the Association contributed extensively to materials in the TRC. The materials disseminated through the Center (which was located at the Executive Office) included manuscripts, modules, syllabi sets, curriculum development materials, discussions of specific teaching skills such as lecturing, guidelines for training graduate students, and other information that shapes effective teaching. (See Appendix 20 for a detailed list of TRC products offered in 1990.)

- The teaching workshop series consisted of seminars conducted throughout the year on a variety of topics of interest to teachers of sociology. Designed to enhance teaching skills, the workshops were directed by the Field Coordinators with the advice and input of the Director of TSP. Workshop topics included discussions on teaching sexism and racism, and on substance abuse and prevention; and sessions on applied sociology, starting local research centers, academic leadership for chairpersons and deans, integrating internships in sociology programs, and using computers in teaching. (Appendix 20 contains a list of all workshops conducted in the series from 1980–91.)

- An ASA Teaching Resources Group (TRG) had members who were available for evaluating and advising departments seeking to improve their sociology programs. Hans Mauksch and Gail Woodstock, University of Missouri-Columbia, coordinated the first TRG Workshops in 1980–81. By the end of 1990, the TRG, which was also self-supporting, offered administrative reviews, diagnostic services, and self-improvement services. In 1990, site visits to more than a dozen campuses during the year were organized, calling upon a pool of some 60 scholars especially trained for these visits.

Both the Teaching Workshops and the TRG were largely financially and administratively independent of the Executive Office (site visit expenses were borne by the institution which hosted the event), although the Director of the TSP (Howery) was on the ASA staff, and budgets for the workshops were approved by the ASA.

In 1988, a Departmental Services Program was established at ASA to improve the distribution of ASA services and publications to departments through a nonvoting departmental membership in the Association. Packages of resources and materials were offered to sociology departments at discounted prices in a simplified ordering process. Brochures and other materials were also prepared and disseminated on ASA publications, resources, and services available to departments.

In 1992, the TSP became part of the Association's Academic and Professional Affairs Program (APAP) (see Chapter 2).

Other Projects on Education

Throughout the 1980s, ASA also focused attention on improving the quality of sociology education at the high school, undergraduate, and graduate levels. Stimulated by reports such as *A Nation at Risk* by the President's Commission on Excellence in Education, ASA collaborated with other social science associations and the National Council for Social Studies (NCSS) in outreach efforts aimed at the high school level "to transform the teaching of sociology and the other social sciences via a rigorous, more scientific approach to the social studies." (D'Antonio in *Footnotes*, August 1990:2)

ASA members also participated in discussions with AAAS leaders in evaluating Project 2061, an effort still ongoing by AAAS to rethink all facets about the teaching and curriculum of the physical and social sciences and mathematics. To assist the ASA to monitor and provide input to these new initiatives for sociology and the social sciences at the K-12 level, a new Task Force on Sociology in the Elementary and Secondary Schools was formed which included Paul Gray (Chair), Joseph DeMartini, Dean Dorn, Carla Howery, Paul Lindsay, Douglas Snyder, Jerold Starr, and Donna Wendel. The Task Force was charged to "examine and strengthen the role of the ASA in the areas of secondary and elementary education and the teaching of sociology at the precollege level." It presented its report to Council and was converted by Council to a standing committee on August 27, 1991.

In 1985, ASA participated in two national conferences on the "The Improvement of Undergraduate Education" at Wingspread in Racine, WI. The impetus for the conference was several national reports on the status of undergraduate education in the U.S. and, especially, the works of Ernest Boyer, President of the Carnegie Endowment for the Advancement of Teaching. The ASA participants included approximately 40 sociologists who reported on lessons learned from the TRG experiences.

In collaboration with eleven other disciplines, ASA was involved from 1988 to 1990 in an initiative to examine the undergraduate major. Sponsored by the Association of American Colleges (AAC), this three-year project on "Study in Depth" was designed to address issues such as the core concepts of disciplines and the sequencing of courses. A Task Force, consisting of Carla Howery, Paul Eberts, Zelda Gamson, Theodore Wagenaar, Kathleen Crittenden, Robert Davis, and Catherine Berheide was appointed in 1989 "to assess current practices and make recommendations on the undergraduate major in sociology." Council endorsed ASA's report, which was published as *Liberal Learning and the Sociology Major* (Washington, DC: American Sociological Association, 1990), authored by Eberts et al. (Summaries of the report were published in *Footnotes* in January, February, and August 1991.) The report offered recommendations and guidelines for strengthening the undergraduate sociology major.

Efforts were also undertaken to assess graduate education. Under the leadership of 1989 ASA President Joan Huber, a Task Force on Graduate Education in the Year 2000 was established by ASA Council in 1988 to examine issues, trends, and curricula in light of new findings in research methodology and theory, major research directions, and recruitment needs. The Task Force consisted of Joan Huber (Chair), Michael Aiken, Lois DeFleur, Mayer Zald, Kenneth Land, Barbara Heyns, Stanley Lieberson, William J. Wilson, and William D'Antonio and worked closely with graduate department chairs. (See also Chapter 2.)

Professional Development Program (PDP)

A high priority during the 1980s was placed on advancing programs relating to "Sociological Practice," a term used to refer to sociologists who worked in business, government, non-profit associations, or who were self-employed. This term was used, according to D'Antonio, because no other single term like "applied' or "policy-oriented," adequately described the professional activities of sociologists in these work settings (*Footnotes*, August 1991:12).

ASA activities focused on expanding and enhancing the employment opportunities of sociologists working outside of the academy through three major programs: the Professional Development Program (PDP), the Certification Program, and the Public Information Program. To guide the work in this area, Council appointed four Ad Hoc Committees: the Committee on Certification of Sociologists; the Committee on Trends in the Occupation of Sociologists; the Committee on Restructuring Professional Opportunities in Sociology; and the Committee on Federal Standards for the Employment of Sociologists. There was also a special Task Force on Sociology and the Media, the interests of which overlapped with those of the other committees.

Sociological Practice: 1981–86

In December 1981, a major workshop was held on "Directions in Applied Sociology," which signaled the importance of and the new commitment of ASA to sociological practice. Sponsored by the Committee on Professional Opportunities in Applied Sociology, and chaired by Howard Freeman, the workshop was held in Washington to a capacity audience. ASA Presidents Peter Rossi (1980) and William Foote Whyte (1981)—both of whom considered themselves applied sociologists—strongly supported ASA moves in this direction. The 1981 workshop and the volume emanating from it, *Applied Sociology* edited by Howard E. Freeman, Russell R. Dynes, Peter H. Rossi and William F. Whyte (Jossey-Bass, 1983), provided the inspiration for much of the growth and development in this area during the 1980s.

Bettina Huber directed the programmatic activities relating to sociological practice at the Executive Office from 1981 to 1986. She led efforts to prepare materials on job opportunities; organize professional development workshops; conduct surveys and analyze data trends of members who were employed in business, government and non-profit associations; and design seminars for federal government personnel officers on the potential for sociological skills. Huber was also responsible for the Certification Program at the Executive Office.

Congressional Fellowships were also established to give sociologists the opportunity to put "theory into practice, and bring her/his scholarly knowledge to bear on a major issue confronting a congressional committee." (*Footnotes*, March 1983:4) Carol Weiss (Harvard University) and William R. Freudenburg (Washington State University) were appointed ASA Congressional Fellows in 1983, and Raymond Russell received a fellowship in 1984 at the U.S. General Accounting Office.

In 1985, Council approved the establishment of the ASA Distinguished Career Award for the Practice of Sociology with Conrad Taeuber as its first recipient in 1986.

Sociological Practice: 1986–91

In 1986, on the recommendation of the Committee on Sociological Practice, Council authorized the appointment of an Assistant Executive Officer to head a program to advance and better serve the needs of sociologists working in practice settings. Council viewed this as an act "to institutionalize the practice of sociology." Stephen Buff was appointed the first Director of the Professional Development Program (PDP) in July 1986. The Committee, chaired by Ruth Love, Bonneville Power Administration, had been at work for more than a year on an action plan for this new program that would focus on:

- Developing and disseminating career materials;

- Working with sociology departments to modify curricula so that graduates would be prepared for a wider range of job opportunities;

- Working with media to demonstrate the value of sociology and sociological skills;

- Making connections for sociologists with potential employers at all levels of government, business, industry and non-profit settings; and

- Serving as a general catalyst to help un- and underemployed sociologists find new venues for employing their skills.

The work of PDP was coordinated by the ASA Committee on Federal Standards for the Employment of Sociologists. The major forms of outreach of the PDP were seminars and other presentations (mostly at federal agencies), publications, and resource materials. See Appendix 21 for a detailed list of PDP projects, but from 1986 to 1990, major program activities included:

- Sponsoring 14 seminars at 18 federal agencies aimed at informing federal officials about the research and work skills of sociologists; for example, William Darrow (Centers for Disease Control) and Rosemary C. R. Taylor (Tufts and Harvard Universities) spoke on the AIDS epidemic for the U.S. Public Health Service; and John Kasarda (North Carolina-Chapel Hill) spoke before Branch Chiefs at the U.S. Department of Housing and Urban Development (HUD) on "Dual Cities: People and Jobs on a Collision Course;"

- Publishing *The Internship Handbook* (with TRC), and "*How to Join the Federal Workforce and Advance Your Career*" along with other career materials and resources;

- Preparing a document for new standards for the classification of jobs in the federal government, which were adopted in 1989 and updated the 1960s federal standards for the employment of sociologists;

- Cooperating with CAFLIS, the Coalition of Associations for Foreign Language and International Studies, whose programs aimed at foreign language study and international education were of interest to many in sociology; and

- Working with the New York-based Sociologists in Business to produce a video on corporate sociologists in the advertising, banking, insurance, communications, and consumer research industries.

Certification Program

The Association had grappled with issues relating to certification for nearly 30 years before Council officially launched the Certification Program in 1985. Several years earlier, in 1979, ASA responded to a revived interest in the issue by creating a Committee on Certification to explore establishing a program of certification. A report to Council in 1981 indicated that, "some sociologists feel that they are being blocked from entering some fields due to the lack of certification in sociology. Most frequently cited was the field of mental health where other disciplines [notably psychology] have established licensing laws which restrict the practice of others." (Council Minutes, January 1981) Council, however, raised questions about the extent to which sociologists were being excluded from jobs because of lack of certification; and noted its reluctance to deal with certification issues in its meetings during 1981 and 82.

A report outlining the need for certification of PhD and MA sociologists was presented to Council on September 3, 1983. In January 1984, after nearly three years of work, Council approved a Certification Program and created a Committee on Certification consisting of Edgar F. Borgatta (Chair), Otto Larsen, Katherine Marconi, Barbara Williams, and Mayer Zald. It was charged with drafting a set of procedures for certifying sociologists at the MA and PhD levels. The procedures were subsequently presented to state and regional representatives during the 1984 Annual Meeting in San Antonio. Council also directed that the consequences of certification on the social and behavioral sciences be further studied, and that a clearinghouse be established for collecting information on certification for use by state monitors.

In the interim report of August 1984, the Committee concluded that the primary purpose of ASA's certification program should be to "provide an additional qualification that will assist our graduates in dealing with the pressures of a highly competitive job market without adversely affecting academics or other sociologists who are not certified." (Kennedy, *Footnotes*, November 1994:4) The Committee also recommended that six certification committees be appointed for various broad specialty areas (demography, law and social control, medical sociology, organizational analysis, social policy and evaluation, and social psychology).

Ultimately, there was very little demand for certification. The August 1990 report of the Ad Hoc Committee on Evaluating the PhD Certification Program recommended that, because of low interest (only 62 persons had been certified in the first four years of that program), the "Oversight Committee be designated as the sole body to maintain and administer the program. This simplified structure would serve as a more cost-effective strategy in place of the existing seven committees." (Council Minutes, August 14, 1990)

Public Information Program

A Public Information Program was established in 1985 to promote public understanding of sociology and the work of sociologists. In 1932, the American Sociological Society had formed a committee to consider means for disseminating important sociological research findings. Although it had only a two-year life span, ASA implemented some of this committee's recommendation more than 50 years later (Howery, *Footnotes*, January 1985:1–2).

The Committee on Public Information, composed of Claude S. Fischer, William C. Martin, J. Ronald Milavsky, Rosalie Schram, Bernard Roshco, Lawrence J. Rhoades, and Michael Useem, presented a report to Council in January 1986 focused on the need to develop a public information program aimed at promoting an understanding of the discipline based on "scientific merit and practical value" and on improving the image of the profession of sociology among policymakers, funding officers, the media, and others who shape public opinion.

The Public Information Program aimed to achieve its goals by coordinating with COSSA and other social science associations in sponsoring joint press conferences and other similar events, cultivating the Washington press corps (especially the wire services), monitoring ASA publications for topics of general interest, expanding and improving media coverage of the Annual Meeting, recognizing the professional contributions of sociologists whose work appears in the media, training sociologists to deal more effectively with the press, and emphasizing media coverage beyond the newspaper story.

Minority Fellowship Programs

The ASA has supported minority students through various programs, activities, and events continuously since the mid-1970s. The main programmatic activities in support of minority students during the 1980s were the: (1) Minority Fellowship Program (MFP), which was launched in 1974 with funds primarily from NIMH to support training of minority sociologists in mental health, (2) Cornerhouse Dissertation Grants (funded from 1974–86), (3) training fellowships in clinical work funded by an NIMH grant (1979–84), and (4) the Minority Opportunity Summer Training (MOST) Program of summer institutes for minority undergraduates funded by the Ford Foundation beginning in 1990.

The largest of these programs was the MFP, with about $550,000 authorized each year from July 1984 through July 1989. By its 10th anniversary in 1984, MFP had funded 219 minority students, of whom 72 had obtained their PhDs (Appendix 23). The MFP program was under the direction of Paul Williams (1981–85) and Lionel Maldonado (1985–90).

Precarious Position of the MFP

The MFP was in a precarious position throughout much of the 1980s because of the drastic cuts in social research programs by the NIMH. The tenuous situation of the MFP led Council to consider new strategies for broadening the base of financial support for the program. MFP Council Liaison Michael Aiken presented the following goals for MFP to Council on August 30, 1984: "(1) a concerted effort to broaden the financial base of the MFP program beyond NIMH; (2) expansion of the program so that by the end of the decade there will be 20–25 new entrants annually and a total of 100–120 students receiving support; [and] (3) establishment of a task force to assist the MFP Committee in achieving the two objectives just outlined."

Council approved the general goals as stated, and in 1985 appointed a Task Force consisting of Charles Willie (Chair), Margaret Andersen, James E. Blackwell, Bonnie Thornton Dill, Richard O. Hope, Cheryl Leggon, Clarence Y. H. Lo, Lloyd H. Rogler, William Sewell, and Howard Taylor. Lionel Maldonado who had been appointed Director of MFP that year was also on the Task Force, and Charles Bonjean succeeded Valerie Oppenheimer as Council Liaison in 1986. The Task Force met several times, developed strategies for new funding sources, and contacted foundations for funding the MFP, however, with little success.

In 1986, ASA received a $27,000 planning grant from the Ford Foundation to review MFP and chart new directions for the program. The Ford Foundation also recommended that the Task Force focus its attention in several areas that have "historically plagued" many minority fellowship programs, including recruitment of undergraduate minority students into predoctoral studies, retention of students in graduate programs, and support in launching careers in the form of a postdoctoral component. Ford suggested that a fellowship program that incorporated all of these elements might appeal to foundations, and even serve as a model for other programs *(Footnotes*, March 1987:10). With Council's approval, the MFP Task Force refocused its attention on revamping the MFP program.

MOST I

In January 1988, Council restructured the MFP to allow for expanding to undergraduates and post-doctoral initiatives, and authorized ASA's direct financial support for the director and administrative assistant, so they could devote full time to the expanded program. In 1990, under the leadership of MFP Director Lionel Maldonado, ASA launched the new initiative, named the Minority Opportunity Summer Training (MOST) Program, consisting of summer institutes for minority undergraduates. The purpose of the new program (which in 1993 became known as "MOST I") was "to promote quality training in sociology as a means to attract undergraduates of color to graduate education. ASA built the institutes around three key approaches: relevant and rigorous curriculum, research-based training, and faculty mentoring of undergraduates." (Levine, Rodriguez, Howery, Latoni-Rodriguez 2002:7)

MOST I was funded by a two-year award of $185,000 from the Ford Foundation, which covered most of the costs for the first two institutes at the University of Delaware and the University of Wisconsin at Madison in 1990 and 1991. The Maurice Falk Medical Fund also gave $20,000 to help pay the travel costs for the faculty of the Institutes, and the American Sociological Foundation made its first grant in the amount of $10,000 to help cover other institute-related activities. The program was limited to 15 students per session at each university. MOST I continued with summer institutes in the summers of 1992 and 1993 at the University of Michigan and the University of California-Berkeley, and later evolved into the second MOST Program—a key ASA initiative during the 1990s, funded by the Ford Foundation.

Other Funding Sources

In addition to the NIMH funding, the MFP also received $10,000–15,000 each year from the Cornerhouse Fund in support of dissertation research for minority students. A *Footnotes* article in October 1985 noted that, "[s]ince 1975, the Cornerhouse Fund has contributed $172,000 to the Minority Fellowship Program. Grants from the Fund have supported 61 students, 45 of whom have received their doctorates." (October 1985:5) The article also reported that seven new Sydney Spivack dissertation awards from the Fund were made in 1985 and 1986. The Cornerhouse Fund discontinued its funding to MFP in 1986. As noted above (see Cornerhouse Fund), in 1991, all remaining monies in the Fund were awarded to the ASA to support sociological initiatives related to public policy in the Spivack Program (see Spivack Program in Chapter 2).

As ASA moved to improve the MFP, it worked vigorously to obtain new sources of support to compensate for the loss of NIMH funding. Assistance came in various forms. Graduate departments in which ASA fellows were enrolled gave tuition and fee waivers and/or remissions, as well as some matching stipends. A contribution of $10,000 by members ensured continued dissertation support for 1986 and 1987. Sociologists for Women in Society (SWS) established a dissertation fellowship, which provided funds (1986–87); and Alpha Kappa Delta (AKD), the Association of Black Sociologists (ABS), the Eastern Sociological Association, Southwestern Sociological Association, the Mid-West Sociological Society, and the Mid-South Sociological Association made contributions to MFP. NIMH also awarded ASA a supplement of nearly $25,000 that enabled MFP to make six dissertation grants for the 1987–88 academic year.

Maldonado noted in 1987 that the special drive helped to keep the program stable at 22 fellows a year, about half the size of ASA's stated goal of support for 40 students per year. To keep MFP stable beyond 1987, ASA increased its financial support of administrative costs to 40 percent for 1987 and 50 percent for 1988 and thereafter. Maldonado reported site visits to 11 campuses in 1988 to explain program guidelines, recruit applicants, develop closer ties between departments and the ASA, and press for permanent funding arrangements for ASA fellows.

MFP was reviewed formally in 1989 by an NIMH-appointed panel, and earned a near-perfect priority score of 115. MFP was again renewed for three years by NIMH at the level of $350,000 annually, and was supplemented by tuition and stipend support from many of the universities cooperating in the program (D'Antonio, *Footnotes*, August 1990:2). This grant also provided some support for the Program Director and the Administrative Assistant, as well as for special dissertation awards. Maldonado reported restoration of the full amount of the 1992 NIMH grant to graduate fellowships following cuts in 1991.

7. OTHER ASA PROGRAMS AND ACTIVITIES

ASA continued to promote and advance collaborative relationships with regional and other sociological associations, to develop sources of support for sociologists—such as the Teaching Endowment Fund, and the Fund for the Advancement of the Discipline (FAD)—and to strengthen programs that focused on students. In addition, ASA directed considerable attention to activities on international issues. This section describes the Honors and FAD Programs and ASA's participation in international programs and activities as illustrative of some of these other Association commitments.

ASA Honors Program

On August 13, 1989, Council approved the Honors Program as an official program of the ASA. Founded in 1974 by John H. Shope of Salisbury State College as a undergraduate teaching demonstration for introductory sociology, the ASA Honors Program was not an official function of the ASA until 1989. Indeed, its name derived from the Program's focus on the participation of undergraduates in the ASA Annual Meetings, and for the honor and recognition received by the outstanding students who were selected for the Program. Professor William Brown directed the Program in 1978 and 1979 and Burton Wright of the University of Central Florida (UCF) was Director from 1980 to 1989.

At the suggestion of then ASA President William Foote Whyte, Honors Program students were invited to become participant-observers at the 1981 Annual Meeting in Toronto. Students attended Annual Meeting sessions, kept detailed accounts of impressions and insights, and wrote a formal paper about their experiences. Program participants were expected to pay their own way (including tuition to UCF) and received transfer credits at their home institution.

In December 1988, Wright met with Executive Office staff and suggested that ASA formally adopt the Honors Program after his retirement the following year. In January 1989, Council appointed an ad hoc committee to further explore the issue, and later that year, voted its formal approval. A subcommittee of Council was appointed to oversee the Program, which was administered by the Executive Office. No appropriations were requested from ASA for the Program.

Fund for the Advancement of the Discipline (FAD)

Origins

At its June 1973 meeting, Council established a Committee on the Problems of the Discipline (POD) to ". . . facilitate efforts by small groups of sociologists (probably three to six persons) to meet periodically, to exchange ideas, and to produce working papers . . . focused on basic theoretical and methodological issues in sociology . . . ." (Council Minutes, June 1973). It consisted of Hubert T. Blalock (Chair), Matilda White Riley, and Gary T. Marx, and became a full Subcommittee of Council by 1977. The idea for such an effort emanated from a Council subcommittee in the early 1970s co-chaired by Blalock and James Davis, which explored possible committee initiatives on core problems of the discipline.

At the same June 1973 meeting, Council created a special Fund for the Advancement of the Discipline (FAD) at the request of the Executive Officer as a means whereby contributions could be made by persons, including the assignment of book royalties, to support projects approved by the POD Program. Royalties from books by Blalock launched the Fund, but income from other sources (including a membership drive) contributed as well. By October, 1981 FAD had grown to nearly $85,000 (Rossi Report, August 1982).

The Committee on POD began to administer a Small Grants Program in 1974, implementing the ideas expressed by Blalock and Davis in 1971. From 1974 to 1979, however, the funding for this Small Grants Program came from general ASA operating funds and not from the restricted FAD funds. Indeed, according to the Rossi Report, Blalock had put consistent pressure on Council to use general operating funds for the small grants program so that FAD funds could grow. FAD funds, however, were appropriated in 1979 for startup of the new journal *Sociological Theory* (Rossi Report 1982).

In 1980, Council approved the allocation of $8,000 from FAD for each of three years for the POD Small Grants Program. Subsequently, funds from the FAD program were allocated to the Small Grants Program from 1982 to 1987, when new support was available from an award of $45,000 by the National Science Foundation in support of a small grants program for 1987–89. Since 1987, ASA has matched the NSF awards in support of the Program—which then became known as the ASA/NSF Small Grants Program, and since the early 1990s, popularly known as the FAD Program. (See Chapter 2.)

FAD in the 1980s

Council affirmed that the small grants program supported by FAD was established with the explicit goal of advancing the discipline rather than the profession of sociology, and that the uses of FAD be restricted for "workshops, seminars or mini-courses whose aim is to upgrade the scholarly and research skills of ASA members as appropriate uses of the Fund." (Council Minutes, September 9, 1982) Criteria for funding small grants under FAD were also discussed in considerable detail at the 1982 Council meeting (and again in February 1985). A proposal was also made to establish a Committee for the Advancement of the Profession, but the idea was not formally implemented.

From 1980 to 1990 up to eight grants were made under the POD Program each year—with the exception of 1983 and 1984 when FAD funded three Congressional Fellows. The POD awards were made for a wide range of research projects and conferences, including, for example: conceptual problems in the field of collective behavior, survey approaches to community organizations, research on the welfare state, equality and inequality in China, urban theory and policy, ethnicity and race, high school sociology, ideology and social organization, and case studies and organization analysis.

From 1980 to 1990, FAD was also used to support other types of ventures as well. In August 1982, Council allocated $25,000 from FAD in support of the Consortium of Social Science Research Associations (COSSA). FAD funds ($8,000) were also used to begin work on indexing the ASA journals.

International Issues and Human Rights

ASA focused attention on international connections in a number of ways during the 1980s, including through: (1) Annual Meeting themes and events, and support for foreign scholar participation; (2) formal and informal representation of ASA in international organizations and at international conferences and events; (3) actions of ASA Council, committees, and sections; (4) initiatives implemented through the Executive Office to establish collaborations with foreign scholars and provide assistance when solicited by sociologists in other countries; and (5) leadership and participation of many individual members of ASA in professional activities on cross-national issues.

ASA also addressed human rights violations of scholars and others through various Council and Executive Office actions, including resolutions, policy statements, and campaigns to raise awareness of and protest these situations.

Annual Meeting Events

President Melvin L. Kohn particularly focused on international connections through the theme "Cross-National Research As An Analytic Strategy" for the 1987 Annual Meeting. In his first Council meeting on September 6, 1986, President Kohn said "that his one substantive mission for the coming year was to strengthen the ties between U.S. and world sociology . . . emphasizing the strategic advantages of cross-national research and bringing to the attention of U.S. sociologists the value of the work being done by fellow sociologists in other countries." To support travel for scholars from Eastern Europe and the Third World, ASA obtained funds from NSF, the International Research Exchanges Board (IREX), and other sources. ASA also provided a contingency fund of $10,000 for travel for foreign scholars, but Kohn noted on August 20, 1987 that this fund was not needed.

Formal Soviet-U.S. exchanges began at the 1985 ASA Annual Meeting, and were solidified in other ways over the next several years through joint ventures described more fully below.

Participation in International Organizations

The International Sociological Association (ISA), the major international organization of sociologists, holds its meetings every four years. Delegations representing ASA attended these meetings (in Mexico City in 1982, New Delhi in 1986, and Madrid in 1990). Individual members presented papers and/or served in organizing functions. ASA members also participated in activities of the International Institute of Sociology (IIS), which holds meetings every two years, and is organized along more fluid lines.

ASA obtained funds from NSF (and from the Smithsonian for the 1986 meeting in New Delhi) to help defray the cost of member travel to the meetings. ASA's relationship with the ISA reflected certain complexities and tensions. For example, questions arose in 1990 regarding an ISA statement condemning racist doctrines, but also asserting that, "sociologists who do not endorse the above statement are not welcome at the Congress." (D'Antonio, *Footnotes*, March 1990:2) Alejandro Portes, the ASA's new delegate to the ISA thought that, although the resolution was commendable, the last sentence amounted to a loyalty oath restricting freedom of expression of scholars, and requested guidance from Council on how to proceed. While Council took a strong stand against Apartheid, it voted its strong opposition to the sentence that was de facto a "loyalty oath."

ASA Committee Actions

The ASA has had committees focused on international issues since 1965. From 1975 to 1990 the Committee on World Sociology (which became the Committee on International Sociology in 1990) was actively engaged in projects and, in 1991, created "area liaison coordinators" for ten world regions.

In 1990 in a report on Exchanges with Foreign Scholars, Craig J. Calhoun, Louis W. Goodman, and Melvin L. Kohn presented Council with a "preliminary report on the whole range of international relations of the ASA and issues arising from the internationalization of sociology. The report detailed existing ASA capacities and experience in the international field, noting the role of the Committee on World Sociology, ASA Sections, formal and informal representation to various other organizations and agencies, and activities within the Executive Office. It also highlighted the dramatic increase in visiting foreign scholars and the ways in which ASA could facilitate the flow;

similarly the importance of integrating international knowledge into U.S. sociology was noted." (Council Minutes, January 1990) Council took several actions relating to the Committee on World Sociology and reaffirmed the direction in which the Subcommittee was moving.

Other Forms of Collaborations

ASA members participated extensively in international conferences and other forms of collaborations. For example, in 1984, Alice Rossi headed a delegation to China that included William Parish, Nan Lin, and Shelby Stewman to establish contact with sociologists there. In 1990, Barry Wellman, Stanley Lieberson, and Thomas Pettigrew attended a small international workshop in Bulgaria on the ethnic crisis in Bulgaria.

ASA also supported evolving relationships with sociologists in the Soviet Union and other Eastern European countries. In a program jointly sponsored by the ASA and the International Research and Exchange Board (IREX), and in cooperation with the Soviet Sociological Association, a series of five seminars brought together Soviet and U.S. sociologists to discuss the feasibility of the exchange of lecturers and graduate students and collaboration in research projects. These cooperative efforts involved a number of graduate departments in the United States, and in the fall of 1989, 17 Soviet graduate students entered U.S. graduate programs. In March 1990, a Soviet sociologist and four students from Russia, Lithuania, Estonia, and Latvia addressed a gathering on Capitol Hill. Especially after the fall of the Berlin Wall in 1989, joint projects also flourished with social scientists in Poland, Hungary, and throughout Eastern Europe.

The ASA supported the establishment of the U.S. Institute of Peace in 1984. Executive Officers Dynes and D'Antonio participated in coalition planning meetings at the National Peace Academy Foundation in Washington and sociologists James H. Laue and Elise Boulding served on the Foundation's Board of Directors. In 1985, Council also approved William Gamson's proposal that ASA jointly sponsor a conference on "Global Conflict and Cooperation: A Sociological Perspective," with the Institute for Global Conflict and Cooperation at the University of California.

ASA's commitment to advancing interest on international topics was manifested in other ways as well. *Footnotes* featured many articles on international issues and on ASA's (and sociology's) international connections. The December 1987 issue of *Footnotes* included a full-page letter from the School of Sociology at the University in Nicaragua and its petition for assistance. Many ASA Business Meeting resolutions at Annual Meetings raised awareness of international issues, and Council voted on a number of these, including opposition to apartheid, nuclear arms proliferation, and the 1991 Gulf War; and urging the U.S. to remain a member of UNESCO. Concern was raised frequently in Council on restrictions placed by governments on sociologists (and social scientists in general) in pursuing professional and scientific work—including formal protests against the U.S. government for not granting visas to visiting sociologists, or for pursuing policies of surveillance by intelligence agencies at ASA meetings and elsewhere.

Human Rights

The ASA lodged protests on behalf of sociologists in many places around the world for violations of their individual human rights, or for those detained or restricted in pursuing professional, scientific work (e.g., in Turkey, Korea, Malaysia, Yugoslavia, the Soviet Union, Taiwan, South Africa, and Japan). ASA also expressed its solidarity with Soviet scientists and Polish sociologists and raised awareness and a strong voice of protest at the murder of two sociologists in November 1989 in San Salvador. Members also expressed their opposition to human rights abuses generally through resolutions of the ASA Business Meeting—such as those calling for respect of the human rights, civil liberties, and sovereignty of the peoples of Central America and for supporting the sanctuary movement for refugees from Guatemala and El Salvador.

Concern was expressed on the situation in South Africa in the form of anti-apartheid policies and direct calls for the release of Nelson Mandela and all other political prisoners. Council responded directly by specifying in its investments policies that "no investment [would be made] in South African companies" (see discussion under Budgets and Fiscal Policies).

8. ANNUAL MEETING

The Annual Meeting grew in size and scope during the 1980s, with increasing levels of activity (i.e., number of instructional seminars, workshops, didactic seminars, and services to graduate students and others). In 1984, with the reorganization of the Executive Office, a Meetings Manager position was created, and Janet Astner was appointed to fill the position. Since 1984, she has had primary responsibility for directing all ASA meetings (with the Annual Meeting by far the largest event), and has directed ASA meetings through this period of growth and major changes in technologies and meetings support systems. During the 1980s, a number of temporary staff, summer interns, and consultants provided support for the Annual Meetings.

Certain issues and concerns relating to the Annual Meeting reoccurred during the 1980s, including: (1) how to present the *Preliminary Program* in the best way possible at the lowest cost, (2) the rationale behind the rotation schedule for Annual Meeting sites, and (3) criteria for site selection (e.g., disqualifying sites if they did not support the Equal Rights Amendment [ERA], or if they had anti-sodomy laws). Indeed, beginning with the 1980s, ASA began to implement policies regarding site selection for meetings based on consideration of factors such as support for the ERA amendment. Considerable emphasis was also placed on improving services in specialized areas including support for childcare, the disabled, and students.

Several Annual Meetings were memorable for the extraordinary challenges they presented. In 1985, three weeks before the meeting took place, a series of electrical fires at the Washington Hilton, where the meeting was to be held, closed down the hotel. A frantic search was made for alternate space over a five-day period, resulting in selection of the Washington Convention Center as the site for the meeting. Transferring operations at the last minute to a new location generated a host of problems and obstacles, especially at a time when technical support systems were not very flexible. However, under the direction of Executive Officer D'Antonio and Convention and Meetings Manager Janet Astner, the Annual Meeting of 1985 was a success—with a record number of sociologists in attendance.

There was also an unexpected relocation of the 1986 Annual Meeting from San Francisco to New York because of the building expansion and remodeling schedules at the San Francisco Hilton, but this occurred with enough advance notice for planning purposes.

Headed by ASA President Matilda White Riley, in 1985, the 1986 Program Committee reconfigured the open submission component of the Annual Meeting Program by reducing and broadening Regular Session topics. The session slots that were opened up by this change were then reserved for use by Regular Session organizers who received a high number of good submissions. This restructuring of the open submission process reached out more broadly to the scientific community and remains in effect today.

Other significant events relating to Annual Meetings in the 1980s include:

- In 1982, Council adopted a resolution that held organizers responsible for the preregistration of participants in their sessions, after discovering that 32 percent of program participants never registered for the 1982 Meeting.

- In 1983, a survey of the membership showed that cost, location, and dates were the three most important variables influencing decisions on whether to attend meetings. Members also indicated a preference for dates between August 10 and 25, and which avoided the Labor Day holiday, and for major tourist spots as sites.
- In 1988, Council reaffirmed its policy to restrict member participation in Annual Meetings to two places in the program.

Chapter 2

The 1991–2002 Period: Transformations and Innovations

1. INTRODUCTION

Background and Context

The period from 1991 through 2002 was a time of major transformation at the American Sociological Association. During this period, ASA elaborated its mission as the national professional association for sociologists, honed its programmatic objectives, and clarified its organizational roles and structure. In large part, major changes emanated by design from strategic planning that took place at ASA in 1992 under the leadership of Felice J. Levine, the 11th Executive Officer. Both the changes that took place and the process that produced them reflected a shift in how the Association did business—with Council focusing on setting policy and broad oversight functions and the professional staff assuming greater responsibility for implementing and achieving Council goals and framing issues that required policy guidance. Over time, this shift produced changes not only in how Council and the Executive Officer worked in collaboration, but also in how staff, committees, and tasks evolved in their functions. During this period, the ASA Council also enacted significant changes in the governance structure of the Association. All of these activities affected and altered ASA in dramatic ways.

Executive Officer Levine led a review of ASA's operations and management in fall 1992, after a one-year period learning first-hand from staff and committees about priorities and challenges. During 1991 and 1992, Executive Office staff also completed a comprehensive Request for Proposals (RFP) for a new computer and software system based on considerable analysis of ASA's work and goals. This examination of technological needs provided the framework for the review of organizational functions and goals known as the strategic plan. The result of this exercise, as set forth below, was presented by Secretary Arlene Kaplan Daniels and Levine to the Committee on the Executive Office and Budget (EOB) in December 1992, meeting with EOB's unanimous and enthusiastic approval. In January 1993, the strategic plan was presented to Council, which also affirmed its support overall and through a series of actions related to specific programs.

In a February 1994 article in *Footnotes*, "Moving Forward for Sociology," Levine summarized the results of the planning. She observed that, over its history, ASA had evolved from an association that, in addition to an annual meeting and a journal, performed secretariat functions (keeping records and sending out communications) to a complex organization that provided a wide range of services (a roster of journals, other publications, meetings, workshops, programs, representation of the discipline) to the membership. Like other scientific and professional societies, ASA was faced with the challenge of defining common objectives, shifting to deliberative planning, articulating goals and operating plans, reorienting resources around key goals, creating an effective organizational structure within the Executive Office, and taking steps (including through the use of technology) to produce business efficiencies and practices. The key objectives for ASA and the Executive Office were defined as "serving sociologists in their work, advancing sociology as a science and profession, and promoting the contributions and use of sociology to society." Ultimately embraced as the ASA mission statement, they provided the framework for defining priorities, annual planning, and specifying six core programs for ASA: Academic and Professional Affairs, Minority Affairs, Applied Social Research and Social Policy (the Sydney S. Spivack Program), Research on the Discipline and Profession, Public Affairs, and Public Information. They also led to other office improvements in the use of technology and the organization of human resources (e.g., establishment of a membership and customer service department).

As reflected in the mission statement, the ASA of the 1990s positioned itself for systemic change to advance the discipline to supplant case-by-case strategies. A fundamental aspect of these changes was the Executive Office staff becoming more proactive in achieving the Association's goals. Testimonies, Congressional seminars, formal and informal meetings with research and science policy leaders, and the establishment of the Department Affiliates Program to facilitate work and communications with sociology department chairs were among the types of activities undertaken to help accomplish the objectives of ASA. The ASA homepage was initiated in 1995, and introduced significant new opportunities for publication, communication, and products and processes related to the Annual Meeting. Even the move of the ASA headquarters in 1998 from a four-story row house to one floor of a recently renovated office building enhanced the capacity of the Executive Office staff to work more efficiently and collaboratively on ASA functions and activities.

Other transformations to ASA systems and practices were guided or approved by Council: The role of the Committee on Freedom of Research and Teaching (COFRAT) was substantially altered in 1994; section finances, administration, and governance were reformed in 1997; the committee structure was dramatically changed in 1998; and the system of dues was essentially decoupled from journal subscriptions in 2001. A major revision of the Code of Ethics took place from 1994 to 1996 and was overwhelming adopted by the ASA membership in 1997. In 1999, Council approved the *Guidelines for the ASA Publications Portfolio*, publishing was considerably enhanced by innovative electronic publishing techniques, and a new ASA-wide journal (*Contexts*) and a first-ever section journal (*City and Community*) were developed and launched.

Finally, although the goal of promoting diversity and inclusiveness in the profession and discipline had been key to ASA for many years, enhanced emphasis was placed on achieving diversity, especially for historically underrepresented groups. (For example, Minority Affairs became a designated programmatic area under the 1992 strategic plan.) In August 1995 and January 1996, Council reaffirmed through two resolutions its commitment to diversity and to the view that excellence and inclusiveness are complementary, not competitive goals. The two statements on diversity read as follows:

> Much of the vitality of ASA flows from its diverse membership. With this in mind, it is the policy of the ASA to include people of color, women, sociologists from smaller institutions or who work in government, business, or other applied settings, and international scholars in all of its programmatic activities and in the business of the Association." (Adopted by Council, August 23–24, 1995) (ASA homepage)

> The American Sociological Association, in its policies and programs, is committed to achieving diversity in the discipline, especially for historically underrepresented groups. The Association encourages a continued commitment to activities—whether through the Minority Affairs Program, Annual Meetings, sections, committees, or other initiatives—that work to accomplish this goal. The Association further commends the principle of diversity across the profession and to the nation." (Adopted by Council, January 1996)

Changes in the American Sociological Association took place in the context of a political, social, and economic climate that might best be described as variable in its receptivity to sociology and the social sciences. This period was marked on the one hand by rescinding of the American Teenage Study by the Secretary of the U.S. Department of Health and Human Services in 1991 and threatened consolidation of sociology departments in Kentucky-wide institutions of higher education in 1993 and 1994, to the establishment of the Office of Behavioral and Social Sciences Research (OBSSR) at the National Institutes of Health in 1995, and a marked improvement in the academic job market for sociologists observable in the late 1990s. And, while Clinton-era politics were generally friendlier to the concerns of the social sciences (the administration was data oriented and interested in research on issues ranging from the environment to race), there were still considerable challenges in the form of policies that could erode the capacity to do quality research (e.g., the Contract with America included proposed legislation to limit research, challenges to funding of social science programs at NSF). During this time, ASA situated itself to address problems and promote opportunities as was appropriate to changing conditions and circumstances.

A pivotal event at the beginning of the new century and millennium was the terrorist attacks in the United States on September 11, 2001, and the rising threats of new forms of terrorism around the world. These events have challenged sociologists and other social scientists to contribute their knowledge and expertise to public understanding of the causes and consequences of such incidences. ASA took immediate steps in 2001 and 2002 to post relevant social science information on the ASA website and to cosponsor a briefing on responses to disasters, risk, and threat, and the Association continues to engage substantially in such efforts (see also Chapter 3).

Revisiting Strategic Planning in 1998

In the summer of 1998, EOB revisited the issue of strategic planning for the ASA. The discussion that ensued is important, both from the perspective of "taking stock" of the programmatic work of the 1990s, as well as for the insights on the future of sociology and the ASA in the short- and long-term. EOB identified a number of challenges to the profession (which could have either positive or negative consequences), including: "demographic shifts in the profession, electronic communication and delivery of our work, international leadership in sociology, funding for research, interdisciplinary and cross-disciplinary work, and deprofessionalization of the academic enterprise. EOB identified the important thrusts for the Association: attention to responsible use of sociology in public policy, to undergraduate and graduate students and their training, to sociologists who are in non-sociology departments." (EOB Minutes June 30–July 1, 1998)

EOB affirmed the importance of ongoing programs and the priorities for future work emphasized by Executive Officer Levine. David Featherman noted positively the transformation and development of programmatic activities over time, and also the use of external funding to develop the most successful programmatic activities. (Excluding awards to the MFP program, about $2 million in funding was awarded to ASA during the 1990s, including from the National Science Foundation, the W. K. Kellogg Foundation, the Ford Foundation, and also smaller amounts from the MacArthur Foundation, the North-South Foundation, and the Soros Foundation.)

2. MEMBERSHIP AND FISCAL STATUS

ASA Membership in the 1990s

Overall membership levels were fairly steady around 13,000 members throughout the 1990s. The student membership category was the major growth category throughout the 1990s, although retention rates for students were lower from year-to-year than for the other membership categories. (Retention rates represent the percentage of members from year-to-year who chose to renew membership.) Regular membership declined somewhat, but retention rates remained high (over 80 percent) during this period. Records show that this rate was considered high when benchmarked against other professional associations.

The ASA Executive Office mounted a vigorous campaign to attract new members to the Association, particularly at times when membership levels were low. Outreach efforts focused on members slow to renew, as well as to members of regional and aligned associations such as the American Association of University Professors, and sections of the American Public Health Association. Members who did not renew their membership were targeted in special personalized campaigns using emails, faxes, and phone calls.

Profile of ASA Members and Minority Participation in ASA

Membership in 2001

The Association began to collect demographic data systematically on its membership in the early 1980s (see Chapter 1). With the implementation of NOAH—a dedicated database management and information system—in the early 1990s, ASA's capacity to report on membership improved significantly, even though nonreporting of certain key information (e.g., race and ethnicity) still presented challenges in related analyses. Reporting up-to-date information on members became even more accessible on an ongoing basis (see following section on Information Technology) after the installation of the Windows based e-NOAH in 2001, but extracting information for research purposes from the NOAH database remained complex and required customized services. Such advances however, made possible generating reports of the membership along various dimensions for administrative and research purposes as required.

A report on ASA membership in 2001 was prepared under the direction of Roberta Spalter-Roth, Director of the Research Program on the Discipline and Profession, and published in *Footnotes* (January 2002:8–9) and on the ASA homepage. The report indicates that ASA had a total of 12,365 members at the end of the 2001 membership year (see Appendix 12 for membership counts by year). Counts in 2001 were overall lower than the years before or after due to an expected attrition in membership associated with the 2001 dues restructuring and due to the comparatively lower attendance at the Annual Meeting in Anaheim. In 2001, most members (53 percent) were in the regular membership category (i.e., those who have full voting rights), followed by student members (30 percent), associates (11 percent), and emeritus members (6 percent).

Although the demographic data (based on the Membership Application/Renewal forms) must be considered with some caution because many members do not provide information on key characteristics, they do provide some indication of the overall composition of the membership in 2001 (see Appendix 13, Tables 3 and 4). Data on the regular members category only show that men were still the majority (55 percent) of these members. Of regular members who reported race/ethnicity, about 80 percent were non-Hispanic white, 5 percent reported their race/ethnicity as African American, 5 percent as Asian American, 3 percent as Hispanic/Latino, and less than 1 percent as Native American. The average age for all regular members was 51 years, and the modal age was 54. For most regular members 85 percent reported a doctorate, 12 percent a master's-level degree, and only 3 percent a bachelors degree as their highest degree.

Most ASA regular members in 2001 who reported their employment status were employed and employed full-time (82 percent). Of these, 80 percent were employed in institutions of higher education; 14 percent worked in federal, state, or local governments, or not-for-profit organizations; and 3 percent either owned businesses that employed others or were independent consultants. The overwhelming majority reported an academic or teaching appointment (73 percent), about 13 percent had a research position and about 7 percent had an administrative position.

The remaining 7 percent were distributed among postdoctoral fellowships, applied, non-research positions, writing/editorial positions, and other work positions.

These data showed significant differences between men and women in income levels, with men earning more than women at the top income categories. Asian Americans, Hispanic/Latinos and Native Americans also were less likely to be in the top income categories and more likely to be in the bottom category.

Trends for the future demographic distribution of ASA members can be seen in looking at the student member category. Relatively large proportions of student members in 2001 were female (65 percent female, 35 percent male). Also, large proportions of non-whites in the total membership were students, although the large nonresponse rate on this data element suggests that these data should be viewed with caution.

ASA Membership Trends

Although there have been changes in definitions of membership and income categories over the past quarter century (and also fairly high rates of non-response on key items on each survey), some estimates of trends in membership on key demographic variables are possible. Comparison of breakdowns on gender and race/ethnicity show a significant increase in women members since 1981. Looking over all categories of membership, women were 33 percent of the members in 1982, 41 percent in 1992, and 52 percent in 2001. Minorities made up less than 10 percent of the membership in 1981, about 15 percent in 1991, and about 20 percent in 2001 (see Appendix 13).

Participation Trends by Women and Minorities, 1982–2002

Following directives of the ASA Council in the early 1980s, the Association also began to collect data on participation of minorities and women in certain areas of its governance (i.e., ASA Council/elected positions, committees, presidential appointments, section councils, journal editorial boards). Appendix 13, Table 5 contains summary data of trends in participation by minorities and women in these areas since 1982. Data for these analyses were compiled from 1982 data presented by Paul Williams in a December 1982 *Footnotes* article, and from the NOAH database for 1992 and 2002 governance activities (prepared for this report). ASA members who serve on councils, editorial boards, in committees, and task forces generally report their race and ethnicity on their membership forms (nonreporting rates on any relevant data element was seven percent or less).

Overall women and minorities have increased their share of positions in all areas of ASA governance over the past quarter century. Minorities comprised 6 percent of Council in 1982, 25 percent in 1992, and 32 percent in 2002. Similar patterns occurred for minorities with respect to representation on constitutional/elected committees (no representation in 1982, 21 percent in 1992, and 35 percent in 2002); in Council, presidential appointments (20 percent in 1982, 21 percent in 1992, and 31 percent in 2002); on editorial boards (6 percent in 1982, 7 percent in 1992, and 23 percent in 2002); and elected section officers (6 percent in 1982, 13 percent in 1992, and 18 percent in 2002).

The analysis of data at these points in time show that women also have increased their representation in all areas, except on Council in 2002. Women, however, made up more than half of all ASA Councils each year from 1991 to 1999. Women now comprise more than one-half of all elected/constitutional committees, and elected section councils, and nearly half of editorial boards and presidential/Council appointments. The Committee on the Status of Women in Sociology presented detailed findings on these and related issues in its 2004 *Final Report* to Council (2004 Report of the American Sociological Association's Committee on the Status of Women in Sociology, *Final Report*, October 22, 2004:24–27).

Budgets and Finances

Audit reports indicate that ASA was financially solid during the 1990s, generally running budget surpluses each year. Investment portfolios reflected the overall market trends, and showed healthy growth throughout the period, with a slight decline as the markets turned downward in the late 1990s. At year end 2000, the revenue of the ASA was $5,134,720 and expenditures $4,891,431. Net assets stood at $8,912,764 (2000 Audit in *Footnotes*, September 2001:16–17).

Investment Portfolio and ASA Reserve Funds

In August 1992, based on a review of the investment strategy over recent years and an examination of a number of investment firms, the Committee on the Executive Office and Budget (EOB) under Secretary Beth Hess decided to change from the Seattle Office of Oppenheimer & Co. to Fiduciary Trust International, Inc. as the manager of ASA accounts. Premised on the value of periodic reexamination of investment management and accordingly based on a resolution of EOB in June 1996, a Subcommittee (consisting of Secretary Teresa Sullivan, Chair, Neil Smelser, David Featherman, and Felice Levine, ex officio) reviewed long-term financial management and investment firms, including Fiduciary International. The EOB Subcommittee scheduled meetings with four firms on December 9, 1996. After the interviews, EOB concluded that Fiduciary Trust International provided a better understanding of how ASA guidelines were being used in handling the ASA portfolio, and that ASA should continue with the current investment firm, but closely monitor the firm's performance and strategy.

A further review of investment policy, asset allocation strategy, and investment management firms was undertaken by Secretary Florence Bonner, Executive Officer Felice Levine, and Deputy Executive Officer Phoebe Stevenson on behalf of EOB in 1999. One impetus was an interest in determining how best to handle the net revenue from sale of the headquarters building on 1722 N Street. Given the shakier state of the economy and the passage of years since the last review, EOB sought this review, which included an independent assessment of the ASA investment portfolio and investment strategies by Robert W. Everett, an investment advisor and Assistant Professor of Finance at the Johns Hopkins University.

At its July 1999 meeting, EOB considered the performance of Fiduciary International, the investment strategy for each of the ASA funds, and the wisdom of a value versus growth investment strategy—the latter being ASA's long-term approach. Everett joined the EOB for this discussion. As set forth in the July 1999 minutes, in January 2000, EOB identified a set of guidelines relating to the Building Fund, decided to continue to purchase only investment grade bonds, clarified policies related to fair labor practices, and specified general parameters for asset allocation. The EOB recognized that the use of a value investment strategy might provide ASA with possible diversification. EOB urged the ASA Secretary and the Executive Officer to interview value managers and potentially solicit proposals that might apply to the Building Fund only. In January 2000, EOB considered value versus growth strategies and proposals for each. EOB concluded that the Building Fund should remain with Fiduciary International and selected an asset allocation that EOB thought would maximize the opportunity for necessary growth in this Fund.

Socially Responsible Investments

An investment policy was defined by Council in 1987 and is monitored by EOB. Two sets of guidelines were articulated at that time (see Chapter 1). During the 1990s several modifications were made to the 1987 policy, such that social responsibility guidelines were further specified as: (1) No funds shall be invested in companies whose economic activity is primarily engaged in defense contracting; and (2) No funds shall be invested in companies with 'notorious' anti-labor policies, deficient records on worker health and safety, or firms whose policies have been prejudicial to minorities. The ban on investing in companies directly involved in or doing business in South Africa was lifted in November 1993. Guidelines were also established for allocation, divestiture, and monitoring of ASA's portfolio.

In December 1997, Council member Joe Feagin raised the issue of proactively pursuing socially responsible investments, but Council members noted that it is easier to craft policies on what not to invest in as opposed to what to invest in. Council also pointed out that ASA would need to decide whether to have categories of industries which to avoid. This issue was raised again in June 1998, but the consensus reached in EOB was that ASA "should not go further down the path to more restrictive (socially responsible) guidelines. Other than the steps already taken (e.g., vote proxies for the companies where ASA owns stock), EOB recommended no further changes in ASA's investment policy." (EOB Minutes, June 1998 and January 1999)

Development Campaign

In 1998, when he was President-Elect of the ASA, Alejandro Portes convened a committee to explore the possibilities of a long-range development campaign for the Association. The goal of such an effort as envisioned by Portes was to "put in place a long-term fundraising effort that would enable the Association to undertake important programmatic work on behalf of the discipline. He thought that a fundraising strategy [planned as part of the Centennial commemoration in 2005] to promote and advance 'Sociology for the New Century' would be the right legacy to leave for sociology and for ASA." (Council Minutes, February 2001)

Council supported Portes' interests in moving in this direction and the initial explorations being pursued. Other issues, in particular the controversy about the *ASR* editorship (see later discussion in chapter), deferred moving ahead on a campaign in 1999. Though Council took several subsequent actions to activate such a Campaign through 2001 and Executive Officer Levine signaled an interest in working on building such a reservoir of resources to advance the discipline, this activity was not a priority in the way that it was for Portes. Council tabled the idea on August 20, 2002 on the recommendation of EOB due to the weak state of the economy as well as consideration that such a campaign linked "to the centennial might not be the best approach."

3. EXECUTIVE OFFICE

Executive Office Staffing

The ASA Executive Office evolved through two major changes over the past two decades: (1) The reorganization of 1984 created a managerial structure which shaped functionality and created the base for professionalizing services offered by ASA (Chapter 1); and (2) As noted in the introduction to this chapter, the realignment of professional functions in the Executive Office resulting from the strategic planning of 1992 further defined staff roles and responsibilities. An aspect of the strategic plan was to create more symmetry and synergism across significant activities within ASA. Thus, in 1993 in addition to articulating six programs, the Annual Meeting and publications activities were more formally featured as central program emphases. In 1993, sociologists who previously were considered Assistant Directors became Program Directors. By 1996, job titles changed from Manager to Director for Janet L. Astner (Meeting Services) and Karen G. Edwards (Publications), thus completing the transformation to creating a tier of senior director-level staff.

The enormous changes in information technologies and their application in almost all areas of Association activity since 1980 also dramatically altered how the ASA does its work. As part of implementing the strategic plan, for example, the integration of technology in membership services (membership, order fulfillment, benefits and other queries) made possible a Membership and Customer Services unit under a single umbrella. While this transformation began in 1990 with a program assistant with computer-based skills being promoted to Membership Manager, by 1994 staffing further altered to hire a manager with database management skills. Other administrative and operational functions were also enhanced. For example, the financial operations of ASA became professionalized by upgrading the position of Bookkeeper to Controller, also in 1994. Similarly, efforts were made to enhance the operations of and support to committees and sections by clearer demarcation of a Governance Coordinator position.

Most significantly, while the Association has substantially increased its services and professional activities, the number of staff persons has held fairly steady since the early 1990s: At the end of 2000, the ASA Executive Office staff consisted of 23 persons compared with 22 persons at the end of 1990. (The Executive Office Staff as of January 1, 2005 is listed in Appendix 30.)

Felice J. Levine served as the 11th Executive Officer of the Association from August 1, 1991 to May 15, 2002. She succeeded William V. D'Antonio and was appointed Executive Officer-designate in May 1990 until she joined the ASA staff in August 1991. Levine was Director of the Law and Social Science Program at the National Science Foundation before becoming Executive Director of the ASA. In the fall of 2001, Levine announced her resignation as Executive Officer to become the Executive Director of the American Educational Research Association (AERA) in Washington, DC. She was succeeded by Sally T. Hillsman in May 2002 (Chapter 3).

During the 1990s, three new professional positions were created:

- Phoebe H. Stevenson was appointed Deputy Executive Officer for finance, administration, and planning effective August 1, 1994. (She remained in that position until 2002.) In this restructuring, Deputy Executive Officer Carla B. Howery was to focus on programs and program planning. Howery was appointed Deputy Executive Officer in the fall of 1990 to succeed Lionel Maldonado by Executive Officer William D'Antonio in consultation with Executive Officer-designate Felice Levine.

- Along with establishing program emphases in Public Affairs and Public Information in 1993 came an alignment of duties and ultimately staffing. In 1995, Edward Hatcher was hired as the first Director of Public Affairs and Public Information and held this position from 1995 to 1997. Executive Officer Levine, who had led these functions from 1993 to 1995 with a special assistant, resumed doing so in 1997 without director-level staff, though a Program Assistant was hired in June 2000, and independent consultant Katherine Rosich coordinated public information functions from 1998 to 2001. Lee Herring was hired as Director commencing employment in April 2002.

- The position of Director of the Research Program on the Discipline and Profession was held by Carla Howery up to 1995, by Cynthia Costello in 1995 and 1996; and Roberta Spalter-Roth, 1997 to the present (2005).

Other professional staff during the 1990s included:

- The Academic and Professional Affairs Program (APAP), established in 1993 on the foundations of the Teaching Services Program and the Professional Development Program of the 1980s, was directed by Janet Mancini Billson in 1993 and 1994 and by Carla Howery since 1995.

- The Sydney S. Spivack Program in Applied Social Research and Social Policy, a new program element established in 1992, was co-directed by Carla Howery and Executive Officer Levine from 1992 to 2002, with a special assistant from 1993 to 1996 and other program assistants providing support thereafter.

- The Minority Fellowship Program and the Minority Opportunities through Summer Training Program (MOST) was directed by Tahi Mottl (1991–92) and Lionel Maldonado (Interim Director in 1992 from California State University-San Marcos). By 1993, these initiatives were grouped into the broader program rubric entitled the Minority Affairs Program (MAP). The MAP Directors were Florence Bonner (Interim Director in 1993 from Howard University); Ramon Torrecilha (1993–94, Torrecilha from the Social Science Research Council through the 1994–95 academic year); Havidán Rodríguez (1995–97; Rodriguez from the University of Puerto Rico-Mayagüez through the 1997–98 academic year); Edward Murguia (1998–2000); and Alfonso R. Latoni-Rodríguez (2000–2). Jean Shin served as Acting Director in 2002 and 2003, and Mercedes Rubio was appointed Director in August 2003. (Appendix 9 contains a list of all Directors of the Minority Fellowship Program from 1974 to the present.)

ASA also had two visiting sociologists on staff in the late 1990s. Patricia White, Program Director in Sociology at the National Science Foundation, spent a year at ASA (1997) under an Intergovernmental Personnel Act (IPA) arrangement to work in areas relating to the advancement of the discipline. John Kennedy, Director of the Center for Survey Research at the University of Indiana also spent 1997 working on a number of governance and policy issues key to ASA (e.g., examination of the certification program, on committee restructuring). In addition, between 1999 and 2002, the staff included three postdoctoral fellows: Jan Thomas (1999–2001), Sunhwa Lee (2000), and Stacey Merola (2001–2).

Information Technology (IT)

A defining issue of the 1990s was the dramatic and rapid change in the area of information technology (IT). ASA built capacity in IT applications by appointing professionals to plan and develop IT functions, implementing new technologies and systems to improve delivery of services, and adapting these systems to improve communications among sociologists and others.

Phoebe Stevenson brought background and expertise to this function throughout much of the 1990s—first as a consultant, and from 1994 to 2002 as a Deputy Executive Officer. In addition, external consultants, especially those from Computer Strategies Inc., and contractual arrangements with JL Systems, Inc., Association Links (the latter led by the primary technology staff from the American Psychological Association), and Spectrum Systems (for email support and innovations) enabled ASA to built on substantial experience relating to membership associations and to create new systems. Over time, staff skills were enhanced and staff was hired with computer-based skills and responsibilities. By winter 2002, ASA hired its first Director of Information Technology.

1993–94: NOAH, LAN, and Email service

The first major technology-related transformations of the 1990s took place in 1993. This installation included faster and more powerful computers with all workstations in the Executive Office linked in a local area network (LAN). Key to the new office automated technology was the installation of NOAH, a specialized association database and management software system developed by JL Systems in Annandale, VA. For the first time, ASA had a system specifically designed for the activities and functions of membership associations—including a link to financial record keeping and reporting through Open System. The installation also included a powerful document organizer called PCDOCS that permitted sharing documents easily and a search facility and backup system for archiving documents.

The cost of the full system including hardware, training, and consultancies was approximately $300,000. In 1992, ASA retained Computer Strategies, Inc. led by Fran Craig to assist staff in writing the RFP and selecting the firm to provide the hardware, service, and support. In 1993, Phoebe Stevenson, then with Computer Strategies, provided management and oversight of the installation of the full project.

Other innovations followed rapidly. Council approved the development of an electronic bulletin board for sociology department chairs (Chairlink), which was launched in May 1994. Also, ASA made a transition to have email through Microsoft mail at all work stations. And, the introduction of a FAX server also allowed receipt of faxes at staff workstations. In January 1995, Council moved to establish committees that would further explore issues such as electronic publishing and to advise ASA on the use of high technology for professional communications more generally. Barry Wellman was appointed Chair of the Advisory Group on Electronic Networking (also included Earl Babbie, Howard Becker, Kathleen Carley, Roxanne Hiltz, Rob Kling, Marc Smith, Lee Sproull, John Walsh, and Phoebe Stevenson). The Subcommittee on Electronic Publishing was comprised of Dan Clawson, Adrian Rafferty, Teresa Sullivan, Barry Wellman, and Felice Levine.

1995–96: ASA Homepage and Electronic Publishing

A major new phase of technological innovation began in 1995 with the launching of the ASA website. President Hallinan encouraged the Executive Office "to continue working with aligned associations in their experiences with technology and to continue to explore an even wider range of electronic communications." (Council Minutes, August 23, 1995)

In April 1996, the *Employment Bulletin* (*EB*) was published online with print copies available to members and subscribers. In early 1996, the Advisory Committee on Electronic Networking and the Committee on Publication's Committee on Electronic Publications met and discussed goals and objectives, which (for both groups) generally were to: encourage informal electronic scholarly discussion among sociologists, facilitate discussion among interest groups, enhance the ASA's dissemination of information, develop sociologists' ability to participate electronically, develop electronic means of publication, develop digital sociological libraries, develop standard forms of referencing online "publications," and ascertain members' capabilities and desires (*Footnotes*, March 1996:10).

The report of the Advisory Group on Electronic Communications, chaired by Barry Wellman, was presented to Council in January 1996. Council discussed guidelines for access to ASA members' electronic addresses, and concluded that members should be given the option to indicate their willingness to have their email addresses published or released to inquirers. Council also discussed the possibilities for electronic and Internet access at the Annual Meeting, but considered it not feasible. At its August 19, 1996 Meeting, Council also asked the Executive Office to contact all sections offering them the opportunity to have a homepage and listservs related to their area of interest. Council encouraged the Advisory Group to continue to bring forward ideas.

Major changes were also occurring in electronic publishing. At the January 1996 Meeting, Council approved a move to explore and negotiate an agreement with the Mellon Foundation for the electronic delivery of ASA journals. The delivery system, eventually known as JSTOR (Journal Storage), initially included back issues of all ASA journals, except *Teaching Sociology*, with a moving five-year wall to become accessible. *ASR*, *CS*, and *JHSB* were the first journals to be digitized and released (see Publications for further discussion)

By the summer of 1996, the ASA homepage was updated and expanded to include information on the Annual Meeting, important initiatives (e.g., the revision of the Code of Ethics), membership information, briefings on important legislative matters (e.g., The Family Privacy Protection Act known as H.R. 1271), links with section homepages, announcements of new ASA publications, the online version of the *Employment Bulletin*, and forms to which members could respond (e.g., call for nominations to ASA committees). The fax-on-demand capability was also well received and utilized by the membership.

1997–2000: Systems Upgrades and Web Enhancement

As information and computer applications grew in number and complexity (and the existing system approached the end of its usefulness), it became clear that enhancements and upgrades would be needed to the overall system in order to continue to operate efficiently. Based on recommendations of EOB and a budgetary allocation by ASA Council in January 1997, new computer equipment was purchased and the transition to an upgraded system was made in the spring of 1997. The equipment was purchased through ASA's operating revenues, from which $110,000 was approved for this transition.

By June 1998, ASA entered into an agreement with the APA in which the APA would act as an "invisible" host for the ASA website through which it would provide journal management software and secure online financial transactions where individuals could join, renew membership, purchase publications, register for the Annual Meeting, and so forth. The enhanced website also included a secure member-only restricted area with member emails, department directories, and abstracts of the articles from ASA journals with keyword and text-search capacity.

Throughout 1999, enhancements continued to be made to the homepage and other information systems. By January 2000, the Great Plains Dynamics, a new accounting system that was Y2K compliant was installed and the website redesign was completed, with the member-only area of the website launched that month. By January 2000, listservs for all sections were operating effectively; officers were communicating by email on closed announcement lists, and section members were receiving regular electronic communications. Sections also had the option of operating open discussion listservs; and ASA members could verify and update their own membership information online.

During 2000, a secure server was installed to facilitate online membership applications and renewals and registration for the Annual Meeting. As recommended by EOB and approved by Council in August 1999, the online *Preliminary Program* became the primary source of detailed information for the 2000 Annual Meeting. A program summary was published as an insert in the May 2000 edition of *Footnotes* (with print copies available on request from the Executive office). Starting in 2000, members no longer received a printed copy of the Preliminary Program.

2001–2: Major Enhancements to NOAH and the ASA Homepage

Throughout 2001, ASA introduced other major improvements in its information technology systems. An upgraded e-NOAH membership and contact database system was installed in the Executive Office in the spring of 2001. This new Windows-based version of the now-familiar database offered major enhancements—including the use of Internet portals to support e-commerce online, which also gave members the capacity to view and change information on their records. The upgrades included new desktop PCs to use the new system (the last round of hardware update was in the spring of 1997).

Major enhancements also occurred on the ASA homepage, which in some areas complemented the upgrades in the NOAH membership database. In January 2001, Hal Warren, Chief Executive Officer of Association Links (and also on the senior technology staff at APA), reported to Council on ASA website innovations and short- and long-term plans for the ASA website development. The major website developments included: (1) Windows web-based version of *Tracker*, an annual meeting organizer/proceedings applications that could receive online submission of abstracts and papers; (2) an electronic member announcement system, tables of contents and abstracts for ASA journals; and (3) a web-based annual meeting program backed by a robust search engine that would permit many different types of searches and sorts, and would have the capacity (among other innovations) to produce personal schedules.

By the summer of 2001, most of the systems enhancements were fully installed: The conversion of the new membership database and management system was completed, and the refinement of the systems was in progress. In 2001, Deputy Executive Officer Stevenson reported on the steady increases in the utilization of the ASA website: In the fourth quarter of 1999, there were 131 unique visitors per day; this rose to 486 per day in the same period in 2000, and to 565 per day in the second quarter of 2001. ASA also continued to expand Internet-based applications on the website across most programmatic areas and in functions related to the Annual Meeting. EOB members commented on the positive improvements of the online *Preliminary Program* for the Annual Meeting—most thought it more user-friendly to read and to search, and found the personal scheduler a welcome new feature.

The ASA leadership demonstrated both a willingness to expand the use of the new technologies for enhancing communications and increasing productivity, as well as a sensitivity to those who might be adverse to or intimidated by these innovations. In January 2000, based on an initiative arising from President Feagin's concerns about a segment of members feeling alienated, and his expressed interest in utilizing the Internet to enhance communication among sociologists, EOB approved launching an ASA Member Forum on the ASA website in the member-only restricted space to encourage members to discuss issues of importance to the discipline and Association. While these fora did not engage much member participation, they signaled ASA's interest in stimulating such exchange. The topics for Member Forum discussion included:

- Where is sociology headed in the 21st century?
- The challenges of feminist thought for sociology
- The challenge of race and racism for a sociology of U.S. society
- Thinking ahead about "Cities of the Future" (2001 Annual Meeting Theme)

Sale of the 1722 N Street NW Building

In the summer of 1998, ASA sold the rowhouse on 1722 N Street NW in downtown Washington, DC, which it owned and which had been its headquarters since 1970. This possibility had come up in 1981 and again in 1993 as other social science associations along with ASA considered collaborating on the lease or purchase of office space. Based on EOB and Council analysis of the advantages and disadvantages of relocation, in January 1994, Council approved putting the Executive Office building on sale and relocating to new quarters. The presence of a strong offer and a growing sense of the wisdom of the Executive Office relocation in Washington, DC led to the sale of the property in the summer of 1998. After design and remodeling of the new space, the Executive Office moved to the 7th Floor of the 1307 New York Avenue NW Building in December 1998.

The 1722 N Street NW building had many charming features, but was generally ineffective as office space. Originally built at the turn of the 19th century as a residence, the building was becoming increasingly costly to secure and operate. The ASA staff was spread out over five floors (with no elevator), making interoffice communication difficult. Also, there was no accessibility for persons with mobile disabilities. The costs for remodeling the building were assessed to be considerable.

ASA sold the 1722 N Street building to the Accrediting Council for Continuing Education and Training (ACCET), a smaller non-profit organization. Since ASA owned the building free and clear, all net procedures from the $1.275 million sale could be placed in the House Fund. (Although these resources were not formally restricted for only housing use, it was assumed that the primary purpose for these funds was to ensure support for necessary office costs, including to allow reentry into the sales market if that seemed wise toward the expiration of the lease.) EOB authorized the Executive Officer to proceed with a long-term, 10-year lease arrangement in the 1307 New York Avenue building, which was purchased by four higher education groups—National Association of State Universities and Land Grant Colleges (NASULGC), the American Association of State Colleges and Universities (AASCU), the Council for Advancement and Support of Education (CASE), and the American Association of Colleges for Teacher Education (AACTE). The expectation was that the anticipated operating costs and essential improvements on the 1722 N Street NW building and interest income and growth from the House Fund beyond inflation would essentially cover the annual lease cost.

4. GOVERNANCE: BYLAWS, ETHICAL STANDARDS, AND POLICY CHANGES

As noted in Chapter 1, ASA Council has the authority to set policies for the Association within the framework established by the ASA Constitution and Bylaws. The Bylaws also allow for the membership to act on behalf of the Association by bringing resolutions in the form of referenda to the membership (see Article II, Section 8). From 1991 to 2002, ASA Council took a number of steps to clarify policies and the policymaking process and also brought issues to the membership for their vote, several of which involved Bylaws changes. During this period, no matters were brought directly to a vote of the membership through a referendum process.

ASA Bylaws Changes

According to the ASA Constitution, amendments to the Constitution and Bylaws of the Association may be proposed by Council or by a petition of at least three percent of the voting members of the Association; amendments to the Constitution must be approved by a two-thirds affirmative vote of voting members of the Association in a referendum (Article IX), and amendments to the Bylaws by a majority affirmative vote, also submitted to the voting members of the Association (Article VIII).

Several important changes were made to the Bylaws of the American Sociological Association from 1992 to 2001. All such changes were made following Council resolutions and recommendations, and, with one exception noted below, all were approved by the membership in referenda held for this purpose. Appendix 15 contains a detailed summary of all modifications to the Bylaws made since 1980, including a definition of each amendment, dates and nature of Council action, and dates and outcomes of membership referenda.

Several types of actions and events resulted in changes to the Bylaws. In two cases, alterations were made to bring provisions of the Bylaws into conformity with changes made to other institutional policies: (1) In February 1992, Council made changes to the *Organizer's Manual* aimed at promoting diversity in nominating Program Committee members. A Council subcommittee was also appointed at the time to recommend alterations in the minor inconsistencies that had emerged between the ASA Bylaws and the *Organizer's Manual*. (2) In January 1997, following the revision of the Code of Ethics, Council recommended a number of changes in the ASA Bylaws based on suggested alterations from the Committee on Professional Ethics (COPE), the Executive Office, and ASA legal counsel. Proposed changes included, for example, the inclusion of the Committee on Professional Ethics as a constitutional committee and clearer definition of conditions of membership (including the requirement to comply with the provisions of the Code of Ethics). Also, at that time, members voted on a Bylaws change to eliminate the emeritus membership category and clarified guidelines for section formation and operations.

Based on a January 1996 Council resolution, the membership voted in the spring 1996 referendum to eliminate the emeritus membership category and to incorporate those members in the regular income categories (the change to the Bylaws on this point was approved by the membership in the spring 1997 referendum referred to above). However, following a survey of lapsed emeritus members in 1998, ASA Council voted in February 1999 to reestablish the emeritus category. The measure to reinstate the emeritus membership was approved by the members in a Bylaws change in spring 1999, and became effective in the 2000 membership year.

The most sweeping Bylaws changes took place beginning in 1998 with Council action taken to restructure ASA Committees (see discussion below). Based on Council resolutions passed at the January 1998 meeting, nine amendments to the Constitution and Bylaws required to accomplish the restructuring were submitted to the membership for a vote in the spring of 1998. These included proposed actions such as to eliminate the Committee on Committees (COC), to reduce the Committee on Nominations to 11 members and eliminate elections by districts, to change the status of the Committee on Sections and the Committee on Awards to Constitutional committees, and to remove ASA journal editors as members of the Committee on Publications. All proposed amendments (see Appendix 15) except one were approved by the membership (the proposal that the Committee on Publications be appointed by Council on recommendations of the President rather than elected by the voting members of the Association failed in the membership referendum). Subsequently, based on a resolution brought forward at the 1999 Business Meeting, Council appointed a subcommittee to examine the discontinuation of COC, which ultimately recommended that COC be reinstated. A special member referendum in October 2001 to reinstate the COC and so alter the Bylaws was passed, and, in 2002, the COC was again elected by the membership.

The final Bylaws change through 2002, related to section governance. In January 2000, Council approved a change to the composition of the Committee on Sections by increasing its membership to nine members to also include "three members elected for three-year terms by current section chairs from among current section chairs according to section membership size. All terms will be staggered." This change to Article V of the Bylaws was approved by the membership as part of the spring ballot. *(Footnotes,* September/October 2000:15)

ASA Code of Ethics

A major revision of the ASA Code of Ethics was undertaken from 1994 to 1996. During that time Council reviewed several draft versions, and in January 1997, endorsed the revised Code of Ethics. The ASA membership approved the revised Code in the spring of 1997.

The Committee on Ethics, consisting of John Kennedy (Chair), Sue Hoppe, Anthony Cortese, Joyce Miller Iutcovich, Barbara Melber, Eleanor M. Miller, Helen Moore, Bernice Pescosolido, and Bette Woody as well as Council Liaisons, Cheryl Townsend Gilkes and Ida Harper Simpson, and staff liaisons, Felice J. Levine and Cynthia B. Costello worked intensively for more than two years to produce a revised Code. The membership was kept informed of revisions through articles in *Footnotes* and on the ASA homepage; and members, section officers, committees and other groups (e.g., department chairs at the Chairs Conference) were afforded extensive opportunity to provide input, comment, and feedback in the summer and fall of 1996. The 1997 Council scheduled time to review the revisions at its August 1996 Meeting, and ASA President Neil Smelser also reported that he and Vice President Charles Willie had served as commentators at a special session on the Code during the 1996 Annual Meeting.

The goal in undertaking the revision was to make for a more informative and useful Code of Ethics by fleshing out key components and addressing issues heretofore unaddressed. For example, more systematic attention was paid to research, teaching, service, and practice; new material was added on conflicts of interest, data sharing, and the issue of confidentiality was broadened to cover sociologists in all facets of professional work as well as limitations on confidentiality guarantees. Also, the enforcement procedures were revised to improve and better specify the processes as well as the steps involved in filing and handling a complaint. ASA legal counsel, who brought interest and expertise in professional ethics, provided useful guidance in revising the Code and the enforcement procedures.

Amicus Briefs

Over the years, the Association has joined in legal actions in cases of significance to sociology and the profession. As noted in the previous chapter, in January 1991, based on a report prepared by Executive Officer D'Antonio and Executive Officer-designate Levine, Council affirmed a process for determining whether to participate in filing an amicus brief. As with policymaking more generally, and as stipulated in the Bylaws, the Executive Officer consults with the President and Secretary on matters of policy and may jointly act on behalf of the Association, conduct a ballot by mail, or defer action to the next Council meeting. Councils were reflective in making determinations about whether to participate in amicus briefs. In 1991, in the *Exxon Valdez Case*, the Committee on Sociological Practice urged ASA President Stanley Lieberson to write to the presiding judge to express ASA opinion in this case involving a suit filed by Exxon against Impact Assessment Inc. (IAI), a private social research firm hired to poll Alaskan citizens on oil spill damages. Exxon and the owners of the Valdez had asked for a court order to impound all of IAI's research instruments and data. The issue of participating in amicus briefs was referred by Council to a Subcommittee chaired by Wendy Baldwin to examine the issue more fully. At the January 1992 Council meeting, the Subcommittee recommended that no further action was needed by Council at that time.

Throughout the years, the Association was strong in its support of the ethical standard of confidentiality of research information. For example, as described in Chapter 1, ASA filed a brief in the case of Mario Brajuha, a graduate student in sociology whose field notes were subpoenaed in 1984 by a federal court. In 1993, another case emerged involving scholar's privilege and a potential conflict with ASA's Code of Ethics. Richard (Rik) Scarce, a doctoral student in sociology at Washington State University, who was conducting a long-term study of animal rights activists, was held in contempt of court and jailed on May 14, 1993 when he refused to reveal confidential information about his sources to a federal court. (See: *James Richard Scarce v. United States of America* 5 F.3d 39 [1993]). He remained incarcerated until October 18, 1993. Scarce cited the ASA Code of Ethics, which affirms the obligation of confidentiality. After a mailed ballot of Council, ASA filed an amicus curie brief in April 1993 when the case went up on appeal to the Ninth Circuit. The ASA argued that, "social science inquiry is dependent upon guarantees of privacy and confidentiality and that the ethical and societal values underlying social science standards support recognition of a qualified privilege from disclosure." (Levine, *Footnotes*, August 1993:2)

In considering the *Scarce Case*, Council again raised the issue of the need to develop a policy to guide the Association in determining how to respond when members request support involving legal action. A Subcommittee of Council consisting of Barrie Thorne (Chair), Ida Simpson, and Janet Chafetz was appointed to consider the need for a legal defense fund, and if appropriate, a guiding policy. Thorne "later reported a committee consensus that the emphasis of the Association's position should be on the importance of and adherence to ethical guidelines. ASA should continue to take an active interest in ethical and legal issues involving human subjects and should periodically review its ethical guidelines. However, ASA cannot be responsible for either the informal or formal contracts and arrangements made between researchers and their subjects or clients. The Committee also did not think it would be wise to set up general guidelines or a standing committee to review specific legal cases. It did recommend that a general statement be written that might apply to all cases, although each case brought to the ASA would, of necessity, be handled in an ad hoc way. A concern was also expressed that an ASA legal defense fund would encourage frivolous law suits." (Council Minutes, January 1993)

ASA Policy Statements

In 1993, Council decided to reexamine the process by which it took policy positions. In January 1993, Myra Marx Ferree, Chair of the Council Subcommittee on the Business Meeting, reported that there needed to be greater clarity regarding the consideration and disposition of resolutions adopted at the Annual Business Meeting. Two issues were key in leading to this reexamination: First, Council sought to specify a process that would allow for issues coming before it to be based on a deliberative process, not just flowing from issues that surfaced at the Annual Business Meeting. Second, Council sought clearer articulation of what resolutions should entail. In August 1993, the Subcommittee further reported back to Council, leading Council to adopt a new policy on a two-year trial basis. The key elements of this policy include:

- Resolutions can arrive via the Business Meeting, from ASA sections and committees, or from individual ASA members who solicit 50 signatures to accompany their requests.
- Resolutions can come any time during the year.
- Resolutions should show direct relevance to sociology as a discipline or profession or be grounded in the substantive expertise or knowledge of the discipline.
- Resolutions must include documentation to guide Council's understanding.
- The proposed resolution must include specific suggestions about what Council action is requested.

The goal was to have in place a process that would support the possibility of the Association taking policy positions, but only those that build on sociological knowledge and expertise. The policy was officially adopted in 1996. From 1993 to 1998, only a few resolutions were submitted to Council.

In August 1998, Council temporarily suspended the use of the guidelines in place for ASA taking positions on public policy matters. Council also appointed a Subcommittee on ASA Policymaking and Resolutions chaired by Patricia Roos, to review ASA policymaking. In January 1999, Council provisionally accepted the Subcommittee's report and recommendations, which concluded that the Association should only take policy positions on issues related to ASA's mission as a learned society or pertaining to how ASA operates as an organization. In advancing this policy, Council emphasized that the Association offers members many vehicles for connecting sociology to public policy in their work from the ASA Annual Meeting Program and the Spivack Program in Applied Social Research and Social Policy to the Fund for the Advancement of the Discipline. Along with provisionally adopting this policy, Council called for a comment period with a final policy to be adopted in winter 2000.

In January 2000, Council asked the Subcommittee to continue its work for another year. Since Past Vice President Roos would leave Council by August, Richard Alba was asked to chair the Subcommittee and report back in winter 2001. Council hoped the additional period would give members the opportunity to express themselves on this issue. In February 2001, the Alba Subcommittee agreed with the Roos Subcommittee on all but one point: The Alba Subcommittee recommended that no limits should be placed a priori on Council's taking policy positions. Consistent with the policy officially adopted in 1996, the Subcommittee recommended that Council should have the latitude to take positions on issues beyond the Association's mission as a learned society, and should do so based on sound and sufficient sociological knowledge. Furthermore, the Subcommittee recommended a procedure whereby Council would appoint an expert subcommittee to provide advice on how to proceed with an issue.

ASA Council adopted the Report and its recommendations. The language of the Report reads as follows:

> In the past, Council has considered member resolutions and other proposed policy statements during its regular working sessions. These discussions have at times generated a sense of uneasiness among Council members who felt that they lacked the expertise to assess the theoretical and evidentiary basis behind various proposals. The subcommittee suggests that, in such cases, the Council employ the model of a review panel in order to develop recommendations for a course of action.
>
> It is especially resolutions pertaining to public policy issues where the credibility of the discipline and the Association is placed on the line and where, therefore, Council needs to be confident that its decisions are made on the basis of solidly grounded knowledge. We recommend that, in such cases, Council appoint a subcommittee from its members to evaluate the scientific basis and the appropriateness of any proposed resolution. Such a subcommittee should be empowered to consult with any non-Council members it deems as having expertise bearing on a resolution. It should also

consider the appropriateness of a resolution for a learned society, to screen out, to take an extreme example, any resolution that takes a politically partisan stance. The subcommittee need not be placed in the position [of] making a simple up-or-down recommendation to Council. Since resolutions that come to Council are advisory, Council may, as appropriate, charge the subcommittee with considering revisions to a motion that might make it more likely to pass scrutiny. Alternatively, it could recommend that a particular topic is better suited to one of the other mechanisms for ASA members to address policy issues, such as the Spivack [Program] series, because, say, the sociological base of knowledge is not sufficiently developed to support a pronouncement from the ASA; a Spivack series report would be an appropriate way to summarize what is and what is not known in a given policy domain. Needless to say, the subcommittee cannot act in Council's stead; only the full Council has the power to pass a resolution on behalf of the Association.

Not every resolution will require the review panel model. It is particularly well tailored to issues where taking a position on public policy issue depends on clear and convincing sociological knowledge or expertise. (Report by Alba Subcommittee to ASA Council, Council Agenda Book, 2001).

5. GOVERNANCE STRUCTURAL CHANGES

During the 1990s, ASA Council modified its award policies and enacted major changes to its governance system by (1) restructuring ASA committees, (2) establishing guidelines for section operations, (3) restructuring dues, (4) decoupling dues from journals, and (5) changing the legal status of the American Sociological Foundation (ASF). Council also made changes to the Committee on Freedom of Research and Teaching (COFRAT) and dissolved the Certification Program.

Awards Policy

During the 1990s, Council undertook several major efforts to examine and adjust Association policies on awards. Major initiatives included:

- In 1992, Council adopted a revision to awards policies relating to the procedures for acceptance of and establishment of new awards. Earlier, in 1991, Council considered the need to: (1) devise a policy for responding to potential donors who would like to establish named awards or grants under the aegis of the ASA, (2) clarify the difference between grants and honorific awards (and in the case of grants, the nature of ASA liabilities), and (3) determine the most appropriate ASA vehicle for reviewing gift offers, since the Award Policy Committee met only once a year. Guidelines were proposed (e.g., to accept "named awards" only if the gift is of $100,000 or more and to accept no gift that entails the expenditure of ASA funds, unless specifically approved by Council). Both the Section Board and the Committee on Sections viewed these revisions favorably and they were adopted in Council on August 24–25, 1992.

- In 1995, Council approved the establishment of an annual Award on Public Understanding of Sociology.

- On August 20–21, 1996, Council modified the timing, nature, and name of certain awards: The Jessie Bernard Award was to be conferred on an annual rather than biennial basis. Council explicitly discouraged conferring two awards, but stipulated that the award could be conferred for a lifetime achievement or a major work. The DuBois-Johnson-Frazier Award would be an annual award, rather than a biennial one.

- In 1997, Council adopted a new awards cycle on a two-year trial basis. On recommendation from the Awards Policy Committee, Council approved changing the cycle for conferring awards (from nomination through selection) so that the process occurred during the year immediately leading up to the conferral of awards, instead of a year in advance. Under the new system, awards committees worked between Annual Meetings, calling for nominations in the fall of each year and making selections no later than June 1. It was anticipated that effective use of electronic mail, conference calls, and other means of communication that became available would support committee work. Yet, some members of Council expressed concerns about the absence of face-to-face deliberation, or the attendant costs to the Association were some committees to request an additional meeting separate from the Annual Meeting. The experiment was ended after one year, because selection committees preferred the practice of meeting face-to-face to discuss candidates and make a selection a year in advance. To phase back to the prior system, two award committees for each year were needed for each award in 1999 (one to select a 1999 winner and one to select a 2000 winner).

- How best to structure the Awards Ceremony was a recurrent concern of both Council and the Committee on Awards. Various strategies to honor awardees, yet limit the amount of time for presentations and acceptance speeches were tried, and despite guidelines set by Council (such as specification of word and time limit), a number of people involved in the Awards Ceremony still exceeded these formats. Council discussed various approaches for improvements, and in 2000 recommended that the Committee on Awards continue to address this issue.

Restructuring of ASA Committees

In January 1998, Council approved a major change in the ASA committee structure by creating a more streamlined system with five components: (1) Constitutional Committees (those that are central to ASA governance operations and functions; in the initial reports and Council recommendations, these Committees were termed "Constitutional"—even though the actual modification was to the Bylaws and not to the Constitution), (2) Awards Selection Committees, (3) Status Committees, (4) Advisory Panels, and (5) Task Forces. Under this new model, ASA Councils could create task forces to address specific issues that require the attention of the Association. (See Appendix 16 for specific committees and task forces.) This restructuring had the greatest effect on entities that previously were standing committees but were not reclassified as (1) through (4) above. Those standing committees that could identify issues or activities under their aegis appropriate to a task force could request of Council to be reconstituted as a task force.

The reorganization was intended by Council to create a more dynamic and flexible committee structure that was better aligned with the work of Council, that was more responsive to the changing needs and demands of the discipline and Association, and that used the volunteer talent of the membership in a more optimal way. This effort created long-term committees specified in the Bylaws only for the essential governance functions of the Association. For all other entities, Council would specify the charge; specify how it served the Association; and the process for reviewing its charge, activities, and continuation.

Background

In January 1998, then Past-President Neil Smelser noted that there had been a "proliferation of committees in ASA without clear guidelines as to their mission and charge as well as to when committees and task forces should be formed and discontinued . . . [and he] believed it would be worthwhile to initiate a review of the committee structure of the Association." Indeed, concerns had been expressed for years about certain aspects of the committee structure. Some committees met regularly and performed vital tasks, while others met infrequently or were poorly attended. The committee structure had evolved into a complex organization that was seen by Council as "rigid, bureaucratic and costly to administer." Members also found it frustrating to join committees for which there was no meaningful work (*Footnotes*, March 1998:1).

In January 1997, Council decided to conduct a comprehensive review of the committee structure and process, and appointed a Subcommittee of Council for this purpose consisting of Linda Waite

(Chair), David Snow, Cheryl Townsend Gilkes, and Neil Smelser. The Subcommittee worked intensively from August 1997 to January 1998 to study the committee structure and to obtain comments and input from existing ASA committees and members.

Restructuring of Committees, January 1998

In January 1998, the Subcommittee on Committee Restructuring presented its recommendations, and Council approved the proposed system of five types of committees: Constitutional Committees, Awards Selection Committees, Status Committees, Advisory Panels, and Task Forces. As noted above, the most significant change in the reorganization took place with respect to certain standing committees, a number of which were eliminated without further activity and four requested spin-off Task Forces.

Task Forces are to be established and appointed by Council for specific tasks and fixed terms (generally no more than two years) based on advice from the membership, sections, officers, staff, or Council itself. All existing committees not identified in the revised committee structure were eligible to become task forces—which, at the time of the reorganization included Committees on: Sociological Practice, Sociologists in Government and International Agencies, Employment, Sociology in Elementary and Secondary Schools, Teaching, Hate Bias on Campus, National Statistics, International Sociology, COFRAT, ASA/AAAS Relations, and Archives. Council asked these Committees to review their work and submit recommendations by September 15, 1998 for Task Forces. Council was to then make a determination as to whether these Committees had viable proposals for Task Forces.

Overall, the net effect of the committee restructuring in 1998 resulted in the following changes (specific changes to the Constitution and Bylaws required by the restructuring are summarized in Appendix 15):

- The Constitutional Committees were expanded to include the Committee on Sections and the Committee on Awards. The Committee on Membership and the Committee on Committees (COC) were eliminated as Constitutional Committees in 1998, but, as noted below, COC was subsequently reinstated.

- The Constitutional Committees, Awards Committees, and the Status Committees, were to have vacancies appointed by the President and reviewed and approved by Council. The shift to the ASA President for appointments was planned to substitute for the role of the Committee on Committees.

    Elimination of the Committee on Committees was only temporary. Based on a resolution brought by the Sociologists for Women in Society (SWS) at the 1999 Business Meeting, Council appointed a Task Force on the Reexamination of the Committee on Committees and the Committee on Nominations. The purpose of the Task Force was to examine the decision (approved in the spring ballot) to discontinue COC and to modify the Committee on Nominations (CON) to reduce its size and eliminate regional representation. The Task Force recommended that the COC be reinstated in altered form (defined set of committees to recommend to Council) and with a specified composition to diversify CON. A special member referendum in September 2001 reinstated a modified COC, and in 2002, the COC was again elected by the membership.

- The Committee on Nominations (CON) was reduced in size from 16 to 11 members and elections would no longer be held by districts. This change reflected Council's belief that a smaller committee could be more thoughtful about nominations and that at-large elections would allow the members more voting choices. After review by the Task Force on the Reexamination of the COC and the CON, no recommendation was advanced to further alter the Committee. Strategies were outlined to strengthen diversity on the CON and to improve the procedures by which they worked.

- The ASA journal editors would no longer be non-voting members of the Committee on Publications. This change was brought about by a concern that the number of journal editors was much larger than the number of elected members and that their service on the Committee, even without vote, conflicted with the Committee's independent oversight function of the ASA journals.
- Starting in five years, Council was to review the Status Committees to determine if this structure was the most effective method of achieving the ASA's commitment to diversity and inclusiveness in the Association and the discipline. (See Chapter 3 for summary of reviews submitted by the Status Committees.)
- With reporting to Council, the Executive Officer was authorized to establish and appoint members of advisory panels as needed to provide advice and guidance to Executive Office programs and related activities.

Formation of the First Task Forces

In February 1999, speaking for the Subcommittee on Committee Restructuring, Chair Linda Waite summarized the work undertaken during the fall of 1998, and especially the review of reports of committees that were invited to propose Task Forces as part of the transition from their continuing work. The Subcommittee ultimately recommended, and Council approved, the formation of five Task Forces. These five Task Forces had their first organizational meetings at the 1999 Annual Meeting. (Appendix 16 contains a list of Task Forces created from 1999 through 2004.)

Strengthening the Work of CON

In August 2001, the Task Force on the Reexamination of the COC and CON reported that the Task Force considered a number of possibilities regarding the nomination process and the Committee on Nominations (CON), including "(1) that Council members receive a more extensive statement on diversity guidelines; (2) that a task force be reconstituted in four years to review the guidelines and results of implementation; (3) that ASA move forward as soon as possible, to create a relational database so that information about persons who can be potential nominees can be easily created; and (4) that there be some tracking of networks for names, where nominations come from (e.g., *Footnotes*), and any patterns in declination of candidates who are asked to run." (Council Minutes, August 21, 2001) The Task Force recommended (and Council supported these steps) as well as leaving in place the altered structure, previously approved as a Bylaws change by the membership.

Status Committees

Over the past several decades, the Status Committees, including the Status of Women in Sociology (CSWS); Status of Racial and Ethnic Minorities in Sociology (CSREMS), Society of Persons with Disabilities in Sociology; and Status of Gay, Lesbian, Bisexual, and Transgender Persons in Sociology (CSGLBT) have played a vital and dynamic role in advocating for the presence of minorities in the Association and the discipline. Since the early 1980s, a series of Biennial Reports have been produced by the Executive Office under the guidance of the CSWS and CSREMS reflecting analysis of data and trends on the participation and representation of women and minorities in all aspects of the Association and the discipline (see Appendix 13). The CSGLBT and the Society of Persons with Disabilities also had a strong voice in shaping ASA policies in a number of ways, including, for example, decisions relating to site locations for and services at ASA Annual Meetings. All four of these Status Committees have also strongly advocated for an increase in efforts to include women and minorities on the editorial boards of the major ASA journals, as well as on committees, sections, and other governance entities of the ASA.

ASA Sections during the 1990s

ASA sections continued to be a vital part of the Association during the 1990s, and were generally regarded as "an important vehicle for member participation as well as taking on leadership positions." (Council Minutes, August 22, 2001) Many of the same themes that shaped the discussion of sections in the 1980s also existed in the 1990s (e.g., concerns about section role and growth in ASA, their role in the Annual Meeting, their taking policy positions, fragmentation, and internal governance issues). Sections continued to press for more flexibility in setting dues, newsletter allocations, and awards policies. Some sections however, had weak governance structures (e.g., no election of officers) and communications systems (e.g., no newsletters). Council took several initiatives from 1996 to 2000 to set guidelines for section operations and activities in order to clarify some of these issues and to enhance the role and participation of sections within the Association, including clarifying the role and responsibilities of the Committee on Sections (COS).

The discussions on sections also reflected differing views of the role of sections in the Association. On the one hand, there was the model of sections as independent groups; on the other, sections were perceived as a benefit of membership in the parent organization to facilitate interaction in specialty areas. In order to avoid fragmentation, ASA had always operated on the latter model (EOB Minutes, June 1996). The January 1996 Council meeting reached a "consensus that, through sections, the Association has been able to accommodate diverse lines of work and give members an intellectual home. Council affirmed the importance of having a governance structure that is 'of the whole' and not based on representation of interest groups." (Council Minutes, January 1996).

Sections played a key and direct role in a number of ASA initiatives during the 1990s. In 1996 for example, the Section on Sociology of Education organized a series of education policy conferences, and with funding from the U.S. Department of Education, produced a special issue of *Sociology of Education*, "Sociology and Educational Policy: Bringing Scholarship and Practice Together" (1996). In March 2000, Executive Officer Levine along with Pamela Barnhouse Walters and Michael Hout assisted the Spencer Foundation in convening a small research conference on future research directions in the sociology of education that involved leading members of the Education Section. Similarly, Executive Officer Levine and William Avison, Chair of the Section on Mental Health, met with the leadership of the National Institute of Mental Health and prepared a submission on translational research for the NIMH Advisory Committee "on the value of investments in sociology of mental health and how basic science in this area translates into applications." (Council Minutes, August 10, 1999)

Section Growth in the 1990s

At the end of the 1990 membership year, section memberships stood at 13,263 in 27 sections (ASA membership was 12,841). By the end of the 2000 membership year, section memberships had grown to 19,223 in 40 sections (ASA membership was 12,854) (Appendix 14). In 2000, more than 60 percent of ASA members belonged to at least one section, and many belonged to at least two sections. Throughout the 1990s, the sections with the largest number of members were: Medical Sociology, Organizations/Occupations, and Sex and Gender. At its January 2000 meeting, EOB noted that sections were experiencing a generally upward trend, while ASA membership was holding steady around 13,000 members. Appendix 17 contains an outline on Section Formation History, including those sections that were formed and attained full section status during the 1990s.

Significant Events Relating to Sections in the 1990s

Council approved several major reports produced by committees established to study various aspects of section activities during the 1990s: (1) A 1996 subcommittee chaired by Patricia Hill

Collins, explored issues pertaining to the role of and proliferation of sections; (2) A joint EOB-COS (Committee on Sections) Report on Section Finances, Administration, and Governance established guidelines for section operations (giving sections more flexibility with their funds and activities, but making them more accountable), and (3) A 2000 report defined a strategy for section budget allocation.

Council also considered issues pertaining to section formation, continuation, and termination, particularly if section membership dropped below the required number (200) to maintain sections. Council was guided in these areas by the COS, which had the responsibility for advising the ASA on the administration of sections—including on creating and continuing sections, advising Council on section policies and procedures, and serving as liaison between sections and Council.

In August 1996, ASA Vice President Charles Willie, Chair of the Council Subcommittee on Sections, presented the Report on section growth and its implications for existing sections and the Association. The Report noted (among other conclusions) that section growth "since 1992 seems to abide by requirements of the *Section Manual* that 'sections should encompass a reasonably broad area of specified interests' and that the 'overlap' if any, has not been harmful to existing and older sections." (Council Minutes, August 19, 1996) The Willie Subcommittee also recommended several options for controlling the growth of sections, including, that the number of Association members required to form a new section should be increased from 200 to 300.

In January 1997, Council approved the Report on Section Finances, Administration, and Governance that was the result of a joint effort by the COS and EOB. The process involved extensive input from section officers and members, recommendations from Vice President Willie's Council Subcommittee Report, and Council discussion from August 1996. In the summer meeting of 1997, EOB approved a plan to give sections an operating base-budget, but sections were required to prepare a budget and track spending. The more controversial change was perceived to be the guidelines for section formation and continuation, with some sections close to 200 finding it hard to meet the 300-member requirement. The use of qualitative criteria would ensure that sections operate under the guidelines (such as holding business and Council meetings), and would provide some flexibility in determining continuation irrespective of absolute numbers. On EOB's recommendation, in January 1998, Council approved an operating base-budget of $1,000, plus $2 per capita amount. This change became effective in 1999, to be reevaluated after a two-year period. This formula for basic budget allocations was reaffirmed by Council in January 2000, which also specified criteria for adjusting budgets in cases where membership drops below 300 members.

Another important event pertaining to ASA sections occurred in January 2000, when Council approved a resolution to expand the COS to nine members. Council member Paula England, a member of COS, indicated that section officers were committed to this proposed structure because it would place section officers in leadership positions on COS. The resolution, which required a Bylaws change, stated: "Six members shall be appointed by Council for three-year terms based on the recommendation of the President. Three of these members shall be appointed from among the Association membership and three shall be appointed from among the Council members-at-large. Three members shall also be elected for three-year terms by current section chairs from among current section chairs according to section membership size." The change was approved by the membership in a referendum in the ASA 2000 election.

Certification

The certification program at the ASA evolved through several phases over a 40-year history. Interest first surfaced in the 1950s, largely in reaction to the certification programs of the American Psychological Association (APA), but the ASA programs were discontinued in the 1960s. In the late 1970s, a revived interest led to Council's approval of a certification program in 1984 and creation of a Committee on Certification, which devised the procedures for PhD level certification in six areas and a MA level certification for social research.

The Certification Program, launched in 1986 generated little interest, and ultimately only 62 people completed the certification process—nearly half of whom were members of the certification committees themselves (64 other members inquired about certification, but never completed the process). (See Chapter 1 discussion of Certification.)

In 1991, Council decided to continue monitoring the program, and in 1992, the Master's Certification Program Committee was also placed under the jurisdiction of the Oversight Committee (as the PhD Certification Committee had been earlier) due to low demand. The MA Certification Committee had concluded, "certification as a sociologist is being handled by the receipt of an MA or PhD. There may be value in certification of Practical Specialties, however the Sociological Practice Association is doing a good job of that for clinical practitioners." (Kennedy, *Footnotes*, November 1994:4) Eventually the combined committee became the Committee on Certification and Licensure, which undertook a review of both certification programs in 1994. (The Sociological Practice Association [SPA] offers the Certified Clinical Sociologist [CCS], which provides an important credential to practicing sociologists.)

Council voted to suspend the Certification Program on August 24, 1992 because of low interest. In 1998, visiting sociologist John Kennedy undertook a review of the programs, including of its state-level monitoring program, and found that it operated at a minimal level for a number of years as well. Council officially terminated the Certification Program on August 25, 1998.

Committee on Freedom of Research and Teaching (COFRAT)

Created by Council in 1968 to handle complaints involving infringement of academic freedoms by institutions, the Committee on Freedom of Research and Teaching (COFRAT) continued to handle individual cases in the early 1990s. The debate that ensued over the mission, mandate, activities, and goals of COFRAT over much of its 25-year history, however, also followed it into the 1990s.

COFRAT's mandates were quite general, its written guidelines for procedures few in number, and its work largely conducted by volunteer Committee members. Although COFRAT undertook studies (e.g., on initial appointments in the 1970s and on part-time faculty in the 1980s), for the most part, it saw itself in a factfinding role on individuals' complaints against institutions, then making a judgment on cases, and recommending possible sanctions to Council. In a few cases, COFRAT took on a mediation or arbitration role, but these were exceptions. Increasingly, throughout the 1980s, COFRAT found itself in contentious relations with institutions under investigation, at times with the potential of placing ASA at legal risk. Tensions between COFRAT, COPE, and other ASA committees also complicated its work.

With the support of ASA President William Gamson, Vice President Barrie Thorne, and COFRAT senior Co-chair Essie Rutledge, Executive Officer Felice Levine undertook a comprehensive review of COFRAT in the fall of 1993, which resulted in a detailed and extensive report on the origins, history, procedures, and caseload of COFRAT ("The American Sociological Association: The Committee on Freedom of Research and Teaching [COFRAT], December 15, 1993).

On the basis of a discussion of the December 1993 Report, COFRAT recommended that President Gamson appoint a Task Force to address what ASA's role should be on issues of academic freedom. The Ad Hoc Committee was composed of President William Gamson (Chair), Margaret Andersen, Barrie Thorne, Peter Meiksins, John Kennedy, John McCarthy, and Executive Officer Felice Levine.

The Ad Hoc Committee recommended to the 1994 Council that, "COFRAT's mandate should be directed to dealing with systematic violations, rather than individual cases. COFRAT should seek to identify patterns in violations, and no longer adjudicate or act as a fact finding body on specific individual complaints about a department or institution." (Council Minutes, August 8, 1994) The Executive Office was to work with COFRAT and other ASA committees to identify patterns, which required the attention of COFRAT.

Subsequently, COFRAT's monitoring role on issues of academic freedom included situations such as those reported to the 1996 Council on sexual harassment of faculty and on H.R. 2202, "The Immigration in the National Interest Act" of 1995. No action was taken on the sexual harassment issue, but Council adopted a resolution deploring certain provisions of H.R. 2202 "as potentially detrimental to the future of science including the social sciences." (Council Minutes, August 24, 1995) The Association was aggressive in opposing these provisions, including in the pages of *Footnotes* (see Levine, *Footnotes*, January 1996:2) and in a guest editorial written by Executive Officer Levine in *Science*.

COFRAT, however, remained largely inactive. In 1998, as part of the overall restructuring of Committees of ASA, COFRAT, along with several other committees, was asked by Council to review its work and to submit recommendations by September 15, 1998 as to whether it wished to continue as a Task Force. In February 1999, Council did not reconstitute COFRAT as a Task Force.

Dues Restructuring

A major restructuring of the dues was approved by Council at its January 1996 meeting, and subsequently approved by the membership in the spring of 1996. The revision was designed to make the membership dues structure more progressive, to reduce the incentive for the no-journal dues categories, and to "be revenue neutral, meaning that the income to ASA will be no greater or lower than the income generated by the current dues structure." (*Footnotes*, July/August 1996:3)

In the restructuring, the income categories of $40,000–49,999 and $50,000 and higher were subdivided into additional income categories: $40,000–$54,999, $55,000–$69,999 and $70,000 and over. Under the new structure, the lowest income category also changed from "under $15,000" to "under $20,000."

The January 1996, Council also passed a resolution (which the members approved in the 1996 ballot) to eliminate the emeritus category membership. Council had recommended integrating emeritus membership into the regular income-based membership structure because of the varied income levels of retired colleagues. However, in August 1998, after a review of lapsed emeritus members, Council moved to "re-establish the Emeritus membership category for persons who have been ASA members for at least ten years and are retired from their primary employment, with such members receiving *Footnotes* but no journals as part of this membership." (Council Minutes, August 25, 1998) In February 1999, Council voted "[t]o amend the ASA By-laws through a referendum in the 1999 ballot to permit reintroducing the Emeritus membership category." (Council Minutes)

In the late 1990s, EOB also revisited the issue of embedding journal subscriptions into the dues structure, which had first been raised in the early 1990s. This "cafeteria plan" offered options ranging from no journals to two selections for dues at most income levels, but evaluations of this system indicated that it was complex and costly to operate and placed limits on "development of a dynamic publications program." A document entitled, "Discussion Points: Decoupling Journals from Dues" was presented to Council at the August 2000 meeting to highlight key issues and stimulate further discussion. Further data gathering took place in the fall of 2000, and Executive Officer Levine retained Fran Marchbank, a consultant with expertise in publishing and membership in scholarly societies, to advise on this issue.

In February 2001, Council approved recommending to the membership a resolution "decoupling of journals from dues as recommended by EOB such that all ASA members (except Emeritus Members) be required to subscribe to one journal, that the cost to students be further subsidized, and that members be consulted on this change with their approval being sought through a member referendum following the Annual Meeting." Better than 90 percent of voting members approved of this change. Council also urged a periodic review of the progressive dues structure, and asked EOB to conduct such a review over the coming year.

American Sociological Foundation (ASF)

In January 1997, at the request of the Board of Trustees of the American Sociological Foundation (ASF) and with the concurrence of ASA Council, the ASF was dissolved as a separate entity of the ASA. The portfolio of funds, valued at about $450,000 was transferred in the summer of 1997 to two restricted accounts to be used "solely for the purposes that had guided the ASF."

The ASF was created in 1985 to fund projects that supported long-range needs of sociology as a profession and as a discipline (see Chapter 1). Funds were used for minority fellowships, a variety of public outreach projects, and from 1992, a Congressional Fellowship Program.

In 1995, ASF President William Julius Wilson appointed a Subcommittee chaired by Charles Bonjean to review the ASF due to the high costs of maintaining its status as a 501(c)(3) entity. The Subcommittee concluded that the goals of the ASF could be fully realized as a restricted fund within the ASA without the high administrative costs of maintaining a separate 501(c)(3).

In 1996, the ASF Board of Trustees and Advisory Committee agreed unanimously that ASF funds be transferred to two restricted funds: an American Sociological Fund, which would continue the goals of "'improving and promoting sociology's scholarship, teaching and public-service on the long-term basis' and would respond to opportunities to advance the discipline. The Board stipulated that income from ASA investments could be used as 'venture capital' to initiate programs or other innovative activities but not for on-going operational purposes. The Board also stipulated that Council create a second fund to ensure continued support for the Congressional Fellowship." Council unanimously approved the conditions for transferring the funds to restricted accounts, thus assuring that ASF's mission would continue, while the restricted nature of the funds would ensure that the donors' original intent is maintained *(Footnotes,* July 1997:3,6).

6. PUBLICATIONS PROGRAM OF THE ASA

During the 1990s, the Association and its Executive Office worked to strengthen the capacity of the ASA to produce high quality publications and products in the context of a rapidly changing publishing environment. The evolution of the Internet, the launching of the ASA homepage in 1995 (and its subsequent enhancements), advances in information technologies related to publishing, and electronic archiving and retrieval of journals dramatically affected how learned societies such as the ASA publish and disseminate research. The Association continued to place a high priority on publishing materials that set standards for and foster excellence in sociology, to find new ways of marketing and disseminating works to raise the visibility of sociology, and to think creatively about the implications for the future of the new technologies for publishers such as the ASA.

Publication Guidelines

In February 1999, Council approved the *Guidelines for the ASA Publications Portfolio* recommended by the Committee on Publications, thus representing a major shift in publications philosophy for the Association. At that same time, Council also approved a resolution from EOB that journals must operate at least on a break-even basis to be financially viable. In the mid-1990s, the consideration of a journal that might reach larger audiences, and questions from ASA sections of the existing policy disallowing section journals led the Publications Committee under the leadership of its Chair Michael Schwartz and Executive Officer Felice Levine to propose guidelines that could facilitate a dynamic and well-planned publications program.

The *Guidelines* articulated a vision for the publications program and set forth criteria for the periodic reviews of journals and for the introduction of new publications—including for the first time, the possibility of section-sponsored journals. The view of Council was that the language of the *Guidelines* should be clear from the outset that, "the intent was to review new journal proposals, whether ASA-wide or section-proposed, in light of the entire publication portfolio and how a proposal fit into the mix. Council considered intellectual viability in the mix of ASA journals to be key." (Council Minutes, February 1999) Council Members strongly believed that these points should be specifically included in the preamble, and voted its approval for the Report based on these modifications.

Scope of Publication

At the end of 2000, in addition to its flagship journal, the *American Sociological Review* (*ASR*), the ASA published seven other journals: *Contemporary Sociology* (*CS*), *Journal of Health and Social Behavior* (*JHSB*), *Social Psychology Quarterly* (*SPQ*), *Sociology of Education* (*SOE*), *Teaching Sociology* (*TS*), *Sociological Theory* (*ST*), *Sociological Methodology* (*SM*), and the *Rose Series in Sociology* (which until 1995 was titled the *Rose Monograph Series in Sociology*). The ASA also published guides and directories as well as a variety of other research, teaching, and professional materials (Appendix 18). Throughout the 1990s, ASA journals, except the *Rose Series* (see below) and *ST* and *SM*, were published by Boyd Printing Company of Albany NY. *ST* and *SM* continued to be published by Basil Blackwell.

Two special issues of journals were also published in 2000. These included an *ASR* volume on "Looking Forward, Looking Back: Continuity and Change at the Turn of the Millennium," and a *CS* volume on "Utopian Visions from America's Leading Social Scientists." During the 1990s, *SPQ* also published two special issues (1996, 1999), and *JHSB* and *SOE* published extra issues.

The Association also published three books and several reports on social policy issues that emanated from various ASA programmatic activities. An objective of the Spivack Program in Applied Social Research and Social Policy was to undertake activities that could yield book products for wide dissemination linking sociological research to social policy. The ASA published *Social Causes of Violence: Crafting a Science Agenda* by Felice J. Levine and Katherine J. Rosich in 1996, based on an ASA-sponsored conference on "Research Challenges on the Social Causes of Violence," held in June 1993. A conference of social scientists was also convened by ASA in June 1996 on "Social Science Perspectives on Affirmative Action in Employment," leading to the volume on *The Realities of Affirmative Action in Employment* (1997), authored by Barbara F. Reskin. In addition, ASA published six volumes in the *Issue Series in Social Research and Social Policy* (Appendix 25 contains a complete list of Spivack Program publications). Finally, the ASA published the report on the MOST Program entitled, *Promoting Diversity and Excellence in Higher Education Through Department Change*, by Felice J. Levine, Hávidan Rodríguez, Carla B. Howery, and Alfonso R. Latoni-Rodríguez in 2002.

The *Social Cause of Violence: Crafting a Science Agenda*, and the 1981 *History of the American Sociological Association* were also made available in pdf form on the ASA homepage in 2002.

Journals

Several major decisions relating to the establishment or continuation of journals were made during the 1990s: (1) *The Sociological Practice Review* (*SPR*) was discontinued by Council on August

23, 1992 meeting after publication of 10 issues from 1990 to 1992 due to low interest as measured by membership and institutional subscriptions and low submissions, (2) The *Rose Monograph Series in Sociology* was reconceptualized (see below) based in part on the availability of research monographs and the unique niche of ASA publishing them, (3) In 2000, ASA officially launched *Contexts*, a general perspectives journal in a magazine format aimed at wide audiences, and (4) In January 2000, Council approved publication of *City and Community*, an official journal of the ASA Section on Community and Urban Sociology.

The Rose Series in Sociology

The *Rose Series in Sociology* consists of volumes published on sociological issues with support from the Rose Fund, which was established in 1967 through a bequest to the ASA from Arnold and Caroline Rose (Appendix 18 contains a list of all volumes published in the *ASA Rose Monograph Series* and the *Rose Series in Sociology*).

In 1994, on the recommendation of the Committee on Publications, Council decided to reexamine the scope and definition of the *ASA Rose Monograph Series*. In January 1995, Council endorsed a change in the *Rose Monograph Series* to shift from publishing single-study research monographs to "short books that are integrative, accessible overviews of a topic. The intended audience would be all sociologists, across all subspecialties, and a broader audience of other social scientists, policymakers, and others. The *Series* would encourage sociologists as public intellectuals to write lively, professional, state of the art short monographs." (Council Minutes) The first editor of the newly revamped *Rose Series in Sociology* was George Farkas. The Series is edited under the ASA aegis, and the Russell Sage Foundation serves as publisher (since 1996), with ASA continuing to hold the copyright on all published works.

Contexts and City and Community

On August 21, 1998, after a one-year period to develop a prospectus and business plan, ASA Council approved launching a new journal to be published in a magazine format, which was aimed at sharing sociological research with a wide audience. Also, Council authorized the Publications Committee to commence a search for an inaugural editor and, in 1999, appointed Claude Fischer to this post. Fischer and Executive Officer Levine launched an extensive effort to examine publishing options and Levine worked through operational issues involved in the launch, including use of and impact on the Rose Fund. At its August 15, 2000 meeting, Council approved naming the new journal, *Contexts*, which was strongly recommended by the Publications Committee. In consultation with editor-designee Fischer, Executive Officer Levine selected the University of California Press as publisher in winter 2001 with official celebration of this partnership held at the Annual Meeting in August in Anaheim. The first issue of *Contexts* was published in the winter of 2002.

City and Community, a journal of the Community and Urban Sociology Section (CUSS), was also introduced in March 2002—the first, and to date, the only section journal approved for publication by the Committee on Publications and ASA Council. Anthony M. Orum (University of Illinois at Chicago) was the first editor of the new journal, which was published by Basil Blackwell. The journal had been in development for more than a decade, with considerable involvement by the Section membership.

Other Publications

The ASA published a number of volumes each year on curriculum development, departmental leadership, and graduate education, as well as teaching resources materials and guides for the Academic and Professional Affairs Program (APAP) (see Appendix 22 for a complete list of current publications). ASA also continued to publish directories, guides, and reference materials (see Appendix 18), and by 2001, some of these materials were also made available on the ASA homepage (e.g., the *Guide to Graduate Departments*). The *Employment Bulletin* has been published electronically on the ASA homepage since 1996. The Association Newsletter, *Footnotes* was published in at least eight monthly issues each year; issues five years back are also available in electronic format on the ASA homepage.

ASA's Association with Boyd Printing Company

ASA marked an important milestone in its history in 2001 by commemorating 50 years of association with Boyd Printing Company of Albany, NY—a "business relationship nearly unheard of in the often-transitory world of journal printing." (*Footnotes*, May 2001)

In 1951, on the recommendation of the SSRC, Executive Officer Matilda White Riley met with Henry Quellmalz, the President of Boyd to discuss the possibilities for publication of the *American Sociological Review* (*ASR*). In February 1951, Boyd published the first issue of *ASR*. At the 45th anniversary of the ASA-Boyd relationship in 1996, Matilda Riley recalled, "When I took over in 1949, our organization faced financial ruin. Not the least of the problems confronting us was *ASR*, the major item in the budget that cost far more than we could afford. But a fortunate event saved the day—the discovery of the Boyd Printing Company and its president, Henry Quellmalz." (*Footnotes*, May 2001) Thus began a long and extraordinary partnership between the ASA and Boyd, which currently prints six of ASA's journals, *Footnotes*, Annual Meeting program materials, and various other ASA publications.

On January 1985, Quellmalz turned over chief operating responsibilities to his daughter Jane Quellmalz Carey, and became Chairman of the Board. Boyd is a family- and female-owned business (Marion Quellmalz, Henry's wife and Jane's mother, owns Boyd Printing Company; and other family members run other parts of the business). ASA's successful partnership with Boyd continues to thrive with Jane Carey as President.

At the celebration marking the 50th anniversary of the ASA-Boyd partnership, Executive Officer Levine, noted, "For a half century, Boyd Printing Company has provided quality printing and service to the ASA. During that time, the printing business has changed dramatically, but Boyd and ASA have continued to produce journals that set standards of excellence." (*Footnotes*, May 2001)

Electronic Publishing and Access

Beginning in the 1980s, computerized word processing, electronic transfer of data and manuscripts, and other systems and technologies for facilitating publishing were introduced into ASA's publications program. By the mid-1990s, rapid advances in the technologies themselves revolutionized the process for publishing, storing, disseminating, and providing access to "printed materials." These changes also brought more efficient systems for advertising and marketing products and offering related services (e.g., online ordering of books and other items). The following are some highlights of ASA's progress in this area (see also section on Information Technology):

- In January 1995, on the recommendation of the Committee on Publications (COP), Council voted: (1) to request COP to establish a subcommittee to explore issues relating to electronic publishing, and (2) to create a second committee to advise ASA on the use of high technology for professional communications more generally. Barry Wellman was appointed chair of this committee (Council Minutes, January 1995).

- In January 1996, Council approved a recommendation from Executive Officer Levine to explore and negotiate an agreement with the Mellon Foundation for the electronic delivery of

ASA journals on the JSTOR system—starting with *ASR, CS, SOE*, and to the extent possible, additional journals in the future. Executive Officer Levine also chaired an American Council of Learned Societies (ACLS) committee on electronic publishing, which was working on a report on delivery options for scholarly journals.

- The ASA *Employment Bulletin* was published online on the ASA homepage beginning in April 1996 as a free service.

- In April 1998, the NeXT typesetting system software, which had been used by ASA since 1992 was replaced by the Pagemaker software. Beginning with the May/June 1998 issue of *Footnotes* and the June issue of *EB*, these publications have since then been produced within the ASA computer environment.

- After 2000, the enhanced website made possible more advanced applications, including publication of documents, data tables, and graphics on the ASA homepage. Quality scanning made possible the reproduction of previously published and printed material into graphic files for publication on the homepage; and the vastly increased storage space on ASA servers made possible the storage, for example, of several years of editions of *Footnotes*, articles from *ASR*, chapters of books, and so forth.

- By 2001, direct online submission of orders for publications became possible through the ASA homepage. Moreover, these were linked to the newly installed upgraded version of the e-NOAH membership database so that order information could be updated immediately on members' records. Members also had direct access to their own records in member-only restricted areas of the homepage.

- Improved communications systems made possible the posting of press releases, "fax-blasting" or mass emailing of announcements, and increased efficiencies of submissions of manuscripts and articles for publication (e.g., through FTP lines).

Controversy over *ASR*

Flagship journals and whom they serve can become areas of debate within scholarly societies. The issue of representativeness and inclusivity of the *ASR*, which had been debated intermittently since at least the early 1970s, emerged as a major topic for discussion in Council during the 1990s. ASA President Amitai Etzioni noted on August 9, 1994 that, "some ASA members feel that *ASR* has not been representative of the discipline . . . [and he invited incoming *ASR* editor Paula England] to address Council about ideas to diversify content, expand the network of people who submit, and change the look of *ASR*." In 1996, Council Member Feagin, "thought there were concerns about *ASR* among qualitative researchers, theorists, African American and Latino/a sociologists, and some of the quantitative sociologists who do policy analysis." (Council Minutes, January 1996) While he noted that progress had been made, Feagin stressed the need "to move ahead aggressively in opening up *ASR* to more diverse work [and he] advocated for greater representation in deputy editors, editors, and reviewers. He recommended that Council create a committee to develop 'diversity of research' guidelines that would become part of the Association's rules for selection of editors." Council asked the Publications Committee at that meeting "to examine the inclusivity of *ASR* and procedures to enhance a broader representation of work and to report back to Council." Over the next several years, considerable discussion on this topic ensued in Council with a subcommittee and eventually a Task Force established to examine its implications and present recommendations.

A major public controversy emerged in 1999 over the *ASR* editor selection process (see details on the specific dispute below), which had always been accomplished as a confidential act of the Council, based on ranked order recommendations of the Committee on Publications (COP). The situation arose after the Council Meeting in February 1999, when Council rejected the top-ranked candidate recommended by COP for *ASR* editor and instead appointed two other co-editors considered qualified by COP.

The COP expressed strong objections to Council's decision not to support its choice of *ASR* editors, and in June 1999, Michael Burawoy, a member of the Publications Committee, made public a letter of resignation from the Committee in protest of the Council's decision to override COP's selection of editors. In a letter published at the same time, ASA President Portes noted that, "in violation of the existing bylaws of the American Sociological Association, the letter divulges details of the selection process that were meant to be confidential for the protection of colleagues who have advanced their candidacies for editorial positions." (*Footnotes*, July 1999:6)

During the spring and summer of 1999, numerous email messages and listserv commentaries, as well as articles in *Footnotes* were circulated on this topic. At issue were debates on (1) Council's treatment of COP, a democratically elected body, and one of ASA's most important committees, (2) whether Council was invoking the principle of confidentiality appropriately or in such a way that limited membership information about processes underlying Council and COP decision making in this area, and (3) whether Council was less committed than COP to promoting diversity and inclusivity in the *ASR*. Comments in the Business Meeting of the 1999 Annual Meeting regarding the issues of confidentiality and democracy were raised and a resolution was passed to ask the immediate past-editor of *ASR* to continue to serve as editor.

Council took up the issue extensively at its August 9, 1999 meeting. By a narrow vote, Council tabled the motion to ask the immediate past-editor to continue to serve, and instead appointed a joint Subcommittee of Publications and Council to articulate a policy regarding confidentiality and accountability that addressed the interests of candidates as well as the ASA membership. A Subcommittee appointed by President Joe Feagin consisting of Nan Lin (Chair), Michael Hout, John Logan, and Guillermina Jasso was charged with considering the editorial selection process and reporting back to Council.

At the invitation of President Feagin, Professor Eduardo Bonilla-Silva of Texas A&M University and Chair of the Section on Racial and Ethnic Minorities, joined the January 2000 Council meeting to present a statement on behalf of the Section Council regarding the 1999 ASA editor selection process. Bonilla-Silva raised questions about the process, and noted that a petition drive (led by Bonnie Thornton Dill) was in process to have Walter Allen installed as editor of *ASR* when the Camic-Wilson editorship was completed. In the ensuing discussion, Council members emphasized confidentiality in selecting editors, and Bonilla-Silva "suggested that perhaps the whole editor selection process should be more open and not confined only to Council." (Council, January 2000)

Ultimately, in January 2000, the Lin Subcommittee recommended to Council that the principle of confidentiality be maintained in the editor selection process, and Council adopted these principles specified in a four-point set of recommendations. Council's action was consistent with the position of the COP, which had reaffirmed its fundamental commitment to principles of confidentiality for the editor selection process at its meeting several weeks earlier on December 12, 1999.

The debate on the editor selection process generated considerable anger and hostility among some members of ASA. Some of the tensions grew out of methodological and theoretical conflicts. Because Walter Allen, the editor who was originally rejected by Council was African American, charges were made of racism behind the February 1999 decision, despite the fact that one of the two co-editors was also African American. These charges were especially leveled against President-Elect Douglas Massey, who read a letter in Council explaining his position. ASA Vice President Patricia Roos, among other members, decried the demonizing of Massey, the author of a number of important works on race relations in contemporary America.

In the summer of 2000, in response to the controversy over the appointment of a new editor for the *ASR*, ASA Council established a 14-member ASA Task Force on Journal Diversity (TFJD) to examine issues of diversity, broadly defined, in ASA journals. "Major issues examined by the TFJD included the relevance of ASA publications to members' interests, whether ASA publications are too narrow in focus, whether certain methodological approaches and substantive areas are under-represented among published articles, and whether certain kinds of individuals are under-represented among the ranks of authors, editorial boards and editors." (ASA homepage) The Task Force presented its Report to Council in January 2003.

7. CORE PROGRAMS OF THE ASA

As noted in the Introduction to this chapter, strategic planning in 1992 provided a comprehensive framework for delivery of services (portfolio of journals, annual meeting, and programs) by the Association to its membership. The role and responsibilities of the Association for an effective publishing program and highly successful annual meetings were conceptualized as vital to promoting how sociologists do their work. In addition, however, Executive Officer Levine noted that, "national associations like [ASA] have perhaps the unique responsibility of promoting the vitality, visibility, and diversity of the discipline. It is here that our programmatic activities are key." (*Footnotes*, February, 1994:2) The ASA objectives during the 1990s were focused in six core programmatic areas: Academic and Professional Affairs, Minority Affairs, the Sydney S. Spivack Program in Applied Social Research and Social Policy, Research on the Discipline and Profession, Public Affairs, and Public Information.

Academic and Professional Affairs Program (APAP)

The Academic and Professional Affairs Program (APAP) was established during 1993 to signal ASA's commitment to advancing sociology and the development of sociologists across academic settings. Janet Mancini Billson, who had been directing the Professional Development Program, led APAP from 1993 to 1995. She also directed the Government Network Project, an experimental effort that operated from 1992 to 1995 to strengthen the links between sociologists and federal employment opportunities. Carla Howery has been Director of APAP since 1995.

The APAP Program integrated key elements of the prior Teaching Services Program (TSP) and the Professional Development Program (PDP). APAP continued to publish syllabi sets and materials on teaching and careers through the Teaching Resources Center (TRC) and to sponsor workshops, consultations, and department reviews through the Teaching Resources Group—with a name change to the Departmental Resources Group (DRG) to underscore APAP's commitment to strengthening sociology departments. (See also Chapter 1 and Appendices 20–22.) Jeanne Ballantine served as Field Coordinator of the DRG from 1991 to 1994; Edward Kain served as Field Coordinator from 1995 to 1997; and Carla Howery assumed these duties thereafter.

APAP sought to provide important services, but more importantly to undertake initiatives to advance sociology in the academy at all levels of the education process and in all types of institutions. In particular, emphasis was placed on strengthening departments of sociology as the key organizational units engaged in the production of sociological knowledge and in the teaching of and training for sociology. Reflecting this ambition, APAP worked more proactively and directly with sociology departmental chairs and others in academic leadership roles.

This objective for systemic change received the strong support of Council. *Footnotes* articles as early as October 1992 ("Enhancing the Stature of Sociology in the Academy"), March 1993 ("ASA Meets with CSU Chairs"), and December 1993 ("ASA Focuses on the Academy") by Executive Officer Levine reported to the membership on the foundations of the APAP Program. The aim was to expand from primarily individual case delivery of services and problem solving to define a new role for ASA in relation to sociology departments (especially chairs and directors of graduate study) aimed at promoting the health and well-being of the discipline. The establishment of a Department Affiliates Program and Chairlink to facilitate routine communications with chairs; an Annual Chairs Conference for two-year, four-year and graduate degree conferring institutions with agendas directed to short- and long-term issues; and data collection about sociology departments, training, students, and graduates to enhance planning were all initiated or in place by mid-1994.

Other specific APAP initiatives during the 1990s contributed to this fundamental agenda. These include the following:

- A key APAP activity was close collaboration with the Minority Affairs Program (MAP) Program on ASA's Minority Opportunities Through School Transformation (MOST) Program aimed at advancing excellence and inclusiveness through curriculum and climate change, research-based training, mentoring, and outreach (see MOST Program).

- In 2001, Council established the Task Force on the Advanced Placement (AP) Course in Sociology, which has created guidelines and curriculum materials for an Advanced Placement high school course and has also assembled other teaching materials. With Caroline Hodges Persell, (Chair), the Task Force has worked to encourage the College Board to develop an AP exam, course, and teacher training. The Task Force has also worked closely with the National Council on Social Studies on these projects. Since August 2002, the ASA has also offered a High School Affiliates Program to link ASA with social studies departments.

- ASA developed a project with Professor William Frey of the University of Michigan to work with departments on Integrating Data Analysis (IDA) into the sociology curriculum. Executive Officer Levine and Frey were Co-Principal Investigators on this Social Science Data Analysis (SSDAN) project designed to build research-based skills "early and often" in sociology students with an emphasis on Census data. ASA received $417,241 from NSF for a three-year award for this project. In 2003, upon Levine's departure, Howery assumed responsibility as Principal Investigator of the ASA team.

- The Carnegie Academy for the Scholarship of Teaching and Learning (CASTL) collaborated with ASA to identify scholars in teaching and learning in sociology. The Carnegie Academy "works with disciplinary associations to maximize the impact of the scholar's work, to disseminate scholarship on teaching and learning, and to identify disciplinary culture that pertains to this work." (Council, February 2001) Nine sociologists were selected from 1999 to 2001 to conduct projects on various issues relating to teaching and learning as part of this venture.

- A workshop on the Scholarship of Teaching and Learning in Sociology was held from July 20–23, 2000 at James Madison University. With support from CASTL and James Madison University, "48 sociologists met to discuss 'what we know' and 'what we need to know' on six topics: on teaching and learning styles, assessment of faculty, use of technology in teaching, curriculum, community academic partnerships, and the institutional context." (Council Minutes, February 2001)

- ASA worked with the Council for Undergraduate Research (CUR) to include more sociologists as members and more sociological research in their publications and meetings. With ASA's encouragement, CUR expanded its programs to include memberships for sociology and other social sciences.

- ASA participated in a project with the American Association for Higher Education on use of peer review in teaching sociology. Initially supported from the Carnegie Foundation for the Advancement of Teaching and Learning, this effort involved synthesis of "empirical work and useful advice" by a team of sociologists.

- In 1998, a report was prepared on part-time work as an outgrowth of a conference on "The Growing Use of Part-time and Adjunct Faculty," held in September 1997.

- With five other disciplines and with funding from the Atlantic Philanthropies, ASA took part in the Preparing Future Faculty (PFF) project to develop models for preparing future faculty. Four sociology departments (competitively selected) participated in the project: North Carolina State University, Texas A&M University, University of Nebraska-Lincoln, and Indiana University. The project concluded in December 2002 with a Capstone Conference.

- At the K-12 level: Based on a review by APAP of practices in nine states, the ASA Council in January 1995 passed a resolution (supported by ASA's Committee on Sociology in Elementary and Secondary Schools) recommending that, "secondary teachers must have nine credit hours of sociology course work in order to be fully qualified to teach courses called 'sociology . . .'" Council at this time also approved initiation of discussions on an Advanced Placement exam in sociology, and on development of course standards for the 12th grade elective in sociology (Council Minutes, January 1995). ASA continued to work with the Educational Testing Service and the College Board in developing a model course for a Grade 12 elective that could serve as the basis for an AP course.

- In 1994, a Task Force on Campus Hate Crimes and Bias-Related Incidents was established by Council to reduce hate-motivated or bias 'crimes' on college campuses. This committee produced a hate crimes resource book and a list of actions which faculty can use to intervene in a campus crisis. This Task Force working with the Committee on Teaching compiled materials illustrative of what sociologists can use to prevent or de-escalate acts of bias and bigotry. A report *Teaching About Ethnoviolence and Hate Crimes* (Second Edition), was compiled by Howard J. Ehrlich and Regina Fidazzo (2000). In 1999, Council created a Task Force on Current Knowledge on Hate/Bias Acts on College and University Campuses with Leonard Gordon, Chair, that presented its final report to Council in January 2002.

- Stimulated by Ernest Boyer's book, *Scholarship Reconsidered*, ASA appointed a Task Force on Scholarly Dimensions of the Professional Work of Sociologists to participate in a national project on "Defining Scholarly Knowledge." (The Task force later became known as the Task Force on "Recognizing and Rewarding the Scholarly and Professional Work of Sociologists.") Funded by the Fund for the Improvement of Postsecondary Education (FIPSE), the Pew Charitable Trusts, and the Lilly Endowment, the project involved about forty disciplines. The objective was for each discipline to produce a set of guidelines for evaluating a broader set of professional activities. ASA's Report, prepared by a Task Force was presented to Council in January 1998. Council "agreed on the importance of encouraging discussion of faculty work and faculty evaluation . . . [and] thought the issues should be discussed but that Council should not endorse or adopt the report." (Council, January 1998)

- In 2001, ASA Council decided to revisit the ASA report on the undergraduate sociology major published in 1990 as *Liberal Learning and the Sociology Major* by appointing a second Task Force "to update and expand upon the original report and its recommendations." The new Report, "*Liberal Learning and the Sociology Major Updated: Meeting the Challenge of Teaching Sociology in the Twenty-First Century*, by Kathleen McKinney, Carla B. Howery, Kerry Strand, Edward L. Kain, and Catherine White Berheide was published in 2004 by the ASA.

- The Task Group On Graduate Education (TAGGE) chaired by Joan Huber issued a Report in March 1992 on a number of issues relating to departments of sociology. Council approved the Report on August 24, 1992, and also appointed a Subcommittee consisting of William Gamson (Chair), David Featherman, Myra Marx Ferree, Jill Quadagno and Doris Wilkinson to examine its implications and frame a discussion for initiatives. The Subcommittee concluded that, rather than orientation toward one "core" in graduate education, a range of approaches and ideas ought to be explored; it therefore examined strengths of various departments, and how these might be modeled as "promising practices" for other departments. In January 1994, a Committee on Graduate Education was appointed by Council for a three-year period "to look at graduate education and identify the special strengths of departments, with the goal of preparing a report on 3 or 4 programs which are doing exceptional work on particular issues."

From 1994 to 1996 subcommittees were appointed by Council to address various aspects of the graduate experience (e.g., preparing graduate students as teachers, sociological practice programs, recruiting and graduating students of color, effective mentoring, and professional ethics). The first reports were issued in 1996 on "Teaching Sociology Graduate Students to Teach Sociology." Subsequent reports were issued by the Committee, including on the "Successful Practice in Master's Programs in Sociology," and on "Models for Professional Socialization of Graduate Students." (All reports are available on the ASA homepage.)

Minority Affairs Program (MAP)

ASA commitment to a diverse discipline led to conceptualizing its specific minority initiatives as elements of a broader Minority Affairs Program (MAP). By the end of 1992, the strategic plan articulated this fundamental objective by characterizing it as Minority Affairs. During the 1990s, the MAP Program consisted primarily of two main components: (1) The Minority Fellowship Program (MFP) funded primarily by NIMH to support predoctoral training of underrepresented minorities in the sociology of mental health and, (2) the Minority Opportunities Through School Transformation (MOST) Program, funded by the Ford Foundation to effect systemic change in sociology departments in order to achieve excellence and inclusiveness in education for *all* students. The MOST program was completed in 2002.

MAP reflected ASA's fundamental objectives that transcended specific activities or projects. A high priority was placed by ASA on expanding the diversity of the profession and on enhancing opportunities for minorities throughout the discipline. The MFP and MOST were described by Executive Officer Levine as, "quite major initiatives whereby the Executive Office plays a pivotal role (a) in ensuring a next generation of well trained minority sociologists, who can be leaders in the field, and (b) in producing systemic changes in how the discipline addresses issues of mentoring and multiculturalism in building faculties of the future." (*Footnotes,* February 1994:2) ASA also worked to build productive alliances with the Historically Black Colleges and Universities (HBCUs) during this time.

The Minority Fellowship Program (MFP)

The Minority Fellowship Program (MFP) of the ASA has provided financial support to minority scholars pursuing graduate studies in mental health continuously since the Program was launched with (primarily) NIMH support in 1974. Since that time (up to 2004), more than 1,200 minority students have received support for graduate training (Appendix 23). By the 25th Anniversary of the MFP, which was celebrated at the 1999 ASA Annual Meeting, 214 Fellows had received PhDs. Effective August 1, 2000, MPF Fellows supported by the NIMH Training grant received a stipend award of $15,000 per year.

ASA received two new awards from NIMH for the MFP Program during the 1990s: $2.5 million was awarded to cover the period from September 1, 1994 to July 31, 2000 (an increase of almost $500,000 over the previous cycle), and $2,688,000 was awarded to cover the period from August 1, 2000 to July 31, 2005.

During the 1990s, ASA continued to seek additional sources of support for minority student training. In order to diversify training for minority students of color in sociology, the MAP Program used resources from the ASA's restricted MFP Fund to support non-mental health predoctoral fellows. While only a few such fellows could receive ongoing support in any one year (leading to only one or two new starts), use of this funding stream allowed ASA to provide predoctoral fellowship support outside of the NIMH award. The MFP Fund consists of member contributions (it was the largest proportion of member individual contributions) support from such organizations as the Sociologists for Women in Society (SWS), Alpha Kappa Delta (AKD), and the Association of Black Sociologists (ABS), as well as royalty gifts.

During the 1990s, ASA added explicit training components to the predoctoral training program in addition to the stipend and informal networking opportunities that Fellows receive. These activities included Proposal Development Workshops held in Washington, DC, the Summer Research Initiative (which placed Fellows at research sites with major ongoing studies in mental health or in methods training courses at the Inter-university Consortium for Political and Social Research [ICPSR], or similar programs), and specific training activities during the ASA Annual Meeting. Also, in 2000, the MFP Program added an orientation training workshop to introduce incoming Fellows to the Program and to the sociology of mental health as a day event before the start of the ASA Annual Meeting.

Minority Opportunities Through School Transformation (MOST)

In 1988, under the general umbrella of the MFP, ASA undertook a program of summer institutes to recruit and attract minority students to sociology. Funded by an $185,000 grant from the Ford Foundation, MOST I (as this initiative was termed as it ended in 1993), consisted of four successful summers of institutes of coursework, research experiences, and mentoring on two university campuses each summer: at the University of Delaware and the University of Wisconsin-Madison in the summers of 1990 and 1991, and the University of California-Berkeley and the University of Michigan-Ann Arbor in 1992 and 1993.

The Minority Opportunities through School Transformation Program officially commenced in the fall of 1993 with a period to plan, recruit, and select departments. In May 1994, the MOST Program launched its work with a workshop of all participating MOST coordinators and department chairs. Ultimately, 11 departments participated for the full duration of the Program, including seven at primarily undergraduate institutions (Augusta State University, Grinnell College, Pitzer College, University of Puerto Rico-Mayagüez, Southwestern University, University of Texas-El Paso, and William Paterson University), and four at PhD conferring institutions (University of California-Santa Barbara; University of Nebraska-Lincoln; Pennsylvania State University; and Texas A&M University).

The Ford Foundation made two awards in support of MOST: The initial grant of $415,000 covered the period from October 1, 1993 through September 30, 1998, and was renewed in 1999 with a $485,000 award covering the period of October 1, 1999 to July 31, 2002.

MOST focused on activities that aimed to produce systemic change at the academic departmental level, to improve access and opportunity for students of color, and, in general to change "business-as-usual" practices of departments in order to achieve excellence in education for all students. With leadership from the national MOST team in the Executive Office, ASA worked intensively with departments over the eight-year life of MOST to introduce sustainable change in curriculum, climate, outreach to diverse populations at undergraduate and graduate levels, research-based training, and mentoring.

A review of program outcomes in the participating institutions conducted at the completion of the program in 2002 showed that the number of courses containing diversity content increased, the percent of graduating minority majors nearly doubled, proportions of underrepresented minorities as graduating majors increased (with many students advancing to graduate study), and the number of minority faculty increased significantly.

On June 6–7, 2002, a Capstone Conference was held in Washington, DC as a culmination to the MOST Program. Nearly 100 leaders in education and on diversity issues gathered to reflect on the achievements of and lessons learned from MOST, and to identify approaches that might be used to transport MOST to other disciplines and institutions. While MOST was located in sociology departments, a key objective was to find ways to transport the MOST model to other social and behavioral sciences and to other fields. A report on the MOST Program entitled *Promoting Diversity and Excellence in Higher Education Through Department Change*, by Felice J. Levine, Hávidan Rodríguez, Carla B. Howery, and Alfonso R. Latoni-Rodríguez was published by the ASA in 2002.

The Sydney S. Spivack Program in Applied Social Research and Social Policy

The Spivack Program in Applied Social Research and Social Policy was established as a core program within the Executive Office in 1992. According to the proposal that was submitted to the Trustees of the Cornerhouse Fund in 1991, the Program envisioned by ASA would "take the lead in enhancing the visibility, prestige, and centrality of applied social research and the application of sociological knowledge to social policy." (Proposal for the Sydney S. Spivack Program in Applied Social Research and Social Policy, January 1991:1) In doing so, the program aimed to build on the substantial advances that had been made with respect to promoting applied sociology and sociological practice during the 1980s.

Origins of the Program

As described more fully in Chapter 1, the Trustees of the Cornerhouse Fund informed the ASA in 1989 that the Fund would cease operations, that remaining funds would be gifted, and that ASA would be invited to submit a proposal on how it would expend these funds. The ASA proposal to establish a continuing program named in honor of Sydney S. Spivack (instead of expending the resources on a single major project) was accepted by the Trustees in early 1991, and the gift to the Association was formally announced on August 26, 1991 at the Annual Meeting in Cincinnati. In taking this unrestricted gift and placing it in an ASA Council-designated restricted Fund, the ASA established a program that in the short- and long-term could continue to pursue activities that addressed the connections between sociological research and important issues of social policy. The basic gift from the Cornerhouse Fund establishing the Spivack Program was $750,000, with a small additional amount (approximately $25,000) transmitted after the Fund was fully dissolved.

The initial Spivack Advisory Committee chaired by Joan Waring (which also included Ivar Berg, William Hoffman, Marvin Olsen, Harriet Presser, Wendy Baldwin, William V. D'Antonio, Manuel de la Puente, and Cheryl Leggon) was appointed by Council to guide the work of the Spivack Program (including the Committee's offering its own initiatives). Various operational models and programmatic ideas were presented for launching the program at the first meeting of the Advisory Committee in November 1991. In July 1992, the Committee decided on a "staged" strategy for topics, including invited papers on policy issues—which would serve as a catalyst for workshops, Congressional briefings, press conferences, and so forth. Phyllis Moen wrote the first paper on "Work and Family Linkages," which was the subject of the first Congressional Briefing on December 10, 1992 and a media briefing on February 1, 1993 (see Appendix 25). In 1993, Council clarified that the Spivack Program was a core program within the Executive Office and allocated full authority over the Program budget to the Executive Office once an annual budget was approved by Council.

The Spivack Program in the 1990s

Inaugurated in 1992, the Spivack Program is a core program of the Association. As it evolved during the 1990s, it consisted of four basic components: (1) a series of policy briefings aimed at Congressional staff, Administration officials, representatives of non-profit associations, and the media, (2) other special initiatives that sought to integrate research and public policy through educational forums, (3) a Congressional Fellowship Program that provided support for a sociologist to work on a Congressional staff or Congressional agency, and (4) a Community Action Research Initiative (CARI) that provided an opportunity for sociologists to bring social science knowledge, methods, and expertise to bear in addressing community identified issues and concerns.

THE CONGRESSIONAL SEMINARS AND POLICY INITIATIVES

Through 2002, the Spivack Program sponsored about a dozen Congressional seminars and other social science briefings on policy topics. To disseminate the results of these briefings more widely, the substantive contributions of each were published in ASA's *Issue Series in Social Research and Social Policy*. Several Spivack Program workshops and conferences were also conducted to apply sociological knowledge to issues of societal importance or with potential policy consequences. Workshops, for example, were held on "Research Challenges on the Social Causes of Violence" (June 1993); "Initiative on Genocide and Human Rights" (November 1993); "Rethinking the Urban Agenda" (May 1994); and "Social Science Perspectives on Affirmative Action in Employment" (June 1996). A volume, *The Realities of Affirmative Action in Employment*, authored by Barbara F. Reskin was produced from the June 1996 Conference. (Appendix 25 contains a complete list of Spivack Program initiatives and related publications.)

THE CONGRESSIONAL FELLOWSHIP

The ASA has supported a Congressional Fellowship each year since 1993 (a complete list of Fellows is included in Appendix 26). The Congressional Fellowship supports a PhD-level sociologist as a staff member in a Congressional office, committee, or agency for an intensive six-month period. This experience provides an opportunity for a sociologist to apply sociological knowledge to important issues and to learn more about the policy making process. The Fellowship is funded in part by the American Sociological Foundation, and is part of the Spivack Program in Applied Social Research and Social Policy. The year 2004 stipend for the Fellowship is $15,000.

AAAS/ASA MASS MEDIA SCIENCE FELLOWSHIP

With the American Association for the Advancement of Science (AAAS), the ASA sponsored a summer fellowship for sociologists from 1997 to 2003 to enhance their skills and training in public communication and working with the media. The Fellow was placed in a major media outlet, in addition to orientation seminars with other AAAS Mass Media Science Fellows. The Program was discontinued in 2003 due to the high costs of this Fellowship and the low numbers of sociologists who applied as candidates. The Spivack Advisory Committee thought that other efforts at preparing social science writers and sociologists who would engage in media work would be more effective. (The AAAS/ASA Fellows and their assignments are listed in Appendix 27.)

COMMUNITY ACTION RESEARCH INITIATIVE (CARI)

Since 1995, the ASA has awarded up to seven fellowships each year under the Community Action Research Initiative (CARI) Fellowship Program. These awards are made in support of sociologists engaged in projects that bring social science knowledge, methods, and expertise to bear in addressing community-identified issues and concerns. Grant applications are encouraged from sociologists seeking to work with community organizations, local public interest groups, or community action projects. Projects have included work with groups involved with: health and culture in the African-American community, jobs and support groups for the homeless, women domestic workers, health conditions in the Latino population, immigrant workers rights advocacy programs, and childcare programs. Up to $2,500 is awarded for each Fellowship to cover direct costs associated with doing the community action research.

The Research Program on the Discipline and Profession

The Research Program on the Discipline and Profession was formally established in 1992 to advance knowledge and information about sociology by improving routine data collection, undertaking studies and issuing reports of significance, and making data accessible to others with research interests in the profession. These goals have been accomplished by conducting several types of surveys, compiling relevant data from secondary sources, building and maintaining databases from ASA membership information and other sources, and disseminating research findings in various formats and through a variety of venues.

Since its inception, research results have been routinely published in *Footnotes*, shared with departments and chairs, and presented at regional and Annual Meeting workshops and at other professional societies and conferences. By 1999, with the evolution of the ASA website, substantially more information, data, and analyses from the Research Program were published on the homepage. Also in 1999, ASA introduced the *Data Brief* and *Research Brief* series containing summary analyses and highlights of information on the discipline and profession. Initially published as print documents, this series became an integral part of the website after several years. (See Appendix 24 for a listing of publications produced by the Program.)

During the 1990s, the Research Program activities were directed by Carla Howery, Cynthia Costello, and (since 1997) by Roberta Spalter-Roth. Other staff in the Research Program has included a Program Assistant (who also performed other programmatic functions), and from 2000–3, two Postdoctoral Fellows. In 2002, William Erskine joined the staff as a Research Associate in the Program.

A major achievement of the Research Program from 1991 to 2000 involved systematizing the data collection processes in several areas:

- **The Survey of Graduate Departments of Sociology.** This Survey was conducted annually between AY 1991–92 and 1997–98 of the universe of graduate sociology departments in the United States. The individual sociology department is the unit of analysis in this survey. In 1999, the Research Program in consultation with department chairs, undertook a review of information needs of departments, and in AY 2001–2, the graduate departments were surveyed again (with this assessment taken into consideration) along with a sample survey of BA-only departments. Since 1994, the Survey was conducted as part of the process to collect information for the *Guide to Graduate Departments*, and the *Guide* has also included a section with analysis of data on graduate departments. Data are compiled on approximately 2,300 departments, and include institution and department name, type of degree or courses offered, chairperson, mailing address, phone number, and number of sociology faculty (Preface to the 1999 Guide).

- **ASA Membership DataBase.** A database on ASA members has been extracted annually since 1999 for research purposes from ASA's NOAH membership database. These data are derived from information provided on membership and renewal forms each year and are entered into the NOAH data base. A "public use" data file containing characteristics of FY 2000 members was created from these files in 2001 for use by the Committee on the Status of Women (CSWS) and the Committee on the Status of Racial and Ethnic Minorities (CSREM). An analysis of the 2001 membership was also published on the ASA homepage, and in the January 2002 issue of *Footnotes*.

- **PhD Tracking Survey.** In 1997 and 1998, ASA took part in a multidisciplinary survey of employment experiences and career paths of the 1996–97 cohort of new PhDs. The study was conducted as a collaborative project of a number of scientific societies, including ASA, under the auspices of the Commission on Professions in Science and Technology (CPST), with funding from the Sloan Foundation and the National Science Foundation. A 72 percent response rate was achieved in the survey, which focused on employment information during the week of October 13, 1997. Several ASA *Research Briefs*, including "New Doctorates in Sociology: Professions Inside and Outside of the Academy" (2000), "Gender in the Early Stages of the Sociological Career" (2000), and "Minorities at Three Stages in the Sociology Pipeline" (2001) were published from this study. In 2001, a brief follow-up survey was conducted, and with 14 professional societies, ASA developed plans to conduct a follow up of the cohort of PhDs, five to six years after they received their PhDs.

- **Secondary Data Compilation and Analysis.** Data relating to sociology and sociologists (including comparative data on selected social science disciplines) have been compiled from various sources, including the National Science Foundation (NSF), the National Center for Education Statistics (NCES), College and University Professional Association for Human Resources (CUPA-HR), and the *Chronicle of Higher Education*. Analyses based on these sources were presented on the ASA homepage.

Public Affairs Program

Council has consistently supported and encouraged ASA participation in activities that enhance the visibility and role of the discipline of sociology and the profession. In February 1992, Council specifically affirmed "the Public Affairs Program as a high priority initiative and endorse[d] efforts by the Executive Office to explore how this [would] fit with ongoing commitments." Discussion in Council focused on the need to undertake such activities in different arenas—particularly as collaborative efforts with other organizations before Congress and federal agencies.

While ASA's efforts built on the commitment to and advances in public information activities of the 1980s, initiatives after 1993 took on new forms following the realignment of Programs as outlined in the strategic plan. "Public Affairs activities reflect our recognition that advocacy, education, and representation are integral to our goals of advancing sociology as a field and discipline, and promoting the contributions and uses of sociology in society," wrote Executive Officer Levine in 1994 in describing the objectives of the Program *(Footnotes*, February 1994:3). The Public Affairs and Public Information Programs were planned as efforts that support and undergird substantive programs (such as the Spivack Program) as well as key goals of the Association.

In pursuing these objectives, ASA has worked closely with other scientific and aligned organizations, particularly the Consortium of Social Science Associations (COSSA), the National Humanities Alliance (NHA), and the American Council of Learned Societies (ACLS). Also, the Association joined and participated in other coalitions such as the Coalition for National Science Funding (CNSF)—routinely sponsoring an exhibit of an NSF-supported sociological project at the CNSF exhibition held each spring on Capitol Hill on scientific projects funded by NSF.

During the 1990s, the ASA undertook initiatives to educate about and speak on behalf of sociology (and the social sciences) by (1) responding to legislation, (2) supporting the National Science Foundation on budgetary and other issues, (3) contributing to the work of the Census 2000 through participation in key committees, (4) promoting sociology in health issues, (5) participating in activities related to protection of human subjects in research, and (6) engaging in or testifying on behalf of agencies and programs vital to ASA and sociology. The ASA also took various actions in response to the terrorist attacks in the United States on September 11, 2001. The following are illustrative of some of these initiatives:

Responding to Legislation

ASA routinely monitored federal legislation (especially legislation with adverse effects for social science research) and, with other scientific and learned societies, responded to such initiatives in various ways. For example, in 1996, ASA led a "Research and Privacy Coalition" of more than 30 groups in opposition to H.R. 1271 ("the Family Privacy Protection Act of 1995") which was passed as part of the GOP agenda on the "Contract with America." The Act required parents to give written consent before their children could participate in almost all federally-funded research. The Coalition strongly argued that this measure would have a chilling effect on research on minors and mobilized action against it. Executive Officer Levine testified before the Senate Committee on Governmental Affairs on behalf of the Coalition in opposition to H.R. 1271 on November 9,1995. On June 19, 1996, the Coalition organized a Senate staff briefing and press conference on Capitol Hill to urge defeat of the bill. The profile that ASA and related groups gave to this issue sufficiently delayed Congressional action that it was supplanted by other topics until it resurfaced in the context of reauthorization of the Elementary and Secondary School Act (ESEA) in 2001.

Supporting the National Science Foundation

ASA participated in activities aimed at strengthening the role of the National Science Foundation as a key federal agency supporting social science research. In the early 1990s, Executive Officers D'Antonio and Levine were actively engaged in the process to establish a separate directorate for the social and behavioral sciences at the NSF, and, throughout the 1990s, Levine continued to work closely with the NSF leadership and the NSF Sociology Program on expanding opportunities for the social sciences. NSF Sociology Program Director Patricia White spent a year starting in March 1997 visiting at the ASA Executive Office to work on special policy issues.

Executive Officer Levine testified on Appropriations for the National Science Foundation, before the U.S. House of Representatives (Committee on Appropriations, Subcommittee on Veterans Affairs, Housing and Urban Development and Independent Agencies) on behalf of ASA on three occasions: in April 1999 (for FY 2000 Appropriations), in May 1997 (for FY 1998 Appropriations), and in May 1996 (for FY 1997 Appropriations).

ASA also supported the NSF Data Infrastructure Initiative, a year-long planning effort launched in the summer of 1997 to examine the investment in data infrastructure—for example, the General Social Survey (GSS). ASA sponsored workshops and meetings, and published articles in *Footnotes* on the initiative to raise awareness of the issue and provide opportunity for contribution to this planning effort. Executive Officer Levine was invited to present at a meeting held by the National Research Council on this issue.

Supporting Census 2000

In January 1995, Council passed a motion urging that ASA seek greater involvement with the U.S. Bureau of the Census. The Executive Office subsequently explored ways that sociology and ASA could have a greater role in the Census. In December 1995, then Department of Commerce Secretary Ronald Brown appointed Executive Officer Levine to the newly reconstituted Advisory Committee for the Census 2000 (renamed the Decennial Census Advisory Committee). Executive Officer Levine was an active member of the Advisory Committee, chairing the Statistical Estimation Subcommittee and serving on a small writing team that drafted the Committee's major report.

Promoting Sociology in Health Issues

ASA brought a sociological perspective to the field of health through various efforts at the U.S. Department of Health and Human Services (DHHS), the National Institutes of Health (NIH), and the National Academy of Sciences (NAS).

A major challenge for social science research occurred in 1991 when DHHS Secretary Louis Sullivan rescinded an award by the National Institute of Child Health and Human Development (NICHD) to the University of North Carolina for support of the American Teenage Study. The award had been made after peer review and approval by the NICHD Advisory Council and the NICHD Director. ASA Council (in response to a request by the Sociology of Population Section), passed a resolution strongly opposing the "totally egregious and unprecedented action of HHS Secretary Louis Sullivan in rescinding an approved grant . . . .This action is a serious threat to the integrity of the peer review process and the independence of scientific thought, and represents political intrusion into scientific research. We direct the Executive Office to publicly oppose this action, and to take all appropriate steps to have the study reinstated." (Council Minutes, August 27, 1991)

ASA played an important role in emphasizing the social sciences at the National Institutes of Health (NIH): In 1993, ASA urged that social science be explicitly included in the title of the newly created Office of Behavioral and Social Science Research (OBSSR) and worked as an active member of the coalition to establish this Office. ASA also worked closely with the OBSSR throughout the 1990s on a number of initiatives, including a jointly sponsored Science Writer's Workshop in June 1997 (see below).

ASA sought to increase the visibility of sociology at NIH by, (for example), providing extensive comment on the restructuring of peer review at NIH, and by submitting a detailed statement to the NIMH on the importance of investing in sociological work. The ASA also helped in planning and implementing a major conference with the NIH, "Toward Higher Levels of Analysis: Progress and Promise in Research on Social and Cultural Dimensions of Health," which took place on the NIH campus in June 2000. This conference was the first time NIH focused on the social sciences in this area.

Executive Officer Levine testified before a U.S. House of Representatives Subcommittee on Appropriations on Fiscal Year 1998 Appropriations for the National Institutes of Health on April 16, 1997. ASA also submitted written testimony on the National Institutes of Health to the U.S. Senate on May 1, 1997.

Participating in Activities on Protecting Human Subjects in Research

The ASA has participated in activities relating to protection of human subjects since the late 1970s when the Executive Office and the ASA Standing Committee on Regulations of Research responded to U.S. Department of Health and Human Services revisions to procedures on standards for human protections in federally-funded research. In the two decades that followed, ASA became involved in the issue in a number of significant ways, including the legal cases of Mario Brajuha (see Chapter 1) and Richard Scarce, which focused on protection of confidential information provided by research subjects. In the mid-1990s, the ASA Committee on Ethics considered related issues extensively in the course of the major revision of the ASA Code of Ethics (approved in 1997).

In January 2001, then Secretary of the U.S. Department of Health and Human Services (DHHS), Donna Shalala, appointed ASA's Executive Officer Felice J. Levine to the National Human Research Protections Advisory Committee (NHRPAC). Levine was one of only two social scientists on NHRPAC. The Committee was charged with providing expert advice and recommendations to the DHHS departmental officials on a broad range of issues and topics pertaining to the protection of human research subjects. Levine was Co-chair of NHRPAC's Social and Behavioral Sciences Working Group. She also testified before the Committee Assessing the System for Protecting Human Research Subjects of the Institute of Medicine (IOM) of the National Academies (on behalf of COSSA and the ASA) on January 31, 2001.

The ASA Response to the Terrorist Attacks of September 11, 2001

Following the terrorist attacks on September 11, 2001, the Association issued a public statement on the tragic events, disseminated relevant materials to members of the Congress and other policy makers, and posted lists of experts from sociology who were available for consultation and interviews. "The Statement of the American Sociological Association on the Terrorist Attack,

September 11, 2001," noted that, "Sociologists have made contributions in different areas that can add significantly to public understanding of these events and to healing communities and our nation." Sociologists added their knowledge and expertise to the public discussion on the causes and consequences of such events, and several Congressional briefings sponsored by the Spivack Program were held during 2002 on related issues (see Appendix 25). Terrorism and related themes were highlighted at the 2002 Annual Meeting (see Chapter 3).

In the months following the attacks of September 11, 2001, the federal government began removing or restricting access to certain public datasets that were vital to researchers, policy makers, professionals in public health and the environment, industry, and others. With consultation and expertise provided by ASA's Section on Environment and Technology, and acknowledging the sensitivity of these issues in light of security issues surrounding the September attacks, ASA Council passed a resolution in January 2002 on "Access to Public Data." The Resolution urged that rationale for such restrictions be specified, "that recognized scientific, academic, and citizens organizations engaged in lawful use of such data be granted access to such information through data access provisions; and that an advisory committee on public access to environmental and public health data be formed . . . to guide government agencies in maximizing reasonable public access." (*Footnotes*, February, 2002:9)

Other Public Affairs Initiatives

ASA also collaborated on actions with other aligned associations in areas of mutual concern and especially on issues affecting the social sciences, humanities, and education. Some of these other initiatives included:

- In 1997, a project was undertaken in response to a request from the Office of Science and Technology Policy (OSTP) in support of President Clinton's Initiative on Race, "One America." Of all the scientific and learned societies, ASA alone responded to this call from OSTP. With the Spivack Program, ASA sponsored a research workshop on the Race Initiative in April 1998, actively sought to engage sociologists and other social scientists in this project, and undertook preparation of research papers on various issues relating to race, racism, and race relations. ASA was awarded $87,640 from the W. K. Kellogg Foundation in 1998, and $54,300 from The Ford Foundation in 1997 for the project.

- With the National Humanities Alliance, ASA joined the effort to protect the National Endowment for the Humanities (NEH) from sharp budget cuts or total elimination due to the House GOP plan to balance the federal budget.

- The ASA joined colleagues from the American Psychological Association (APA) on the Human Capital Initiative in the mid-1990s; and in 2000, began support for the Decade of Behavior (2000–10), a multidisciplinary effort led by the APA to focus attention on the potential for contribution by the behavioral and social sciences on meeting significant challenges of society.

- The ASA was involved in collaboration on several major projects on violence. Executive Officer Levine was invited to attend the federal Interagency Violence Research Working Group, and served on the Advisory Board of the National Consortium on Violence Research (NCOVR) and the National Television Violence Study.

- On behalf of COSSA, Levine provided testimony on Appropriations for the Office of Justice Programs, U.S. Department of Justice, before a U.S. House of Representatives Subcommittee on Appropriations three times: on April 17, 1997 (for FY 1998); April 17, 1996 (for FY1997); and on May 11, 1993 (for FY 1994 Appropriations).

Public Information Program

First established in the mid-1980s, the Public Information Program of ASA continued to expand media coverage of sociology during the 1990s. The strategic plan of 1992 envisioned two goals for the Public Information Program: (1) to respond to media inquiries with timely and relevant information, including referrals to experts on specific issues, and (2) to initiate press briefings and other actions that inform and educate about sociology. Topics emanating from the substantive programs such as the Spivack Program were viewed as particularly appropriate for nurturing media interest in sociological issues. There was a close alliance between Public Affairs and Public Information initiatives with the same members of ASA's small staff often engaging in one, the other, or both forms of activity.

At the 1993 Annual Meeting, a public information consultant was engaged to enhance coverage and to involve the media in the meeting by initiating a special media panel. Edward Hatcher was appointed Director of Public Affairs and Communications in 1995 and served until 1997. Katherine J. Rosich, a Policy Analyst Consultant to the ASA on Spivack projects, continued the work of coordinating the public information functions from 1998 to early 2002, when Lee Herring joined the staff as Director. In July 2000, Johanna Ebner, a recent graduate of American University in Sociology and Communications was hired as a Program Assistant in Public Information. Ann Boyle, the AAAS/ASA Media Fellow for 1998, and Rachel Gragg (who had completed a term as Congressional Fellow) provided professional support in the public information area during the 1998 and 1999 Annual Meetings respectively.

Considerable emphasis was placed in the Public Information Program on enhancing forms of communication with the media:

- Requests for information by media were routinely referred to sociologists with expertise in a given area. These events also generated ongoing contacts with some members of the press.

- Press releases were written on articles from ASA journals (*ASR* and *JHSB* as well as special editions of *ASR* and *CS*) and were posted on the news wires (these were routinely filed on newswires: Newswise and the AAAS news service, Eurekalert).

- Events held under the auspices of the Spivack Program or special public affairs initiatives were also covered in press releases and posted on the newswires (e.g., ASA held a briefing at the National Press Club on research related to the Family and Medical Leave Act in 1993, and also on the action against H.R. 1271 in 1996). The media was invited to all Congressional briefings and Spivack Program initiatives and to the MOST Capstone Conference in June 2002 (special media packets were prepared for these events).

- A Science Writer's Workshop sponsored jointly by ASA and OBSSR was held on June 30, 1997 on "Families, Youth, and Children's Well Being," featuring Linda Burton, Donald Hernandez, and Sandra Hofferth (proceedings were published in the ASA *Issue Series in Social Research and Social Policy*).

- The ASA Annual Meeting was a high priority for the Public Information Program. A major effort was made to contact or invite national and local media to the meeting, packets of special materials were prepared, and a media office was set up at the Annual Meeting to provide services and support to members of the press who attended. Press releases on plenary sessions, presentations, selected papers, and other special events at the Meeting were prepared and posted on the newswires. Each year one or two press conferences were also held during the meeting: In 1998, a press conference was held at the release of *The Realities of Affirmative Action in Employment*, by Barbara F. Reskin. A press conference on "Cyberspace and Everyday Life," with Barry Wellman, Keith Hampton, and Marc Smith at the 2000 Annual Meeting generated dozens of media stories around the world in the weeks following the Annual Meeting.

8. OTHER PROGRAMS AND ACTIVITIES

Fund for the Advancement of the Discipline (FAD)

The Fund for the Advancement of the Discipline (FAD) continued to provide support in the form of small grants for projects that advance the discipline of sociology. Supported by the American Sociological Association through a matching grant from the National Science Foundation, the goal of FAD is to nurture the development of scientific knowledge by funding small, groundbreaking research initiatives and other important scientific research activities. FAD awards provide scholars with seed money for innovative research that has the potential for challenging the discipline, stimulating new lines of research, and creating new networks of scientific collaboration. The award is intended to provide opportunities for substantive and methodological breakthroughs, broaden the dissemination of scientific knowledge, and provide leverage for acquisition of additional research funds. The maximum amount of each award is $7,000 (2004 levels). (ASA homepage)

The first NSF award to ASA in support of a small grants program was made in 1987 (see Chapter 1). During the 1990s, the National Science Foundation made the following awards to the Program: in 1990, $60,000 (covering the period from September 1, 1990 to February 29, 1996); in 1994: $60,000 (for September 1, 1994 to August 31, 1997, including a supplement of $20,000); in 1997: $161,526 (for July 15, 1997 to June 30, 2001, including a supplement for June 2001), and in 2001: $165,000 (for February 15, 2001 to February 14, 2004).

From 1991 to 1997, the Program was directed by Executive Officer Levine, and from 1997 to 2002, by Felice Levine (the Principal Investigator on the NSF grants) and Roberta Spalter-Roth, with the assistance of Andrew Sutter. A FAD Advisory Panel (composed of members of Council) participated in making award selections.

From 1987 to 2001, 622 proposals were submitted to the FAD Program and 184 scholars received awards. The Program is limited to PhDs (or the equivalent degree), and grantees come from a broad spectrum of colleges and universities, all academic ranks, and a range of years since they received their PhDs (Spalter-Roth, in *Footnotes*, March 2001).

International Activities

The ASA has a long history of commitment to international issues. The Association addressed such issues in a number of ways, including by: (1) sponsoring activities at the Annual Meeting featuring international themes and topics, (2) participating in the International Sociological Association (ISA) and other international organizations and events, (3) initiating activities through ASA committees and sections, (4) collaborating and networking with other professional organizations relating to specific area studies (e.g., Latin America), (5) hosting visiting foreign delegations, (6) responding to requests for assistance from sociological associations in other countries, and (7) featuring articles on international events in *Footnotes*, and in other ASA publications. The ASA has also responded to human rights violations (see Human Rights), and to efforts in response to international conflicts and acts of terrorism.

Task Force on the International Focus of American Sociology

In August 1999, a Task Force on the International Focus of American Sociology (TFIFAS) was appointed "to provide the Association with a comprehensive review of the international focus of the Association . . . [and] to undertake specific activities that reinforce this strong commitment." (Council Agenda Memo, August 1, 1999) The members of the Task Force were Michael Micklin (Chair), James McCartney, Cathy Rakowski, Saskia Sassen, Brent Shea, and David Wiley. The TFIFAS submitted its final report to Council in 2003.

As part of its mandate, the Task Force examined the *Annual Meeting Programs*, committee activities, and ASA teaching materials for international content. The analyses of program content showed a generally increased attention over the years to international issues at the Annual Meeting. Committees also increasingly addressed international topics. However, levels of participation in ASA meetings by foreign sociologists (especially by non-Europeans) were found to be low, in part due to the lack of available funding. Teaching materials also generally had a low degree of international material. Finally, the Report assessed external funding sources that could enhance the participation of non-U.S. scholars at the Annual Meeting and recommended that ASA should reconstitute a committee dedicated to international issues.

Annual Meetings

Annual Meetings in 1993 ("Transition to Democracy") and 1997 ("Bridges of Sociology") were among those during the 1990s with a strong emphasis on international themes. In 1993, ASA President Lipset continued the practices of Presidents Melvin Kohn and James Coleman by inviting foreign scholars (especially those with Caribbean and Latin American interests) to participate on the program at the Annual Meeting in Miami. Funding was also obtained to support travel to the meeting by sociologists from the former Soviet Union, other Eastern European countries, and several developing nations. With President Neil Smelser, the 1997 Annual Meeting in Toronto was intentionally inclusive of most geographic regions of the world. The meeting theme was on the bridges between countries and between disciplines, and great efforts were made to include Canadian sociologists, with two thematic sessions assigned to the Canadian Sociological and Anthropological Association.

International Sociological Association (ISA)

The ASA continued to participate in meetings and activities of the International Sociological Association (ISA), the major worldwide organization of sociologists. The ISA meetings, which are held at regular four-year intervals, took place in Madrid, Spain in 1990 (the Twelfth Congress, as the ISA meetings are known); Bielefeld, Germany in 1994 (Thirteenth Congress); and in Montreal, Canada in 1998 (Fourteenth Congress). The ASA received block travel grants from NSF in support of travel by U.S. sociologists to the ISA meetings (with the exception of the Montreal meeting, for which funding was not requested, because it was considered to be no different than travel to an ASA meeting).

The ISA-ASA relationship was complex and reflected certain tensions. Over the years, ASA Council and other ASA members criticized certain aspects of the ISA governance, organizational, and operational structure. ASA long argued for a more democratic system with individual dues and individual voting by members. However according to the ISA Bylaws adopted in January 1994, ASA dues to ISA were increased—but each country would continue to have one representative in the Council of National Associations, regardless of the size of the country or the number of members it has in ISA. Discussion in Council during 1994 focused on these changes, including whether ASA should continue to be an institutional member. In August 1994, however, Council voted to continue its affiliation with ISA and to review it on an annual basis (given the governance issues of ISA), and to enhance coordination by having the ASA delegate to ISA serve as a member of the Committee on International Sociology.

In 1997, the Russell Sage Foundation awarded ASA $25,000 to fund the ISA-ASA North American Conference on "Millennial Milestone: The Heritage and Future of Sociology," which was planned and coordinated by Council member Janet Abu-Lughod, and took place on August 7–8, 1997 in Toronto, Canada. A manuscript based on the conference, "Continuities and Cutting Edges: Sociology for the Twenty-First Century," edited by Janet Abu Lughod was published by the University of Chicago Press in 1999.

Other International Organizations

The ASA also has a working relationship as part of the Consortium of Affiliates for International Programs of the AAAS. In 1992, former Executive Officer William D'Antonio was elected President of the International Institute of Sociology (IIS). Founded in Paris, France in 1893, the IIS (distinct from the ISA), is an organization of scholars sharing theoretical and research interests *(Footnotes,* March 1992:6).

Other activities relating to Internationalization of Sociology

Over the years, ASA has focused attention on international issues in many other ways. The ASA, for example, has been asked to lend its support on behalf of sociological associations in developing countries or those emerging from totalitarian regimes (e.g., In 1992, by the Albanian Sociology Department). The ASA also hosted delegations from a number of countries (e.g., of Chinese students in October 1997; as well as from Russia and other countries).

President Coleman also addressed the "rapid internationalization of sociology and what role the ASA should play to improve communication and collaboration. He also sought comments on the need to stimulate greater interaction among international sociology associations. Among items discussed were the current structure of the International Sociological Association, the role of the Committee on International Sociology, the role of the ASA/NSF Small Grants Program in funding proposals aimed at enhancing international networking, and foundation support." (Council Minutes, January 1992)

The ASA additionally provided coverage of international issues in *Footnotes,* through its homepage, and through other publications. A regular *Footnotes* feature to the mid-1990s "International News and Notes" covered a range of topics, including international funding and teaching opportunities, news about research programs (such as the International Social Survey [ISS] Program of NORC), and so forth. President Coleman proposed this idea "to provide better visibility for the activities of overseas colleagues and to facilitate better communication in general. Although no formal motion was made, the editors indicated that they were sympathetic to the suggestion of highlighting international issues." (Council Minutes, August 27, 1991)

Human Rights

Over the past several decades, the ASA has spoken out in defense of human rights generally, but especially on behalf of scholars who have been arrested, convicted, and incarcerated for activities relating to their scientific and scholarly work. ASA has long argued that restricting the academic freedom of sociologists and other scientists is certain to have a chilling effect on other independent scholarly investigations. Since the late 1990s, ASA has also advocated a strong U.S. governmental response to the infringement of academic freedoms as critical to promoting democracy in nations under study, since the "free production and circulation of knowledge [is] vital to both science and democracy." (ASA Press Release on "Addressing Human Rights Violations of U.S. Scholars," August 19, 2001)

Actions by ASA have been in the form of resolutions of ASA Council, letters of appeal or protest on behalf of those detained, articles in *Footnotes* (and, more recently, on the ASA homepage), op-ed pieces, press releases on ASA positions, and in general public announcements to mobilize action at the grassroots level in support of the victims. Since the mid-1980s, ASA has worked closely with the American Association for the Advancement of Science (AAAS) Human Rights Action Network (AAASHRAN) in coordinating appropriate responses on specific cases.

Human Rights Issues in the 1990s

The Association took up issues regarding human rights from a broad sociological perspective as well as from the context of potential suppression of rights of research scholar. For example, ASA also initiated efforts to further understanding of social conflicts that lead to massive human rights violations. In November 1993, under the leadership of ASA President Gamson, a Spivack workshop was held on "Initiative on Genocide and Human Rights,"which addressed the need to "mobilize social science associations and funding organizations to respond to situations of genocide and mass deaths, such as that now occurring in the Bosnia-Serbia conflict. [Gamson] said that there was an agenda, as well as research roles, which go beyond the current activities of such organizations as Amnesty International." (Council Minutes, January 1993)

In the late 1990s, a series of human rights cases emerged involving sociologists detained in Egypt and China that led to ASA's engagement. In June 2000, Saad Eddin Ibrahim, a Professor of Sociology at American University in Cairo who holds both Egyptian and American citizenship, was arrested with colleagues from the Ibn Khaldun Center for Development Studies on charges widely believed to be politically motivated. Also, Li Shaomin, a PhD in demography from Princeton and a Professor of Business at the City University of Hong Kong, and Gao Zhan, a PhD from Syracuse University and a researcher studying Chinese women students, were arrested in China in early 2001. ASA raised a strong voice in protest in these cases. (Li Shaomin and Gao Zhan were released by the summer of 2001; Saad Eddin Ibrahim was released in December 2002 and acquitted in March 2003.)

In a unanimous resolution, ASA Council also called upon the U.S. government to strengthen its resolve to protect the safety and well-being of scholars engaged in scientific research in countries where basic freedoms do not exist, and to speak out assertively in support of academic freedom:

> The ASA calls upon the State Department to go beyond merely working behind the scenes to secure the release and departure of social scientists once they are jailed. It is imperative that the State Department protects foreign-born scientists who are naturalized citizens or permanent U.S. residents with the same vigor it would apply on behalf of U.S.-born citizens; that it asserts and defends the values of free scientific investigation of human society, both for its intrinsic worth and for its ultimately positive consequences for the nations under study; that it does not stand passively by while academic freedoms are systematically repressed abroad, and that it must not itself act to curb research and thereby become a tacit participant in repressing those freedoms. (ASA homepage)

ASA President Douglas S. Massey, Vice-President Richard D. Alba, and Council Member Craig J. Calhoun, who is also President of the Social Science Research Council (SSRC), issued a joint statement which noted that the ASA is "very concerned that sociologists are most at risk because the issues they study inevitably touch on the distribution of power and resources in society and the methods they use frequently involve contact with ordinary citizens, as in surveys or observational studies." (ASA Press Release, August 19, 2001)

The ASA Archiving Project

The preservation of sociology's history has been a topic of discussion for decades. Stephen Turner summarized some of these issues in a May 1991 *Footnotes* article on "Salvaging Sociology's Past," in which he described concrete steps taken by ASA to preserve the history of the Association.

In 1983, ASA donated its records to the Library of Congress, where some 57,900 ASA administrative records and documents from 1931 to 1986 are part of the Manuscript Division Materials of the James Madison Building of the Library. In 1989, supported by a grant from the Fund for the Advancement of the Discipline, Michael R. Hill and Mary Jo Deegan conducted an inventory of the materials and prepared a "finding aid" based on the their assessment of the contents. As Turner notes in the 1991 article, this archive at the Library of Congress, while substantial, is still only a small part of the potentially large body of information that exists on the history of sociology during the 20th century.

ASA Council turned its attention to exploring other approaches for preserving records from the Executive Office, when the Library of Congress informed ASA in 1992 that it would no longer accept the ASA archives. From 1989 to 1993, Council reviewed various proposals for archiving projects, and reached a consensus that Pennsylvania State University's offer should be further explored. Further negotiations were pursued with Penn State while the Committee on Archives worked to establish guidelines for what should be preserved and archived, to define criteria for classification of materials as "restricted" and "non-restricted," to work out procedures for transmission of materials to the archive, and in general, to define specifications to ensure the integrity and security of the ASA archive. The Committee on Archives during this time was co-chaired by Stephen Turner and Lynne Zucker, and also consisted of John M. Goering, Sydney Halpern, Michael Hill, John Stanfield, and Executive Officer Felice Levine.

In September 1997, ASA signed the contract with Penn State to create the ASA archive that affirms "a common commitment to establish, maintain, and provide access to the ASA records, documents, and materials for research and investigation by current and future generations." (*Footnotes*, November 1997:1) State-of-the-art methods were to be used to maintain and provide access to documents. The final agreement also provided for the "appointment of an ASA Archives Advisory Committee, to be named by Penn State and ASA, to make recommendations regarding the ASA archives and its operations. This Advisory Committee would include potential scholarly users." (Council Minutes, August 12, 1997)

The American Sociological Association Archives were dedicated on February 28, 1998 in a one-day symposium focusing on use of archives for scholarly research and on the importance of Jessie Bernard in Sociology.

9. ANNUAL MEETING

During the 1990s, the Annual Meeting continued to be the most important forum for scholarly communication and dissemination of research and ideas by attendees in addition to network opportunities. By 2000, about 600 program sessions were held during each Meeting for the nearly 5,000 registrants. In addition, at each Meeting about 100 book publishers, computer software companies, data/statistics centers, research institutes, government agencies and bureaus, and internet resource providers exhibited books and other materials. The Meeting is open to sociologists, "scholars from disciplines related to sociology, students in all areas of social science, and anyone interested in the scientific study of society." (ASA homepage)

The Annual Meeting Program evolved in length and composition throughout the 1990s, even as the Annual Meeting itself was shortened from a five- to four-day event in 2001. In 1980, the Annual Meeting had 206 program sessions and 3,331 paid registrants; in 1990, 312 program sessions and 3,818 paid registrants; and in 2000, 577 program sessions, and 4,793 paid registrants (Levine, *Footnotes*, January 2002:2). While Annual Meeting Programs reflected membership interest and proposals, during the 1990s, the Association also modified some familiar features or introduced new ideas and services: (1) Regional Spotlight Sessions, which focus attention on the discipline from the perspective of the Annual Meeting locations, were expanded; (2) The Science Policy Forum, a series of sessions that featured representatives of funding agencies in discussion of trends and opportunities for professional support, was introduced; (3) Poster Sessions grew in number; and (4) A variety of other professional sessions, such as the Chairs Conference and meetings for Directors of Graduate Studies, were added.

During this time, the nature and character of workshops changed as well. In 1980, there were eight professional workshops and 10 didactic seminars. By 2000, there were 16 workshops related to the academic workplace (i.e., sessions addressed to leading and managing in the academic workplace), 21 professional workshops (i.e., on topics and issues important to the professional development of sociologists, such as writing grant proposals), and 29 teaching workshops (i.e., those that center on strategies for teaching specific courses). In addition, didactic seminars, held as half-day or full-day events were offered on topics such as new methodological approaches or techniques.

In 2002, some innovations were introduced into the program of workshops at the Annual Meeting. Under the leadership of President Barbara Reskin and ASA Council as well as the strong interest of Executive Officer Levine and APAP Director Howery, the Association more actively promoted workshops and the training component of the Annual Meeting. For the first time, two extended "short-course" workshops, one on Teaching Racial Profiling, and another on Human Research Protections in Sociology and the Social Sciences were offered at the Annual Meeting in 2002 with a credit-granting mechanism. Attendees were required to register in advance for these courses, expected to do some preparation prior to the workshop session, and were offered certificates by ASA to attest to successful completion of these courses.

Other highlights relating to Annual Meetings during the 1990s include:

- The threatened boycott of Miami as a site for the Annual Meeting in 1993 came from African-American leaders over a snub of Nelson Mandela in 1990 and a strong concern about underrepresentation of African Americans in tourist-industry jobs. Both ASA President Lipset and Executive Officer Levine worked closely with boycott leaders in planning a major luncheon plenary at the 1993 Annual Meeting to address the reasons for the boycott and apply sociological knowledge to understanding the situation. The matter was settled prior to the meeting with gains for the African-American community.

- The Association made significant policy decisions aimed at enhancing inclusivity and wide participation at Annual Meetings by emphasis on "assembling a Program Committee to be as fully representative as possible of the diversity of the ASA membership" (Council Minutes, February 1992); through its site selection policies, and through various other structural changes. In 1995, Council affirmed an August 1994 statement "to hold its meetings only in cities where its members are afforded legal protection from discrimination on the basis of age, gender, marital status, national origin, physical ability, race, religion, or sexual orientation." (August 22, 1995) Over the years, ASA also sought to enhance and improve its services to special groups at the Annual Meeting, such as for childcare, persons with disabilities, and for those persons seeking employment.

- ASA has long supported the presence of students and student activities at the Annual Meetings, and in various ways provided support to encourage student attendance. The Honors Program had a strong presence at each Annual Meeting with enthusiastic support from the Association and the Executive Office. Special receptions, roundtables, and other events were held with the student participants in mind. During the 1990s, the Honors Program was directed by David Bills, Duane Dukes, and Kerry Strand.

- Although the impetus for the ASA Policy on Exhibits, Advertising, and Sales emanated from "political advocacy exhibits" at the 1991 Annual Meeting, a Subcommittee of Council (consisting of Janet Chavetz, Chair, Felice Levine, Richard Scott, and Franklin Wilson) was charged with addressing the broader question of policies relating to *all* ASA exhibits, sales, and advertising. The Report submitted by the subcommittee found that, in general, the ASA policies were similar to those of other social science associations, and "offered an affirmative guideline based on three criteria; that any item must be (in brief) a tool of the trade, of benefit to individual members, or of benefit to the ASA. ASA has the sole authority to judge conformity to these criteria and reserves the right to refuse, curtail or cancel any exhibit, ad or sale which does not. The report also outlined internal review and enforcement procedures." (Council Minutes, January 1992)

- In 2000, Council voted to shorten the 2001 Annual Meeting from five to four days on an experimental basis for one year in order to cut costs and potentially increase attendance. A survey of other professional organizations had indicated that a four-day meeting seemed to be the norm. The 2001 Annual Meeting in Anaheim, CA was the first four-day meeting held by the Association. In February 2001, Council voted to continue the four-day meeting on a permanent basis.

- Council also approved participation exemptions for professional service appearances as specified by the Program Committee (e.g., for leading workshop or seminars, or representing an organization in an informational poster session), effective for the 2001 Annual Meeting.

- With improvements in technologies and enhancements to the ASA homepage since 2001, activities relating to the Annual Meeting (including the Program) have been much more visible. The advance of the Internet, use of emails, listservs, and other forms of electronic publishing (such as the online presentation of the Annual Meeting Program with a personal scheduler feature) greatly enhanced communication about the Annual Meeting. Since 1997, the ASA homepage has increasingly become pivotal in disseminating information on the Annual Meeting (e.g., Call for Papers). Annual meeting-related innovations introduced during the first half of 2001 included the online abstracts and papers center (the only place where abstracts and papers can be purchased), online audiovisual request system, and online preliminary program and personal scheduler. (See also Information Technology.)

Chapter 3

Moving Forward at Century's End: ASA at 2002–2004

1. BACKGROUND AND CONTEXT

On the eve of its Centennial year, the American Sociological Association is a strong and healthy organization, well poised to serve its membership, the profession, and the discipline of sociology into the 21st century. Reflecting on the substantial contributions of ASA over its 100-year history, and at the same time looking forward, Executive Officer Hillsman observed recently that the ASA's "operational efficiency, productivity, and program quality (e.g., its publications, annual meetings, academic alliances, minority affairs, research on the profession, policy and media relations efforts), all contribute to the Association's future prospects to continue as the premier representative of professional and academic sociology in the United States." *(Footnotes*, February 2005)

New challenges to the nation, the profession, and the ASA have emerged over the past several years. In this context, from 2002 to 2004, the Association expanded its services, its membership, section activities and membership, and maintained subscriptions to journals and other institutional services at a healthy level. This period culminated in a record-breaking attendance at the 2004 Annual Meeting. The Association addressed a range of challenging science policy issues, including ASA's role as a publisher of scientific journals. The ASA leadership continued to think creatively on how to raise the visibility and relevance of ASA and sociology, to enhance and streamline Association services and operations, and to find new ways to link sociology's contribution to the public good. The Association also launched a program of planning and activities leading to the commemoration of its Centennial in 2005.

Context and Issues

A defining issue for the nation in 2002 was the aftermath of the terrorist attacks on America on September 11, 2001. In late 2001 and throughout 2002, sociologists in general, as well as the Association through its leadership, turned their attention to how they could contribute knowledge and expertise to addressing the problem of terrorism. The ASA Executive Office facilitated this process in various ways, including by disseminating relevant materials and resources and referring sociological experts on key issues to public discussions. The opening Plenary Session of the 2002 ASA Annual Meeting, "The Challenge of September 11: The Social Dimensions of Terrorism," explored the effects of terrorism from religious and cultural perspectives, and a large number of sessions on the 2002 Annual Meeting Program included discussions on other aspects of this issue.

The Association also reacted to policies enacted by the U.S. Government as part of its response to the "Global War on Terror." In January 2002, ASA Council passed a resolution calling for certain measures to ensure public access to data sets that were being removed or restricted by the federal government in the months following the terrorist attacks. Also, an ASA member-initiated resolution against the U.S. invasion of Iraq was approved overwhelmingly by the membership in the spring 2003 ballot.

The ASA Council turned its attention to other national disciplinary concerns as well. Under the leadership of ASA President William Bielby, the ASA continued to focus on the issue of collecting data on race categories. Council decided unanimously to urge California voters to reject Proposition 54, which would have forbidden public agencies from collecting data on the race, ethnicity, and national origin of its citizens. Another member-initiated resolution on opposition to a U.S. Constitutional Amendment banning same-sex marriages was supported by ASA Council and by the vote of the membership in the spring of 2004. In 2003 and 2004, ASA also joined with other professional societies in two amicus briefs deemed vital to sociology and the Association: the ASA brief in the Michigan affirmative action case (2003), and the JSTOR brief in *Faulkner v. National Geographic Society*, a case with important implications for ASA as a scholarly publisher.

The 2004 Annual Meeting, which featured the theme of "Public Sociologies," was the culmination of a year-long effort by President Michael Burawoy to raise professional and public awareness of "sociologies that transcend the academy and engage wider audiences. Our potential publics are multiple, ranging from media audiences to policy makers, from think tanks to NGOs, from silenced minorities to social movements. Teaching is central to public sociology: students are our first public for they carry sociology into all walks of life . . ." (ASA homepage). Held in San Francisco, the 2004 Annual Meeting was the best-attended meeting in the Association's history, with overflowing crowds at the many plenary and regular sessions. President Burawoy worked extensively at outreach before the meeting. He visited regional and aligned sociological association meetings to present information about the topic of the meeting and its special events and programs, and secured a grant to bring to the meeting public sociologists, public intellectuals, and activists from developing countries and the former Soviet Union.

Leadership Changes

The Association marked an important transition in 2002: A new period in ASA's history began with the appointment of Sally T. Hillsman as ASA Executive Officer effective May 15, 2002 to succeed Felice J. Levine. Hillsman, with specialties in crime and justice, came to ASA from the National Institute of Justice (NIJ), U.S. Department of Justice, where she had served as Deputy Director from 1996 to 2002.

Executive Officer Hillsman serves the Association at a unique and special time. As Hillsman noted in her January 2005 column in *Footnotes*, "It is a once-in-a-century privilege to be the ASA Executive in office at an historic moment—the 100th anniversary of this organization." Centennial events will draw attention to past accomplishments, and as Hillsman noted, "the ASA has helped build and support a membership and a discipline that has contributed richly to our society and our world through its scholarship and in intellectual collaboration (and creative tension) with sister disciplines' studying behavior, culture, and society through the economic, political, psychological, cognitive, and natural sciences." *(Footnotes,* January 2005:2) As the Association moves into its Centennial year in 2005, Executive Officer Hillsman is dedicated to working with the membership and the ASA leadership in creating a memorable commemoration of this historic event.

Executive Officer Hillsman's background in research and administration has been demonstrated on pressing issues of electronic publishing, a new ASA website, ethics, Institutional Review Boards (IRBs), and social science funding. Building on achievements in the Executive Office of the past twenty years, she has undertaken a process of refining administrative and programmatic functions that have evolved over the years into a structure of Executive Office departments to improve service and accountability. While these efforts are still ongoing, progress on key fronts indicates continued growth and professionalization of services offered by the Association to its membership.

In collaboration with the science policy community, Executive Officer Hillsman is working to ensure that important science issues are firmly on the nation's agenda. Hillsman brings sociology's perspective to key science issues by implementing policies of the ASA Council on vital science issues, and by participating in a range of joint efforts with the Consortium of Social Science Associations (COSSA) and other learned societies on such matters. These initiatives educate and inform policy makers on the relevance and contributions of the social sciences to national policy issues (e.g., on terrorism and disasters). Collaborative efforts by Executive Officer Hillsman and leaders of other scientific and professional societies have also challenged policies and practices of the U.S. government, which have adversely affected (or have the potential of doing so) the integrity of scientific processes.

A change in Association leadership also took place in 2004, when Arne L. Kalleberg who served as Secretary of the Association from 2001 to 2004, was succeeded by Franklin D. Wilson who will serve as Secretary from 2005 to 2007. Kalleberg's period as Secretary was characterized by his effective leadership in ensuring a smooth transition in the Association's changes in Executive Officers and the Association's development of a new strategy for investing its assets.

2. HIGHLIGHTS FROM COUNCIL ACTIONS: 2002–4

From 2002 to 2004, the ASA Council took action on a range of issues important to sociology and the Association, including (1) issuing statements and resolutions on collecting data on race and ethnicity, (2) signing amicus briefs, (3) voting resolutions stating ASA policies based on member initiatives, and (4) approving other important changes relating to ASA policies and procedures (e.g., on investments, awards, and gifts).

Data on Race and Ethnicity

Statement on Race

The Association took several important initiatives in recent years that emphasize the need for collecting and using data on race and ethnicity to advance sociology and public discourse on social policy. Established by ASA Council in January 2000, the Task Force on the Statement on Race was asked "to craft an ASA statement on race that reflects and draws upon sociological knowledge and expertise." The members of the Task Force were Troy Duster (Chair), Diane Brown (Council Liaison), Manuel de la Puente, Bette J. Dickerson, Deborah K. King, Sharon M. Lee, Felice J. Levine, Suzanne Model, Michael Omi, Willie Pearson, Jr., Ivan Allen, C. Matthew Snipp, Roberta M. Spalter-Roth (ASA Executive Office Staff Liaison), Edward Telles, Hernan Vera, Lynn Weber, David Wellman, David R. Williams, and J. Milton Yinger.

The ASA Council Statement on "The Importance of Collecting Data and Doing Social Scientific Research on Race," based on the Task Force Report, was presented at a press conference at the 2002 Annual Meeting in Chicago. In introducing the work of the Task Force, President Barbara Reskin and Executive Officer Sally Hillsman reiterated ASA's strong commitment to the value and importance of sociological research on race, and to the importance of collecting sound data to enable that process. Troy Duster, the Chair of the Task Force, emphasized the importance of collecting data on race as fundamental to research on the causes and consequences of racial disparities across a wide spectrum of social institutions. He noted that, not to have data on race would preserve the status quo with respect to racial disparities in areas such as health care, labor markets, communities, and schools.

California Proposition 54

The ASA Statement on Race was cited by Council as strong and persuasive empirical evidence for taking a formal position on Proposition 54 in the California election of October 7, 2003. Council voted unanimously to approve a statement which urged California voters to vote "No" to Proposition 54 ("The Classification by Race, Ethnicity, Color and National Origin' [CRECNO]"), which if "approved, would eliminate the ability of California citizens to hold both their state and local governments as well as private entities accountable regarding prohibitions against discrimination on the basis of race, ethnicity, and national origin. Researchers would lack the data to inform policymakers on this critical issue. ASA urges California voters to allow their governmental entities to collect the necessary data to support evidentiary research on race, ethnicity, and national origin." (Council Minutes, August 20, 2003)

Congressional Briefing

In addition to Council actions, an ASA Congressional briefing on "Racial and Ethnic Data: Why we Collect it; How We Use It in Public Policy," sponsored by the Spivack Program, was held on May 28, 2003. A panel of experts, including the Hon. Thomas C. Sawyer (former U.S. Rep. from Ohio) (moderator), Troy Duster, Brian Smedley (Institute of Medicine/The National Academies), and Gerald R. Sanders (Virtual Capital of California, and former San Diego Police Chief) addressed key issues relating to the importance of data on race for policy across a wide number of areas (Appendix 25).

Defense of Scientific Integrity

From 2002 to 2004, several actions taken by the federal government raised serious challenges to the social sciences and to the integrity of the scientific process. Council responded to these situations by passing resolutions placing it on record as strongly objecting to these violations and intrusions by political processes in areas vital to fields of science. As it has done since the 1980s, ASA continued to work in close collaboration with COSSA and other professional and scientific organizations in responding to these situations.

Peer-Review Process

On August 20, 2003, Executive Officer Hillsman reported to Council on an initiative by two members of Congress to defund five National Institutes of Health (NIH) behavioral and social science grants which had been approved in a peer-reviewed process. Four of the five grants under assault addressed aspects of sexual behavior and function. The proposed legislation was defeated by only two votes in the House of Representatives, despite considerable efforts of COSSA, the ASA and other scientific organizations to educate and inform the members of Congress on the significance of the peer-review process for scientific research in all fields. Hillsman noted that an assault on scientific peer review had also occurred in 1991 and 1992 (see Chapter 2), and recommended that Council again take action opposing any attempts to restrict funding for high quality, peer-reviewed research.

Council voted unanimously to approve the following statement: "The American Sociological Association strongly opposes any action by Congress that would restrict the ability of the National Institutes of Health to fund high quality, peer-reviewed research and affirms its support for the ability of NIH to support high quality, public health-related research on sexual function and sexual behavior . . . . The ASA considers such actions to be a serious threat to the integrity of the peer review process and the independence of scientific thought, and represents political intrusion into scientific research. We direct the Executive Office to oppose such actions publicly and to take all appropriate steps to help ensure these studies are not de-funded." (Council Minutes, August 20, 2003)

Appointments to Scientific Organizations

Discussion in Council in August 18, 2004 reflected grave concerns in the science community regarding the U.S. Government's disregard for the independent role of scientific research, particularly as manifested in policies on Executive branch appointments to scientific advisory bodies, and U.S. Government vetting of scientists in international scientific roles. As a result of this situation, the National Academy of Sciences (NAS) engaged in a major effort to develop a report (the third since 1992) on how to improve the process of presidential appointments of scientists to advisory committees and policy positions within federal agencies (the report was to be released after the fall 2004 elections). In addition to the comment to NAS prepared by COSSA, ASA Council approved a statement to be issued on behalf of ASA on this issue. Council also voted to make a public statement on the related issue of government vetting of scientists for international bodies, and to bring this statement to the attention of the National Academy Board on International Science Organizations.

In May 2004, ASA also joined more than 30 other American organizations in science, engineering and higher education in signing a *Statement and Recommendations on Visa Problems Harming America's Scientific, Economic, and Security Interests*. This action was taken in response to the increasingly negative consequences to higher education of recent changes to U.S. visa policies.

Amicus Briefs

The Association joined in two important amicus briefs in 2003 and 2004: *Grutter v. Bollinger* ([02-241] [288 F.3d 732, affirmed.]); and *Faulkner v. National Geographic Society* (294 F. Supp. 523 [S.D.N.Y. 2003]):

Grutter v. Bollinger

The case involved the University of Michigan Law School, which followed an official admissions policy that sought to achieve student body diversity through compliance with the *Bakke* case. The Michigan Law School admissions policy looked beyond factors such as undergraduate grade point average and Law School Admissions Test score in order to ensure that a "critical mass" of underrepresented minority students is accepted for enrollment at its Law School. When the Law School denied admission to Barbara Grutter, a white Michigan resident with an outstanding academic record, Grutter filed suit alleging that she had been discriminated against on the basis of race in violation of the Fourteenth Amendment and the Civil Rights Act of 1964. The case was eventually appealed to the U.S. Supreme Court which held that the Michigan Law School's "narrowly tailored use of race in admissions decisions to further a compelling interest in obtaining the educational benefits that flow from a diverse student body is not prohibited by the Equal Protection Clause or the Civil Rights Act of 1964."

Former ASA President Barbara Reskin led the efforts to prepare an ASA amicus brief in support of the Michigan policy. The ASA brief (also signed by the Association of Black Sociologists, the Law and Society Association, the Society for the Study of Social Problems, and Sociologists for Women in Society) argued that an extensive body of research by social scientists demonstrated that race and ethnicity profoundly affect the life chances of individuals and how they are treated in society. The brief argued that because race shapes experiences of individuals and is a "defining life experience, universities have a compelling interest in considering race when selecting students . . . Research has established that considering race among many other factors produces graduates of all races who become leaders in law, medicine, science, and public life. Declaring student's race out of bounds in admissions decisions would deny admissions officers crucial information to contextualize other life experiences and accurately measure academic performance." (No. 02-241:4)

Faulkner v. National Geographic Society

In 2004, ASA joined JSTOR in an amicus brief in the appeal of *Faulkner v. National Geographic Society*. This case is one of a series that had been filed in recent years by freelance writers and photographers objecting to reproduction of their work in extended electronic forms. The writers and photographers generally contend that publication of original print works containing their pieces in other, generally electronic, formats (such as a CD-ROM) constituted a "revision" of the original publication, and therefore violates the original copyright.

JSTOR approached a number of professional associations in 2003 about joining as co-signatories on its amicus curiae brief in the Faulkner case. The central issue for ASA was that, since ASA holds the copyright for its journal content, it should not be required to obtain a new copyright when it made this content available online, for example, in JSTOR type formats. Executive Officer Hillsman, the Secretary, Secretary-Elect, and the three ASA Presidents (current, Elect, and Immediate Past) consulted with the ASA legal counsel on whether to join in the amicus brief. On June 22nd, 2004, EOB voted unanimously to authorize the ASA to join in the amicus curiae brief submitted by JSTOR to the United States Court of Appeals for the Second Circuit. ASA Council supported this decision.

Member Resolutions

War in Iraq

A member-initiated resolution against the U.S. Government's invasion of Iraq was proposed in the spring of 2003 by a group of ASA members called Sociologists and Political Scientists Without Borders. The resolution was signed by more than three percent of the Association's voting membership, therefore requiring Council under the ASA Bylaws to present the resolution to the full membership for a vote if Council did not endorse it. ASA Council took up the member resolution in a meeting held by conference call on March 31, 2003. Council decided to publish the resolution with contextual material in *Footnotes* (April 2003) and on the ASA homepage in preparation for submitting it to a vote of the full ASA membership. In the spring 2003 ballot, members were given the option to vote on the member resolution, and also to register their views on the war via an opinion question on the ballot. The resolution against the war passed by 66 percent of the voting membership—thus placing the ASA on record against the war in Iraq. In a separate question, 75 percent of the voting membership responded affirmatively to the question "do you call for an immediate end to the war against Iraq?"

On August 19, 2003, ASA Council considered the complaint of James Tucker of New Hampshire and some other ASA members alleging that the member resolution adopted by Council was in violation of ASA's Code of Ethics. Executive Officer Hillsman reported that "COPE had met to examine this complaint and found that it did not meet the standards set out for filing a complaint under the official COPE policies and procedures." Council directed that a letter summarizing the COPE decision and the discussion in Council be sent to Tucker.

Ban on Gay Marriage

On March 26, 2004, a member-initiated resolution was submitted to ASA on a proposed amendment to the U.S. Constitution to prohibit same sex marriage. The Caucus of Lesbian, Gay, Bisexual, Transgender Sociologists, the ASA Family Section, and the ASA Sexualities Section jointly sponsored the resolution that was signed by more than three percent of ASA voting members. Council met by conference call on April 7, 2004 to consider the resolution, voiced strong support for it, and voted unanimously to submit the resolution directly to the ASA membership on the 2004 annual ballot.

A large majority of voting members (75 percent) responded affirmatively when asked, "Do you endorse the membership resolution opposing a constitutional amendment prohibiting same sex marriage?" Recognizing that some members might be opposed to amending the U.S. Constitution to prohibit same sex marriage but would endorse other legislation to ban same sex marriage, Council also voted unanimously to place a separate opinion question on the ASA ballot: "Do you personally favor or oppose legislation that bans same sex marriage?" A large majority (79 percent) of ASA voting members responded that they opposed such legislation. Kalleberg reported that under the ASA Bylaws, the member resolution is now the official position of the Association (Council Minutes, August 17, 2004).

Business Meeting Resolutions, August 2004

Members also introduced two resolutions during the Business Meeting of the ASA Annual Meeting on August 17, 2004. The first resolution on "Graduate Students as Employees," affirmed the rights of graduate students and research assistants to unionize. A motion was introduced for Council approval of this resolution as Council position. After debate on the issue, Council voted to accept the resolution *in principle* recognizing graduate students and teaching assistants as employees. Several members of Council "asked that the minutes reflect that this is a decision of the ASA Council and does not imply support of the membership for this resolution." (Council Minutes, August 17, 2004)

A second resolution on "Labor and ASA Conventions," called on the Association to adopt a policy of union preference in negotiating hotel and service contracts for all meetings organized by the Association. President Burawoy summarized for Council the complexities involved in site selection for meetings, and a consensus emerged that a vote on this issue should be deferred pending consultation with ASA legal counsel.

Other Council Actions/Policy Issues

Collaboration with Aligned and Regional Associations

As noted in Chapters 1 and 2, ASA has placed a high priority on nurturing collaborative efforts with aligned organizations and in developing a strong working relationship with regional, state, and other sociological associations. Appendix 28 contains a list of organizations (including the regional, state, and aligned associations) with which ASA maintains close ties.

In August 2004, Executive Officer Hillsman noted that an ASA priority continues to be "outreach to the aligned associations, looking to the Centennial as an opportunity to embrace the diversity of the sociological community. She commended Michael Burawoy for his outreach effort to the regional and state associations in preparation for the 2004 Annual Meeting." (Council Minutes, August 18, 2004)

In 2004, as part of its preparation for its Centennial year, the Association undertook a project to extend collaboration with state, regional, and aligned sociological associations by broadening the Sorokin lectures. Established by ASA in 1967 with a $10,000 gift from Pitirim Sorokin, the winner of the ASA Distinguished Scholarly Publication Award was invited to present the Sorokin Lecture at a regional sociological association meeting. However, as regional meetings grew in size and complexity, it was apparent that the audience for the ASA Sorokin lecture could be broadened.

In August 2004, Council voted unanimously to expand and revise the current Sorokin Lecture into the ASA Award Winning Sociologists Sorokin Lecture Series, in which any of the winners of major ASA awards in the past two calendar years could be asked to deliver a lecture at a state, regional, or aligned sociological association meeting, or on a campus. The Sorokin Fund and the American Sociological Fund will provide support for up to four such lecture trips in a calendar year beginning in ASA's Centennial Year in 2005 (Council Minutes, August 17, 2004).

Collaborations with Federal Science Policy-Focused Associations

The Association also worked closely with the COSSA (the Consortium of Social Science Associations of which ASA is a founding member), the Coalition for the Advancement of Health Through Behavioral and Social Science Research (CAHT-BSSR), the Coalition for National Science Funding (CNSF), the Decade of Behavior (ASA is represented formally on both the staff committee and advisory committee), the Behavioral and Social Science Coordinating Committee at the National Institutes of Health (BSSR-CC), BSSR-COSSA (coordinated by staff of the White House Office of Science and Technology Policy to keep the research community abreast of issues affecting behavioral and social science research), the Council of Professional Associations on Federal Statistics (COPAFS), the National Humanities Alliance (NHA), and the Coalition for Health Funding. These collaborations help ASA and its Executive Office keep abreast of science issues in the federal policy arena, and when necessary, take collective action on matters of concern to the social sciences. The Executive Officer regularly reports to the ASA Council on these matters and provides Council with the necessary background information to take action as needed.

Changes in ASA Investment Strategies

During 2003 and 2004, led by Secretary Arne Kalleberg, the EOB undertook a comprehensive review of the Association's investment policy and portfolio. As of June 30, 2004, the Association had about $7.1 million in long-term assets invested in a balanced portfolio of fixed income and equity investments managed by Fiduciary Trust International, Inc. Approximately 57 percent of the long-term assets invested by the Association are funds owned by ASA, and may be used by it for whatever purposes Council deems appropriate. The remaining 43 percent are held by the Association and invested on behalf of donors (e.g., the Sorokin Fund, the American Sociological Fund), and may be used by the Association only in accordance with the donors' restrictions.

In January 2004, the EOB interviewed potential new managers on investment strategies, and also created an Investment Committee consisting of Secretary Kalleberg, Michael Aiken, Paul DiMaggio, Lois DeFleur, and Franklin Wilson, and staffed by Executive Officer Sally Hillsman and Controller Les Briggs. Secretary Kalleberg presented an extensive report to ASA Council of EOB's findings and decisions on August 17, 2004. EOB concluded that moving ASA's assets toward far greater diversification as well as using a passive investment strategy would be advantageous to ASA, and selected an investment manager for these funds who invested exclusively in the very large portfolio of mutual funds developed by Dimensional Fund Advisors (DFA).

A priority issue for EOB in analyzing investment strategies and evaluating potential investment advisors was ASA Council's concern since the 1980s with ensuring socially responsible investing. EOB concluded that a passive investment strategy utilizing DFA mutual funds would be consistent with ASA's past position on socially responsible investing, and presented a detailed rationale for its position to Council. ASA Council voted strong support for EOB's decision, finding these actions to be in keeping with its position on responsible investing of ASA funds (Council Minutes of August 17, 2004).

Gifts and Awards

Following his death in 2003, the family of William "Si" Goode, the 63rd President of the American Sociological Association in 1972, offered to make a substantial contribution to the ASA in support of a dissertation grant in his memory. In January 2004, Council voted to accept the gift and establish a competitive travel grant for a PhD candidate conducting cross-cultural or comparative dissertation research to be administered by the Executive Office until the funds are exhausted.

A new award in honor of Lewis A. Coser was also established by the ASA Theory Section in 2004 with gifts from his many friends and colleagues. The Lewis A. Coser Award for Theoretical Agenda-Setting will be bestowed on an annual basis to "a mid-career sociologist whose work . . . holds great promise for setting the agenda in the field of sociology" and exemplifies the "sociological ideals Coser represented." The award is intended to be a prestigious discipline-wide award "that reinforces the centrality of theory in the discipline of sociology." (ASA homepage) The recipient will receive a financial award and present the Lewis A. Coser Award Lecture at a section session at the ASA Annual Meeting in the following year.

In 2003, at the urging of then President Michael Burawoy (and over the objections of the Committee on Awards), Council established a new ASA honorific award, the "Distinguished Coverage of Social Issues in the Media," and referred it to the ASA Committee on Awards to develop the criteria and process for nominations and selections. The first such award is to be made at the 2005 Annual Meeting.

Governance: ASA Council Bylaws Changes

In February 2003, Council voted to make changes to the Bylaws in order to clarify certain sections, resolve inconsistencies and other technical problems, and update certain provisions in light of new forms of communication *(Footnotes*, May 2003:28–9). (See Appendix 15.)

With the 2003 election, members were offered for the first time the option to vote electronically via the internet or to cast their votes by paper ballot as they have done in the past. The Council minutes of August 19, 2003 indicate that a majority of members (54 percent) voted via the internet.

3. GOVERNANCE: STRUCTURAL CHANGES

Sections

Memberships in ASA sections were 21,386 at the end of the 2004 Membership Year—the highest number ever (see Appendix 14). In the first meeting of the 2005 Council, Past President Michael Burawoy commented that Sections are "one of the most wonderful things about the ASA and urged Council to do nothing to tamper with the current Section system. He noted that some Sections would never become large entities, but they were nonetheless vibrant groups that contributed to the value of the ASA." (Council Minutes, August 18, 2004)

How Council should handle situations when a section membership falls below the required 300-member level continued to be a subject of discussion. The Committee on Sections (COS) considered various options for dealing with this issue. At the Council Meeting on August 20, 2002, Lynn Smith-Lovin speaking for COS, reported that as an alternative to small sections, "the committee asked Council to consider the formation of 'interest groups'. Interest groups may not have enough people to constitute an official section, or necessarily want the organizational costs and benefits of full section status, but would like to have a session on the program at annual meetings, and perhaps a room to hold a business meeting." Council endorsed the idea in principle but asked the Executive Office to assess the long-term implications of such a change. In January 2003, Council voted not to move forward with an "interest group" structure because of both policy and administrative concerns with its feasibility.

Over the past several years, three sections attained full section status: Labor and Labor Movements (2002), Animals and Society (2002), and Ethnomethodology and Conversational Analysis (2004). On the recommendation of the Committee on Sections, in August 2004, Council voted to approve a new Section-in-Formation on Evolution and Sociology (see Appendix 17).

On the recommendation of the Committee on Sections, Council also voted to increase the maximum number of awards a section may present each year to five single-category awards per year.

Task Forces and Committees

Council created three new task forces in February 2003: Task Force on the Assessment of the Undergraduate Major, Task Force to Revise the ASA Areas of Specialty, and the Task Force on Bridges to the Real World (that merged with the Task Force on the Institutionalization of Public Sociology, created in January 2004).

Most of the task forces appointed since 1999 (after the reorganization of the ASA Committee structure in 1998 and 1999) completed their work from 2001 to 2004 and submitted final reports (see Appendices 16 and 24). The Task Force on Opportunities Beyond Graduate Education: Post Doctoral Training and Career Trajectories (established in February 2001) was disbanded with no report. The three Task Forces established in February 2003 (and 2004) remain active.

Status Committees

When the ASA committee structure was reorganized, Council also authorized four committees on the status of the following groups in sociology: persons with disabilities; lesbian, gay, bisexual and transgender people; racial and ethnic minorities; and women. Council mandated that the work of these status committees be reviewed "in five years to evaluate how they fit in relation to the Association's goals in these areas." (Council Minutes, February 1999)

The Committee on the Status of Lesbian, Gay, Bisexual and Transgender (LGBT) Persons in Sociology presented an 85-page Report to Council in August 2002 of its findings on major aspects of the professional experience of LGBT people in the discipline. The Committee on the Status of Women in Sociology, presented an extensive preliminary draft of its Report in 2003, and a final Report on August 17, 2004. Members of Council discussed favorably the work of these two committees; Council voted unanimously to extend their work for an additional five years, and requested their Reports be made available on the ASA's homepage.

The Committee on the Status of Persons with Disabilities in Sociology requested an extension to complete its report, as did the Committee on the Status of Racial and Ethnic Minorities in Sociology. Both will submit final reports to Council during 2005.

4. EXECUTIVE OFFICE INITIATIVES

Under the leadership of Executive Officer Sally Hillsman, the Executive Office activities relating to programs and functions are being institutionalized in six departments: (1) Operations and Meeting Services, (2) Publications and Membership, (3) Governance, Sections, and Archives (4) Research and Development, (5) Public Affairs and Public Information, and (6) Information Services and Technology. In addition, three key ASA Programs—the Academic and Professional Affairs Program (APAP), the Minority Affairs Program (MAP), and the Spivack Program in Applied Social Research and Social Policy—continue to serve the membership. The MAP Program Director now also oversees some student activities of the Association, including the ASA Honors Program and the Student Forum.

ASA Departments manage programs and provide services to the Association, its members, and the wider public. Departmental functions encompass the core of programmatic activities in given areas (e.g., the Publications and Membership Department continues to manage the publication program of the ASA, and the Public Affairs and Public Information Department conducts media outreach to raise the visibility of sociology and the Association). However in some areas functional activities were expanded or modified: The Operations and Meeting Services Department coordinates office administration and human resources functions in addition to all functions relating to Association meetings; the Publications and Membership Department directs the publications program of the ASA, and also handles all membership services and conducts outreach beyond the Association. In addition to coordinating activities relating to the Fund for the Advancement of the

Discipline (FAD), the Research and Development Department provides expanded services to ASA Council, committees, and task forces. (See Appendix 29.)

ASA Departmental Activity: 2002–4

Publications and Membership Department

The internet continues to expand and offer new opportunities for disseminating scholarship in sociology. In 2004, ASA began to provide online as well as print access to all ASA journals through Ingenta, a database and access system to scholarly journals. The Association set a goal in 2003 of having "online access to all ASA journal content—past and current—through the JSTOR/Ingenta combination compete within two years. By the 2006 volume year, 2004 and later issues will be available through Ingenta, and 2003 and earlier issues will be available through JSTOR." (Council Minutes, August 19, 2003). This increased access to online journals was made possible by Council's decision to adjust the "moving wall" on ASA journals in JSTOR from five years to two years by 2004.

Sociological Methodology and *Sociological Theory* became available on JSTOR in 2002. In 2003, Council also voted to return all typesetting and editorial functions of *ASR* to the Executive Office by 2004.

Both *Contexts*, the new general perspectives magazine of the ASA, and *City and Community*, a journal of the Community and Urban Sociology Section (CUSS), began publication in 2002 and have been well received. In 2003, *Contexts* was named the best journal in the social sciences by the Association of American Publishers' (AAP) Professional and Scholarly Publishing Division, and as one of the ten "Best New Magazines of 2002" by the *Library Journal*.

After several years of testing, the ASA introduced the Journal Builder software for use by the editorial offices of the ASA journals in 2004. Journal Builder is an online manuscript tracking system that keeps track (and produces reports) on manuscript submission, editorial and production lags, and final decisions on acceptance of manuscripts for publication.

New technologies have also created new challenges in the publication program. In August 2002, ASA Council appointed a Subcommittee of Council and the Committee on Publications on Electronic Publishing consisting of Carol Heimer (Chair), Bernice Pescosolido, William Bielby, Robert Crutchfield, Arne Kalleberg, and Sally Hillsman to examine some of these issues (e.g., the applicability of copyright laws in electronic versions of articles posted on websites, the implications of open access to journals) and ASA policies regarding electronic publication. The Subcommittee presented a preliminary report in February 2003, and continues its work.

Research and Development Department

The Research Department conducted a new survey of sociology departments in 2002 and continued to track a 1996 cohort of 634 PhDs with respect to careers and job opportunities. A Membership Data File has been extracted annually in recent years from the ASA NOAH membership database and continues to provide vital information on membership activities and trends. In addition, the Department compiles information and conducts analyses on sociology and sociologists from other sources (such as the National Science Foundation). Research reports, research briefs, as well as data from these secondary sources are published regularly in various formats by the ASA (see Appendix 24).

ASA's research staff is also developing other projects to advance understanding of the profession and discipline of sociology, for example, a survey of sociologists working outside the academy. Research Department staff has also been working with the National Science Foundation and the

Commission on Professionals in Science and Technology to provide data and analyses for federal efforts to promote the recruitment and retention of women and minorities in the science, technology, engineering and mathematics (STEM) workforce.

FUND FOR THE ADVANCEMENT OF THE DISCIPLINE (FAD)

The Program on the Fund for the Advancement of the Discipline (FAD) was placed under the Department of Research and Development in 2002. FAD is a small grants program designed to support innovative, groundbreaking research and other scientific research projects, and to create new networks of scientific collaboration. FAD is funded jointly by the Sociology Program of the National Science Foundation (NSF) and the ASA (see Chapters 1 and 2). The maximum amount of each award in 2004 is $7,000.

In 2004, the National Science Foundation (NSF) awarded a three-year grant of $165,000 to the American Sociological Association (ASA) to support FAD from August 2004 through July 2007. The current award includes for the first time, funding to disseminate more broadly the work of the FAD grantees.

Public Affairs and Public Information Department

Through its Public Affairs and Public Information Department, ASA promotes and gives visibility to sociology and the Association by participating in the national science policymaking arena, monitoring key national legislative and policy developments affecting sociological research and sociologists, and engaging in efforts to enhance opportunities for sociologists' contributions to policy. The Public Affairs Office also manages the editorial and pre-production of the *Footnotes* newsletter.

Public Affairs activities of the Association from 2002 through 2004 included:

- Sponsoring Congressional briefings, aimed at educating policymakers and the wider public. These included briefings on reactions to terrorism (June 2002), the collection of racial and ethnic data (May 2003), human dimensions of disasters (October 2003), and immigration policy (April 2004) (see Appendix 25).

- Supporting exhibits through the Coalition for National Science Funding (CNSF), an alliance of organizations concerned with the future of the sciences, and the increased federal investment in the National Science Foundation's research and education programs. In 2004, the ASA sponsored the research of Bruce Western and Devah Pager at the CNSF exhibit held each spring on Capitol Hill.

- Participating in the Decade of Behavior initiated in 2000 to bring policymaker and public attention to the importance of behavioral and social science research. The National Advisory Committee selected ASA's nominee, David R. Williams, University of Michigan-Ann Arbor, for the Decade of Behavior's inaugural Research Award. The Decade will sponsor a Congressional briefing in which Williams participates.

- Representing sociology and the social science community on the Secretary of Commerce's Census Advisory Committee. Executive Officer Sally Hillsman represents ASA on the Committee and is participating in efforts to ensure the scientific quality of the 2010 Census, the American Communities Survey, and the further protection of data on vulnerable populations (such as Arab-Americans). Sociologists Robert Hill and Corinne Kirchner are also members of this and related Bureau of the Census committees focusing on issues of racial and ethnic classifications and the inclusion in the census of persons with disabilities.

- Monitoring key national (and some state-level) legislative and policy developments affecting sociological research, sociologists, and the ASA. For example:

- In November 2004, the ASA provided comments in response to the National Institutes of Health (NIH) draft proposal for *Enhanced Public Access to NIH Research Information*. In response to pressure from various sources to provide timely access to publications emanating from government-funded health research, the NIH developed an "open access" plan that would post peer-reviewed scientific manuscripts on NIH's PubMed Central database six months after journal publication. In its comments, the ASA raised a number of questions about the underlying premises of the proposal as well as the overall process through which it was developed. In coordination with other scholarly societies, ASA offered a series of recommendations to NIH for the implementation of the proposed public access plan.

- In September 2003, the U.S. Treasury Department's Office of Foreign Assets Control (OFAC) issued an interpretation of the *International Emergency Economic Powers Act* and the *Trading with the Enemy Act*, with serious implications for the ASA publishing program. These Acts and their amendments were interpreted by OFAC "as meaning that publishers may only publish materials from embargoed countries [e.g., Cuba, Iran, Sudan, and Libya] if they are in camera-ready form and are not subject to 'substantial alteration' which would include peer review, copy editing, design or translation." (Council Minutes, August 17, 2004) Executive Officer Hillsman met with OFAC officials in the fall of 2004 to express the concern of the Association as a publisher of scientific materials, and to urge a reversal of the decision on these restraints on publication. At the end of 2004, OFAC reversed its decision in the area that most threatened ASA by recognizing that journal submissions from embargoed countries that had been peer reviewed and edited by U.S. publications were indeed exempt from embargo. However, legal suits and other actions taken by publishers and authors' associations continue to seek changes to the government's position with regard to other media, such as film.

- Engaging in efforts to advance sociologists' contributions to policy—especially at the national level and across federal agencies and other executive offices. For example, based on efforts by the Public Affairs Office, sociologists Lee Clarke, Kathleen Tierney, and Mansoor Moaddel have been invited by the President's Office of Science and Technology Policy (OSTP) to make presentations on ASA's behalf to the U.S. Department of Homeland Security, other public audiences, and to staff of the President's National Science and Technology Council.

- Working with nearly 10 Washington, DC-based coalitions to advance the cause of social science through advocacy efforts.

Information Services and Technology Department

The Information Services and Technology Department manages the ASA Information Technology (IT) systems and infrastructure. In 2003, ASA Council approved a project to redesign the ASA website to coincide with ASA Centennial year publications and projects. Upgrades were also made to the ASA computer and information system in 2003 and 2004: (1) In late 2003, the internal document management system was upgraded with considerable improvements in storage and retrieval of documents, (2) Throughout 2004, ASA worked with JL Systems to develop an e-commerce system, permitting members to purchase ASA publications and other products directly from the website, and (3) Computer system performance was greatly improved by replacement of both the network server and the servers that provide support for all ASA listservs. (Appendix 29 contains a description of the technical specifications of the new hardware.)

Highlights from Programs of the ASA: 2002–4

The Association continues to serve sociology and Association members through its programs on Academic and Professional Affairs (APAP), Minority Affairs (MAP), and the Spivack Program in Applied Social Research and Social Policy.

Academic and Professional Affairs Program (APAP)

The Academic and Professional Affairs Program (APAP) continues to focus on advancing the discipline of sociology by working with academic departments and department chairs through the Department Affiliate Initiative, the Departmental Resources Group, Chairlink, the Annual Chairs Conferences, and the various continuing education programs at the Annual Meeting. APAP also continues to add to the extensive collection of resource materials produced by members and the Executive Office and distributed through the ASA's Teaching Resources Center (see Appendix 22). In addition, a High School Affiliate Program was established in 2003 to link high school social studies departments to the ASA similar to department affiliates.

From 2002 to 2005, APAP led the NSF-funded project, Integrating Data Analysis (IDA), an effort to build the quantitative literacy and research skills of sociology undergraduate students throughout the entire sociology curriculum of a department. This project was a collaborative initiative with the Social Science Data Analysis Network (SSDAN) at the University of Michigan (see Chapter 2).

In addition to these core activities, APAP was substantially involved in the Task Force on the Advanced Placement Course in Sociology for High Schools, and the Task Force on the Assessment of the Undergraduate Major, both of which delivered final reports to Council on August 18, 2004. The APAP also continued a program of outreach to community colleges and began an initiative on the professional MA degree.

The Preparing Future Faculty (PFF) project was formally completed by APAP with a three-day Capstone Conference on December 5–6, 2002. For more than two years, four sociology departments (along with three other social science disciplines) participated in the PFF project, which was designed to produce various training models and enhance the graduate experience in preparation for faculty careers.

Minority Affairs Program (MAP)

The Minority Affairs Program (MAP) encompasses the core Minority Fellowship Program (MFP), as well as the other programs that provide support to students and minorities, or those that relate to health issues more broadly. The Minority Fellowship Program (MFP), which was established in 1974 with funding primarily from the National Institute of Mental Health (NIMH), continued its program of support to minority sociology doctoral students, with the 31st cohort of students now participating (Appendix 23). In April 2005, the ASA was awarded a continuation of the grant by NIMH for the MFP Program covering the period 2005 to 2010. Also, ASA Council voted unanimously to approve funding for one additional non-NIMH MFP Fellow in 2005 and 2006 from the ASA's general operating funds.

With the consolidation of programmatic activities into departments, the Honors Program and the Student Forum were placed under the direction of the MAP Program Director (along with other student-related activities of ASA).

The Association has long emphasized programs and activities that focus on student members. The ASA Honors Program (see Chapters 1 and 2) and other activities centered on the Annual Meeting, the Dissertation Award, employment and career materials specifically designed for students, and special incentives for students to join the ASA have been created over the past twenty-five years.

In 1999, Council approved the institution of a Student Forum to "strengthen students' connections to the American Sociological Association and the discipline." (*Footnotes* April, 1999:3) Students who join the ASA automatically became a part of the Student Forum and receive special mailings and electronic communications to encourage their participation. These services have been greatly enhanced with a special section for students on the ASA homepage, which, in addition to the Student Forum, now includes newsletters and other special features designed for students.

Spivack Program in Applied Social Research and Social Policy

The Spivack Program continues to sponsor Congressional briefings, and each year, to provide funding to support a Congressional Fellow, and several projects under the Community Action Research Initiative (CARI). Congressional briefings were held on "Reactions to Terrorism: Attitudes and Anxieties" (June 2002), "Racial and Ethnic Data: Why We Collect it; How We Use It in Public Policy" (May 2003), "The Human Dimensions of Disasters: How Social Science Research Can Improve Preparedness, Response, and Recovery" (October 2003), and "A Nation of Immigrants: Current Policy Debates Meet New Social Science Research" (April 2004) (see Appendix 25).

Other Programs and Activities

Support for Individual Sociologists

Over the past several decades, funding opportunities have been available to individual sociologists through a variety of programs offered by the ASA. Funding for these programs was obtained primarily from NSF, various programs of the NIMH, other restricted funds of the ASA (such as the American Sociological Foundation), and ASA membership drives. Over the years smaller amounts (typically for travel and special events) have also been obtained from other sources (e.g., the MacArthur Foundation and the Smithsonian). These programs generally have been administered by ASA in a competitive, peer-reviewed process.

In addition to funding through the Minority Fellowship Program (MFP), the ASA provides support to individual sociologists through the Spivack Program Congressional Fellowships and the Community Action Research Initiative grants (CARI), the Fund for the Advancement of the Discipline (FAD), and the Teaching Enhancement Fund (TEF).

International Activities

On August 19, 2003, the Task Force on the International Focus of American Sociology submitted its final report to Council. The Report noted that while Annual Meeting Programs and committee activities generally showed increased attention to international issues, levels of participation in ASA meetings by foreign sociologists (especially by non-Europeans) were low, in part due to the lack of available funding. Also, the Task Force found that ASA teaching materials generally had a low level of international content (see Chapter 2).

The Association continues to place a high priority on activities on international issues, including human rights. ASA was actively engaged in the case of the Egyptian-American sociologist Saad Eddin Ibrahim who was sentenced on July 29, 2002, by the Egyptian State Security Court to seven years in prison on charges widely believed to be politically motivated (see Chapter 2). ASA worked closely with AAAS's Human Rights Action Network, sent letters of protest to Egyptian officials, and provided information on the case on the ASA website. Saad Eddin Ibrahim was released in December 2002 and acquitted in March 2003. He was a special guest at the 2003 ASA Annual Meeting in Atlanta.

As noted in Chapter 2, in 2002, ASA again obtained a travel grant from NSF to support sociologists participating in the International Sociological Association (ISA) World Congress Meeting, held in Brisbane Australia from July 7–13, 2002. The grant supported partial travel expenses for 33 persons to attend the meeting.

A panel discussion at the ISA entitled "The Internationalization of American Sociology: A Centennial Challenge for the ASA in 2005 and Beyond," featured Craig Calhoun (Social Science Research Council and ASA Council member), Executive Officer Sally Hillsman, Secretary Arne Kalleberg, A. Douglas Kincaid (the ASA representative to the ISA), and Immanuel Wallerstein (Yale University). The session was designed to generate discussion and ideas for a Centennial event featuring an ISA component. At the presidential session on the last day of the ISA meeting. Neil Smelser (University of California-Berkeley) was awarded the ISA's first Mattei Dogan Foundation Prize for a distinguished career in sociology.

In 2004, a grant was obtained from the Ford Foundation to bring public sociologists and activists from developing countries and the former Soviet Union to the 2004 Annual Meeting. The grant provided support for 25 persons from more than a dozen countries to attend the meeting.

5. CENTENNIAL PLANNING

On the occasion of the 75th anniversary of the American Sociological Association in 1980, the editors of *The American Sociologist* (*TAS*) invited past officers of the Association to "comment on the positive and negative accomplishments of the Association, and their hopes for what it might become." (February 1981, Editor's Page) Two volumes of articles were produced from these contributions: the first (February 1981) traced the evolution of the Association through the 1960s, and the second (May 1981), examined sociology's future. It is noteworthy that concerns expressed then about fragmentation, diversity, participation, and egalitarianism continue to the present (albeit perhaps in different forms). Also evident is the recurring nature of some of the debates and tensions—including, for example, on sociology as a profession and discipline; on goals and objectives for the Association; and on how best to optimize infrastructures to serve members, advance sociology, and promote the public good.

A variety of publications are also planned to mark the Centennial in 2005: A Council Subcommittee on Intellectual History, under the direction of Craig J. Calhoun, is preparing an edited volume on the history of sociology in America, which will be released during the Association's Centennial celebrations at the 2005 Annual Meeting. An Advisory Committee was appointed for the project consisting of Andrew Abbott, Troy Duster, Barbara Laslett, Alan Sica, and Margaret Somers.

In addition to this volume on the History of the Association commissioned by Council, *American Sociological Review* editor Jerry A. Jacobs is preparing an Editor's Comment on "ASR's Greatest Hits" to examine the influence of this important journal. *Teaching Sociology* is planning a special issue in honor of the Association's Centennial. The ASA Section on History of Sociology is also preparing a book on *Plural Histories of Sociology*, which will be issued as an ASA Section publication. A light-hearted look on topics about or of interest to sociologists in the form of cartoons from *The New Yorker* Magazine was released by ASA in November 2004. The hardcover volume is branded with ASA's name and includes a special cover cartoon commissioned for the publication and an introduction by President Troy Duster. The volume was produced by CartoonBank.com, a subsidiary of *The New Yorker* Magazine, which holds rights to all images published in *The New Yorker* magazine over the last 75 years.

Centennial Events and Projects

The ASA Council has been planning Centennial events and publications since February 2001, when Council members discussed at length some ways to mark its 100th anniversary. In December 2000, the Committee on Publications formed a Subcommittee to generate ideas about special publications for the centennial, including special issues of journals, "reviews," and so forth. The February 2002 Council launched a process for planning, organizing, and creating initiatives to mark the Centennial.

A Centennial Subcommittee of Council on Public Outreach and Events, consisting of Victor Nee, Roberta Spalter-Roth, Pamela Walters, and Robert Crutchfield, is exploring projects to reach people beyond the ASA regarding how sociology contributes to society. The Council Subcommittee on International Collaborations is considering ways to link events with an international focus to the Centennial celebration. The 2002 International Sociological Association Meetings (ISA) meetings in Brisbane Australia featured a panel discussion titled "The Internationalization of American Sociology: A Centennial Challenge for the ASA in 2005 and Beyond," which was designed to generate discussion and ideas for a Centennial event featuring an ISA component.

In August 2003, Council agreed to co-sponsor a meeting of the ISA Committee of National Associations (CNA) in the United States in conjunction with the ASA 2005 Centennial Annual Meeting. The CNA encompasses the 55 collective members of the ISA national and regional members. At the 2002 ISA World Congress, the ISA Executive Committee approved an initiative to revitalize the CNA, including sponsorship of a meeting prior to the 2006 World Congress in conjunction with the ASA Centennial meeting: This was approved by the ISA Executive Committee in March 2003 and by the ASA Council on August 20th that year.

Douglas Kincaid of Florida International University, ASA's representative to the ISA, and Sujata Patel of Pune University, ISA Vice President for National Associations and Chair of the CNA, have been organizing and fund raising to hold this meeting in South Florida just prior to the ASA Centennial meeting in Philadelphia in August 2005. ASA Council agreed to provide $14,000 in matching contributions and the 2005 Program Committee has provided space in the invited portion of the program for the participation of the CNA attendees who come to Philadelphia. In addition, both the current president of the ISA and the immediate past-president will present at the Philadelphia meeting. The president of the Italian Sociological Association will also make a presentation to the ASA in Philadelphia honoring the ASA centenary.

The Association plans a variety of activities and events in honor of the Association's Centennial. In addition to the publications highlighting the Association and sociology's past, an enhanced ASA website will feature historical records, photos, documents, data, and the volumes on the history of the ASA. A reception on Capitol Hill and media events are being planned, a Centennial Store on the ASA homepage has been set up, and a wide variety of products and instructional resources are being prepared or planned to celebrate ASA's 100th birthday. ASA commissioned a new logo for the Centennial. The Centennial logo appears on stationery, special commemorative stamps, and on a variety of special products and memorabilia available from the Centennial Store on the ASA homepage.

A timeline of important events in the Association and sociology's history is being designed and will be featured on large banners to be displayed at the Annual Meeting (the timeline will also be available on the ASA homepage). The content for the banners was prepared with contributions from sections and others in the ASA. The banners will be created on materials that can be shipped easily so that they can serve as instructional and resource materials on sociology in other venues beyond the Annual Meeting.

A range of other ideas are also being considered to celebrate ASA's 100th birthday, including expanding the Sorokin lecture series, producing film/video presentations and exhibits, and targeting events at regional and specialty sociological associations. Two documentaries created by sociologist Gale Largey, one on the Presentation of Presidents and another on Lester Ward, the first President of the American Sociological Society, will be premiered at the 2005 Annual Meeting.

The Focus of the 100th Annual Meeting

ASA's centennial will be the focus of the 100th Annual Meeting in Philadelphia in August 2005. A Centennial Subcommittee of the 2005 Program Committee chaired by Caroline Persell, and including Troy Duster, Patricia Hill Collins, Jill Quadagno, and Sally Hillsman is at work planning the Centennial program of the 2005 Annual Meeting. The program will focus on the past, present, and future of the discipline of sociology, the ASA, and other aligned organizations within the context of social and historical events of the past century. ASA President Troy Duster has chosen "Comparative Perspectives, Competing Explanations" as the theme for the 100th Annual Meeting. The theme is conceptualized as being broad enough "to address a wide historical sweep, and yet have sufficient focus to provide a framework in which to address key aspects of the social history of the discipline—its contemporary situation and its potential future development."

Epilogue

The American Sociological Association at its Centenary

Mission

Over the last two decades the American Sociological Association (ASA) honed its mission and identity. As the chapters to this volume show, the Association's development has been marked by both stability and change. At its centenary, ASA continues to describe itself on its homepage with the language and vision clarified in 1992:

> Founded in 1905, [the ASA] is a non-profit membership association dedicated to advancing sociology as a scientific discipline and profession serving the public good. With nearly 14,000 members, ASA encompasses sociologists who are faculty members at colleges and universities, researchers, practitioners, and students. About 20 percent of the members work in government, business, or non-profit organizations.
>
> As the national organization for sociologists, the American Sociological Association, through its Executive Office, is well positioned to provide a unique set of services to its members and to promote the vitality, visibility, and diversity of the discipline. Working at the national and international levels, the Association aims to articulate policy and implement programs likely to have the broadest possible impact for sociology now and in the future.

Its mission is defined as:

- Serving Sociologists in Their Work
- Advancing Sociology as a Science and Profession
- Promoting the Contributions and Use of Sociology to Society

The Association is chartered as a 501(c)(3) organization in the District of Columbia with headquarters at 1307 New York Avenue NW in Washington, DC, with an annual budget in 2005 of about $4.6 million.

Key Components of Success

The year 2005 marks the 100th anniversary of ASA's founding, and is therefore the occasion for reflection, commemoration, and celebration. The discussion in the preceding chapters has focused on highlights of Association history over the past quarter century around key topical areas. None of this would have been possible without the evolution of both a strong professional staff and the continued commitment, engagement, and contributions of ASA's members and its elected and appointed leadership.

Like other scientific and professional societies, ASA depends on a spirit of volunteerism by its members to contribute their services and talents to organizational functions. Members serve in leadership positions on Council, on committees and task forces, in sections, Annual Meeting events and activities, and in other ways that advance the organization, the profession, and the disciple of sociology. In a world that has become accustomed to instant emails, listservs, teleconferencing and other rapid forms of communication, it is perhaps worthwhile to recall that only two decades ago, none of these modes of communication existed, and yet the Association was still able to rely on the energy, commitment, and engagement of its members as it can today.

Matilda While Riley is a unique illustration of such professional dedication and support. Riley, who died in November 2004 at the age of 91, served the Association and her profession for more than half a century. She was the first Executive Officer of ASA (1949–60) and served as the 77th President of the Association in 1986. Dating back to the beginning of Riley's career, active and committed sociologists volunteering to work in and for the Association as well as an able, dedicated staff have been a hallmark of the American Sociological Association and the source of its strength and successes.

In a recent column in *Footnotes* (February 2005), Executive Officer Sally Hillsman reflected on the consequences of the strong commitment and engagement of the Association's membership and staff for the past accomplishments and future directions for the Association as it marks its 100th anniversary: "Positive trends in the discipline at the commencement of our second century as a scientific society and professional association contribute to ASA's vision. While I am neither a gambler nor a crystal ball gazer, I predict that ASA's fundamental strength, its integrity of purpose, and its ability to face and meet the real challenges that lie ahead, will carry us vigorously through our next 100 years to the celebration of our bicentennial."

Appendix

APPENDIX 1: CHRONOLOGY OF ASA EVENTS

The Chronology of ASA Events for 1905–1980 is reproduced (with minor formatting changes) from *A History of the American Sociological Association 1905–1980* by Lawrence J. Rhoades (1981), pp. 74–78. The chronology for 1981–2004 is derived from text in this volume.

1905	• American Sociological Society founded
1906	• First Annual Meeting Membership totaled 115
1907	• First edition of *Papers and Proceedings of the Annual Meeting*
1909	• Addressed subject matter of first course in sociology
1910	• Membership totaled 256
1912	• Began exploring research mission of Society
1913	• Initial involvement in social studies curriculum • Began looking at problems of academic freedom
1914	• First amendment to the Constitution
1919	• Participated in the founding of the American Council of Learned Societies • Investigated possibility of publishing a journal
1920	• Membership totaled 1,021
1921	• Presidential control of Annual Meeting reduced • Sections formed to organize sessions for Annual Meeting
1923	• Participated in founding of the Social Science Research Council • Initiated effort to establish the *Encyclopedia of the Social Sciences*
1924	• Urged proper classification of scientific positions in sociology in the federal government • Started an annual census of research projects in sociology • Approved honorary membership for distinguished foreign scholars
1926	• Publication of *The City*, first volume of Annual Meeting papers produced in book form
1930	• *Publications of the American Sociological Society* appeared; included annual proceedings, papers and abstracts of the Annual Meeting, membership list, annual program and Yearbook of the Section on Rural Sociology • Membership totaled 1,530
1931	• Affiliated with the American Association for the Advancement of Science
1932	• Explored means to disseminate important sociological research findings to general public • Issued charters to local and regional groups in sociology

1933	• First revision of the Constitution and Bylaws
	  - Created Administrative Committee
	  - Established a Nominations Committee to solicit nominations from the membership

	- Recognized divisions and sections - Provided for the creation of funds and endowments - Initial investigation into non-academic employment for sociologists
1935	• Issued Certificates of Indebtedness; $10.00 non-interest bearing bonds
1936	• First issue of the *American Sociological Review* published
1937	• Rural Sociology Section became Rural Sociological Society • Affiliated with the International Federation of Sociological Societies
1938	• Began effort to get press coverage at Annual Meetings
1940	• Urged the Civil Service Commission to establish category for sociologists • Began to move toward contributed papers at Annual Meetings • Membership totaled 1,034
1941	• Started involvement in social statistics produced by government agencies
1942	• Annual Meeting cancelled • Second major revision of Constitution and Bylaws - Regional and affiliated societies represented on Executive Committee - Officers elected by mail ballot - Improvement of instruction made an objective of the Society - Program Committee established
1943	• Incorporated under the laws of the District of Columbia • Began involvement in graduate training and recruitment to the discipline
1944	• Annual Meeting cancelled
1945	• Annual Meeting postponed
1946	• Two Annual Meetings held • Decided not to meet in hotels where racial discrimination was practiced • Established membership classification—Active, Associate, Student • Began effort to have social sciences included in National Science Foundation • Protested actions of House Committee on Un-American Activities, as they affected academic freedom • Established liaison with the U.S. National Commission for UNESCO
1947	• District of Columbia Chapter resolution on reorganization of the Society
1948	• First placement service at Annual Meeting
1949	• Executive Office established at New York University • Part-time Executive Officer employed • Employment Bulletin started • Charter member of the International Sociological Association
1950	• Annual Meeting time changed from December to September • *Directory of Members* published • Protested loyalty oath in California as infringement of academic freedom • Reorganization committee recommended new periodical to deal with practice of sociology as a profession • Membership totaled 3,241

1951	• Third major revision of Constitution and Bylaws
	  - Established a 29-member Council
	  - Created position of President-Elect
	  - Established position of Executive Officer
	  - Required referendum to amend Constitution
	  - Reduced term of Past Presidents to three years
	• *Bulletins* of American Sociological Society published; sociology in government programs; role of sociologists, especially in non-teaching positions; financial assistance for graduate students
	• Index to first 15 volumes of ASR
	• Began looking at ethics of research
	• Transferred production of ASR to Henry Quellmalz of Boyd Printing Company

1952	• First award presented at Annual Meeting: Bernay Award for Radio-Television • Accepted funds for Robert MacIver Award • Severed relationships with International Federation of Sociological Societies and Institutes
1953	• First Annual Meeting on West Coast and on a campus • Opened all sessions at Annual Meeting to contributed papers
1954	• Backed tax-exempt foundations supporting social science research during Special House Committee investigation • Society for the Study of Social Problems became an affiliate • Developed first policy on awards • Recommended session at Annual Meeting on teaching sociology in colleges and high schools
1955	• J. L. Moreno gave *Sociometry* to the Society
1956	• Began publishing *Sociometry* • Russell Sage Foundation *Bulletin Series* on applied sociology began • Number of vice presidents reduced from two to one • Certification of psychologists poses threat to autonomy of profession • First MacIver Award presented
1957	• Asia Foundation began grants to facilitate cooperation between Asian and American sociologists
1958	• Mechanism created for "modern" sections • *Sociology Today: Problems and Prospects* published • Section on "The Profession" added to *ASR* • Began negotiating for the *Journal of Educational Sociology*
1959	• Changed name to American Sociological Association • Established "Fellow" membership category • Sought support for a study of graduate training in sociology • Began issuing the Employment Bulletin as supplement to *ASR*
1960	• Russell Sage Foundation funds study of graduate training in sociology • Appointed full-time Administrative Officer • Reached agreement with APA on certification of social psychologists • Membership totaled 6,875
1961	• Approved plans for the development of a code of ethics • Appointed a liaison to the federal government
1962	• Hosted Fifth World Congress of Sociology in Washington • Changed method for electing regional representatives on Council

1963	• Appointed full-time Executive Officer • Moved Executive Office to Washington, DC • Began publishing *Sociology of Education* • Began Visiting Scientists Program in Sociology under NSF grant • *The Education of Sociologists in the United States* published by Russell Sage Foundation • Started to administer Sociology Section of the National Register for Scientific and Technical Personnel under NSF grant
1964	• Sociological Resources for Secondary Schools Projects funded by NSF • *Guide to Graduate Departments of Sociology* published under NIMH grant
1965	• Began publishing *The American Sociologist* • Approved proposal for a *Careers in Sociology* booklet • *Sociology and Rehabilitation* published under grant from Vocational Rehabilitation Administration • "Sociologist" made occupational title on the Civil Service Register
1966	• Began publishing *Journal of Health and Social Behavior* under grant from Milbank Memorial Fund • Alice F. Myers became Administrative Officer • Concern expressed about nature and quality of sociological instruction • Authorized annual publication on methodology in sociology • Began involvement in the protection of human subjects in behavioral research

1967	• Sorokin Lectureship and Award established
	• *Uses of Sociology* published
	• Fourth major revision of Constitution and Bylaws
	   - Created 18-member Council and eliminated Executive Committee
	   - Eliminated representation of regionals on Council
	   - Required committees on nominations and committees to be elected by districts
	   - Established a Committee on Regional Affairs

1968	• Membership voted not to take an official position on the Vietnam War • Urged President Johnson to give all disciplines equal deferment status in the Selective Service System • Created Arnold and Caroline *Rose Monograph Series* • Began exploring legal protection for research sociologists • Opposed anti-riot provisions in grant contracts • Sociology Liberation Movement formed • Caucus of Black Sociologists formed • Radical Caucus formed • First Sorokin Award presented • Moved 1969 Annual Meeting out of Chicago • Created a standing Committee on Professional Ethics • Endorsed the fullest participation of black sociologists in Association affairs • Created a standing Committee on Freedom of Research and Teaching • First volume of *Sociological Methodology* published
1969	• Began *Issues and Trends in Sociology*, a series of readers • Passed resolution supporting funding for NIMH • Published *Careers in Sociology* under grant from Russell Sage Foundation • Endorsed regular surveys of graduate departments urged by Women's Caucus • Opposed use of political criteria for appointment to HEW review committees • Adopted Code of Ethics • Censured members who disrupted 1969 Presidential Address
1970	• Appointed first Executive Associate • Issued Manual on Sections • Membership totaled 14,156

1971
- Began publishing *Socio-Log*, forerunner of ASA *Footnotes*
- Purchased townhouse in historic landmark section of Washington and relocated Executive Office
- First DuBois-Johnson-Frazier Award presented
- First *Rose Monograph* published
- Supported creation of a Council of Social Advisors in federal government
- Made recommendations to departments concerning the treatment of women in the profession
- Established a standing Committee on the Status of Women in the Profession

1972
- Began publishing *Contemporary Sociology: A Journal of Reviews*
- Appointed first Executive Specialist for Race and Minority Relations
- Created standing Committee on the Status of Racial and Ethnic Minorities in the Profession
- Held conference on relationship among sociological research, social policy and graduate training under NIMH grant
- Added didactic seminars to Annual Meeting program
- Supported right of scholars to copy articles under "fair use" doctrine
- Created a Committee on Employment

1973
- Minority Fellowship Program funded by NIMH and NIE
- Created Problems of the Discipline small grants program
- First Stouffer Award presented
- Published *The Status of Women in Sociology, 1968–72*
- Established open nominations process
- Supported workshop on teaching undergraduate sociology
- First Departmental Alumni Night (DAN) Party held during Annual Meeting

1974
- Project on Teaching Undergraduate Sociology funded by FIPSE
- Appointed Director of the Minority Fellowship Program
- Revenues from reprints shared with authors
- Co-sponsors study of confidentiality of social science research sources and data funded by Russell Sage Foundation

1975
- Sydney Spivack Dissertation Fellowships funded by Cornerhouse Fund
- Began Presidential Series based on plenary sessions at Annual Meetings
- Launched Professional Information Series with publication of *The Author's Guide to Selected Journals*
- Created registry of retired sociologists
- *Social Policy and Sociology* published, based on 1972 conference
- Professional workshops added to Annual Meeting
- First *Annual Review of Sociology* published

1976
- Council meetings opened to members
- Strengthened staff and broadened functions of Executive Office
- Teaching Development Project supported by Lilly Endowment grant
- Teaching Projects began teaching workshop programs and established Teaching Resources Center at Oberlin College
- Constitutional referendum defeated
- *Employment Bulletin* converted to separate monthly publication

1977
- Guidelines developed for journals
- Teaching Projects develop Teaching Resources Group
- Testimony given before the National Commission for the Protection of Human Subjects of Biomedical and Behavioral Research
- First Jessie Bernard Award presented
- Published report on the *Status of Racial and Ethnic Minorities in Sociology*
- Testimony given before the Privacy Protection Study Commission
- Cambridge University Press began publishing the *Rose Monograph Series*
- Published Index to *Journal of Health and Social Behavior*, Vols. 1–17

- Spivack fellowships in intergroup relations funded by Cornerhouse Fund
- Journal title changed from *Sociometry to Social Psychology*

1978
- First Spivack Awards presented
- Teaching Resources Center transferred to Executive Office
- Joined coalition organizing clearinghouse on academic freedom
- Published guidelines for initial appointments in sociology
- Created new awards structure
- Referendum moved 1980 Annual Meeting from Atlanta to New York in support of the Equal Rights Amendment
- Began publishing *Directory of Departments*
- Processing fees initiated for journal articles
- Decided not to meet in states that have not ratified the Equal Rights Amendment

1979
- Authorized publication of theory annual
- First Research Skills Development Institute held
- First Common Wealth Awards of Distinguished Service presented
- Minority Fellowship Program expanded to include applied sociology fellowships under new NIMH grant
- Established award for contributions to the teaching of sociology
- Alice F. Myers retired
- Supported brief in Golden Fleece suit before U. S. Supreme Court
- Published *Federal Funding Programs for Social Scientists*
- Teaching Projects held Plenary Conference on Teaching Undergraduate Sociology
- Developed new structural relationship with Sections
- Affirmed civil rights of homosexuals or any other group
- Report issued on the *Status of Women in Sociology, 1934–77*
- Approved insurance plans for members
- Sociologist shared Pulitzer Prize

1980
- Established Teaching Services Program
- Published proposed revision of Code of Ethics
- Teaching Projects designated April as "Teaching Sociology Month"
- Supported survey of membership on functioning of Association
- Fifth major revision of Constitution
  - Term of Vice President changed to three years
  - Created office of Past Vice President
  - Clarified Annual Meeting program planning in regards to Sections
  - Committee on Regional Affairs deleted
  - Incorporated petition guidelines for Members' Resolutions
  - Non-sexist language incorporated
- Privacy Research Award given
- First Distinguished Scholarship Awards given
- Current Membership total: 13,304

1981
- History of the Association published (June 1981)
- National Humanities Alliance (NHA) was founded
- Sections on Political Economy of the World System; Collective Behavior and Social Movements; and on Racial and Ethnic Minorities attained full status
- Jo Ann Ruckel appointed new Administrative Officer
- Federal support for social science research and training was drastically cut
- COSSA responded to budget cuts and set up a Congressional liaison office in DC
- Final research regulations for Institutional Review Boards (IRBs) approved (most social science research exempt)
- Executive Officer Russell Dynes announced resignation in 1982

1982
- ASA membership requirements and dues were restructured
- "Directions in Applied Sociology" workshop held in Washington, DC
- William D'Antonio appointed Executive Officer
- Alva Myrdal received the Nobel Peace Prize
- Council moved to one mid-year meeting
- Report of the ASA's Task Group on Homosexuality published in *The American Sociologist*
- Revised Code of Ethics approved
- Council authorized the Executive Office to collect and publish data on minorities and women
- Report on the "Crisis in the Occupation of Sociology" published
- *The American Sociologist* discontinued

1983
- Procedures for enforcing the ASA Code of Ethics adopted
- Congressional fellows appointed (Carol H. Weiss and William R. Freudenburg)
- Section on Comparative and Historical Sociology attained full section status
- Emeritus membership category approved
- ASA cosponsored Congressional breakfast with the Consortium of Social Science Associations (COSSA)
- *Applied Sociology*, edited by Freeman, Dynes, Rossi, and Whyte published
- Council adopted a *Manual on Policies and Procedures for Awards and Prizes*
- National Academy of Sciences (NAS) held a "Symposium on Knowledge in Social and Behavioral Science: Discoveries and Trends over Fifty Years" to commemorate the Social Trends Report ("Ogburn Report")
- Seminar on medical sociology held in People's Republic of China

1984
- ASA Executive Office reorganized
- ASA submitted amicus brief in appeal in the Brajuha case
- ASA Program Committee increased in size
- Raymond Russell named ASA Congressional Fellow
- Commission on Sociology and Society established and disbanded by Council
- Computer based Index of ASA journals published
- Council established a Certification Committee
- National Institute of Mental Health (NIMH) renewed the Minority Fellowship Program (MFP) grant

1985
- American Sociological Foundation established
- Brajuha case was decided
- ASA Certification Program approved
- Public Information Program created at ASA
- Teaching Endowment Fund established
- Section on Political Sociology attained full section status
- Task Force on Minority Fellowship Program established to explore new sources of funding
- William Ewens named the first Teaching Services Program Field Coordinator
- Soviet–U.S. exchanges began at 1985 Annual Meeting
- ASA purchased *Teaching Sociology* from Sage Publications

1986
- Professional Development Program (PDP) established
- PhD Certification Program launched
- ASA hosted Congressional Seminar on "Work and Family Policies"
- Section on Asia and Asian America attained full section status
- ASA began publication of *Teaching Sociology* (also incorporated The *Teaching Newsletter*)
- Annual *Sociological Methodology* published by ASA
- *Sociological Theory* became a semi-annual journal published by the ASA
- The 15-year *Cumulative Index* was published
- First Distinguished Career Award for the Practice of Sociology made to Conrad Taeuber
- ASA received $27,000 planning grant from the Ford Foundation to review Minority Fellowship Program
- Editor-Designate position created for ASA journals

1987	• Andrew Greeley made $50,000 challenge grant to the American Sociological Foundation (ASF) campaign
• Departmental Services Program established
• The Committee on the Executive Office and Budget (EOB) added current President and Past President as voting members
• *The American Sociologist* was again published by Transactions Press
• *Sociological Abstracts* contracted to publish proceedings of the 1987 Annual Meeting
• Membership survey conducted
1988	• 1989 section dues were set at 8 dollars with a student rate of 5 dollars
• *Guidelines for Employment of Part-Time Faculty in Departments of Sociology* published
• Report of Electronic Sociological Network Committee presented
• Ad Hoc Committee for Research on the Profession established
• Section on Emotions and Section on Culture Section attained full section status
• Electronic addresses used in *Directory of Members* for first time
• Federal government revised Classification Standard for Sociology series (GS-184)
• ASA joined the Coalition for the Advancement of Foreign Languages and International Studies (CAFLIS)
• ASF made its first grant of $10,000 to Minority Fellowship Program
1989	• ASA Council approved revised Code of Ethics
• Washington University Department of Sociology closed
• Eight-district system adopted for elections
• Emeritus membership category adjusted
• Honors Program became an official ASA program
• ASA established Bitnet communications connection through George Washington University
• Dissertation award was established
1990	• Section on Science, Knowledge, and Technology and Section on Sociology and Computers (renamed Communication and Information Technologies in 2003) attained full section status
• Population Association of America (PAA) leased space at ASA Executive Office
• Council approved submission of journals in electronic form
• Task Force on Graduate Education (TAGGE) was established
• MOST I was launched with grant of $185,000 from Ford Foundation
• First issues of *The Sociological Practice Review* were published
• Minority Opportunity Summer Training (MOST I) Program institutes held at University of Delaware and University of Wisconsin-Madison (also in summer 1991)
• ASA hosted visit of Soviet sociologists
1991	• Report on "Liberal Learning and the Sociology Major" published from three-year project with Association of American Colleges (AAC)
• Executive Officer D'Antonio retired
• Felice J. Levine became Executive Officer
• ASA was awarded $750,000 from the Cornerhouse Fund
• ASA protested rescinding of funding of American Teenage Study by U.S. Department of Health and Human Services (DHHS)
• Students achieved the right to vote and hold office in ASA
• Separate directorate established for Social & Economic Sciences at the National Science Foundation (NSF)
• ASA endorsed the Seville Statement on Violence
• ASA passed a resolution opposing the continued exclusion of gays and lesbians from the military based on their sexual orientation
• Council endorsed an American Association for the Advancement of Science (AAAS) statement on scientific misconduct

1992
- Sydney S. Spivack Program in Applied Social Research and Social Policy established from Cornerhouse Fund
- ASA discontinued publication of *Sociological Practice Review* (*SPR*)
- Congressional briefing on work and family held in December
- Guidelines for ASA advertising and exhibits approved by Council
- Certification Program suspended
- Council approved a revised Awards Policy
- ASA participated in national project on "Defining Scholarly Knowledge"
- Minority Opportunity Summer Training (MOST I) Program institutes held at University of California–Berkeley and the University of Michigan-Ann Arbor (also in summer 1993)
- ASA presented written testimony to National Science Foundation (NSF) Commission on the Future of NSF

1993
- Strategic plan developed by Executive Officer Levine was approved
- Executive Office installed new computer systems and membership database (NOAH)
- ASA awarded $415,000 from Ford Foundation for Minority Opportunities Through School Transformation (MOST II) Program
- Congressional Fellowship Program launched
- Section on Alcohol and Drugs attained full section status
- Council adopted guidelines on policy making through member resolutions
- Program on Academic and Professional Affairs (APAP) established
- Media briefing held on family and work at National Press Club in February
- Congressional briefing held on "Social Dimensions of AIDS" in May
- Workshop held on "Research Challenges on the Social Causes of Violence" in June
- Workshop held on "Initiative on Genocide and Human Rights" in November
- ASA filed amicus brief in Richard Scarce case

1994
- Congressional briefing held on "Revitalizing Public Education" in May
- Sections on Sociology of Children and Youth, Sociology of Law, Sociology of Religion, and on Latino/a Sociology attained full section status
- National Institute of Mental Health (NIMH) awarded $2.4 million to Minority Fellowship Program
- National Science Foundation (NSF) awarded $60,000 to the Fund for the Advancement of the Discipline (FAD)
- Task Force on Campus Hate Crimes and Bias-Related Incidents established
- ASA cosponsored Capitol Hill briefing on sexual behavior survey
- Department Affiliates Program launched
- Richard Scarce was jailed from May to October for protecting confidentiality of data
- ASA made a transition in its email system from Bitnet to Microsoft Mail via the internet (bringing email to all workstations)
- Invitational workshops: "Rethinking the Urban Agenda" and "Prevention of HIV and Hatred" held
- Cosponsored with Rural Sociological Association the publication *Sociology in Government: The Galpin-Taylor Years in the Department of Agriculture: 1919-1953*

1995
- ASA launched homepage (www.asanet.org) in November
- ASA led "Research and Privacy Coalition" against H.R. 1271
- The Rose Monograph Series was revamped
- Congressional briefing held on "The Myth of the Entitlement Crisis" in March
- Sections on Rationality and Society (originally Rational Choice), and on International Migration attained full section status
- Community Action Research Initiative (CARI) established under Spivack Program
- Annual Award on Public Understanding of Sociology approved
- Statement on Diversity adopted
- ASA adopted a site selection policy for Annual Meetings focusing on locations that provided guarantees of legal protection from discrimination
- Commission on Applied and Clinical Sociology established by Sociological Practice Association and the Society for Applied Sociology
- ASA participated in Conference Examining Implementation of Federal Education Legislation

1996
- Dues restructuring was approved by Council and membership
- ASA membership voted to drop emeritus membership category
- ASA entered into agreement with JSTOR for electronic publication of journals
- *Employment Bulletin* was published online (as well as in print form)
- Congressional briefings were held on "Basic Science and Transforming the U.S. Economy" (February), and on "Sociological Perspectives on Promoting Safe Schools" (June)
- ASA *Employee Manual* was adopted
- ASA published *Social Causes of Violence: Crafting a Science Agenda*
- ASA sponsored workshop on "Social Science Perspectives on Affirmative Action in Employment" in June
- ASA was awarded grant of $50,000 from NSF to engage in the study of PhD career trajectories
- ASA signed agreement with Russell Sage to publish the *Rose Series in Sociology*

1997
- The American Sociological Foundation was dissolved and funds placed in restricted accounts
- Revised Code of Ethics was approved
- ASA and the Office of Behavioral and Social Science Research (OBSSR) cosponsored a science writer's workshop on health issues in June
- Congressional briefings were held on "Welfare to Work" (March), and on "Youth Violence: Children at Risk" (June)
- Fund for the Advancement of the Discipline (FAD) received $161,526 grant from NSF
- *The Issue Series in Social Research and Social Policy* was launched
- Sections on Mathematical Sociology; Sociology of Sexualities; and Race, Gender, and Class attained full section status
- ASA signed archiving agreement with Pennsylvania State University
- *American Sociological Review*, *Contemporary Sociology*, and *Journal of Health and Social Behavior* were available on JSTOR
- Report on Section Finances, Administration, and Governance was approved by ASA Council
- The Russell Sage Foundation awarded ASA $25,000 for ASA-ISA conference on "Millennial Milestone: The Heritage and Future of Sociology"

1998
- ASA Committees were restructured
- ASA sold headquarters office at 1722 N St. NW and relocated to 1307 New York Ave. NW
- Congressional briefing held on "Immigrant Families and Children" in June
- *The Realities of Affirmative Action in Employment* by Barbara F. Reskin was published
- Certification Program ended
- W. K. Kellogg Foundation awarded ASA $87,000 for project on Race, Racism, and Race Relations
- Workshop held on the President's Initiative on Race in April
- Publications Department moved from NeXT (old Burroughs System) to PageMaker *Footnotes* and *Employment Bulletin* were produced at ASA for first time
- ASA entered into an agreement with the American Psychological Association to upgrade the ASA website

1999
- Emeritus membership category was reinstated by vote of the membership
- *Guidelines for the ASA Publications Portfolio* approved by Council
- Six new task forces were created
- *Continuities and Cutting Edges: Sociology for the Twenty-First Century* was published from ISA-ASA 1997 Conference
- Section on History of Sociology attained full section status
- MOST Program awarded $485,000 by Ford Foundation
- Congressional briefing held on "Hate Crime in America: What Do We Know?" in October
- *Data Brief* and *Research Brief* series were first published
- *Directory of Departments* was made available online
- Student Forum launched
- ASA contributed to revision of OMB Circular A-110
- Controversy over selection of *ASR* editors emerged

2000
- Committee on Sections expanded
- ASA established collaborative relationship with Carnegie Academy for the Scholarship of Teaching and Learning (CASTL)
- Congressional briefing held on "How Neighborhoods Matter" in September
- Minority Fellowship Program (MFP) awarded $2.7 million by NIMH
- Member Forum launched on ASA homepage
- Conference on "Scholarship of Teaching and Learning in Sociology" held at James Madison University
- ASA homepage was enhanced (e.g., member-only area and search tools introduced)
- Section on Economic Sociology attained full section status.
- ASA organized conference on Sociology and Education in March 2000 funded by Spencer Foundation
- Task Force on Journal Diversity and Task Force on the Statement on Race created
- ASA participated in Preparing Future Faculty (PFF) Project
- ASA participated in NIH sponsored study on social and cultural dimensions of health
- Special issues of *American Sociological Review* and *Contemporary Sociology* published for Millennium

2001
- Council approved plan to decouple journals from dues
- Membership voted to reestablish the Committee on Committees
- Alba Subcommittee Report on Policy Making was accepted by ASA Council
- The Annual Meeting changed to a four-day event
- Felice J. Levine was appointed to National Human Research Protections Advisory Committee (NHRPAC)
- Fund for the Advancement of the Discipline (FAD) awarded $165,000 by NSF
- FAD sponsored conference "Toward a Sociology of Sociology: A Research Agenda for the 21st Century"
- Resolution on human rights passed by Council
- ASA installed upgraded MS-windows-based e-NOAH linked to ASA website
- ASA awarded $417,241 by NSF for three years for Integrating Data Analysis (IDA) project
- ASA and Boyd Printing marked 50 years of association
- ASA issued statement on the September 11, 2001 terrorist attacks against the U.S.
- Section on Undergraduate Education changed its name and mission
- Task Forces established by Council on (1) Opportunities Beyond Graduate Education: Post Doctoral Training and Career Trajectories, (2) Contingent Employment in the Academic Workplace, (3) Undergraduate Sociology Curriculum, and (4) Advanced Placement (AP) Course in Sociology
- Executive Officer Levine announced resignation

2002
- Sally T. Hillsman appointed ASA Executive Officer
- Minority Opportunities Through School Transformation (MOST) Program Capstone Conference held in June, and *Promoting Diversity and Excellence in Higher Education Through Department Change* published
- Preparing Future Faculty (PFF) Capstone Conference held in December
- Integrating Data Analysis (IDA) project launched
- First issue of ASA's new magazine *Contexts* published
- *City and Community*, a journal of ASA's Community and Urban Sociology Section (CUSS), was first published
- Section on Labor and Labor Movements and Section on Animals and Society attained full section status
- Committee on Committees was once again elected by membership
- Congressional briefing held on "Reactions to Terrorism" in June
- ASA issued statement on importance of collecting data on race
- Subcommittees of Council on ASA centennial projects appointed

2003
- Members voted and approved resolution against U.S. invasion in Iraq
- Council voted unanimously to urge California voters to reject Proposition 54
- ASA submitted amicus brief in *Grutter v. Bollinger*
- Council adopted resolution opposing attempts of Congress to restrict NIH support for peer-reviewed research

- *Contexts* was named the best journal in the social sciences by the Association of American Publishers' Professional and Scholarly Division
- *Library Journal* named *Contexts* one of the ten "Best New Magazines of 2002"
- ASA Bylaws were updated
- Congressional briefing on "Racial and Ethnic Data: Why We Collect It; How We Use It in Public Policy" was held in May, and on "Policy Implications Regarding Disasters" in October
- Three new task forces were created in February 2003: (1) on the Assessment of the Undergraduate Major, (2) to Revise the ASA Areas of Specialty, and (3) the Bridges to the Real World
- The ASA award "Distinguished Coverage of Social Issues in the Media" was created
- ASA introduced electronic balloting in elections

2004
- Online access to ASA journals became available through Ingenta
- Member resolution opposing a U.S. constitutional ban on gay marriage approved by vote of membership
- ASA signed on to amicus brief in *Faulkner v. National Geographic Society*
- Office of Foreign Assets Control (OFAC) challenge to publishing from "embargoed" countries was resolved in areas relating to ASA journals
- Ford Foundation grant obtained to bring international scholars to Annual Meeting in 2004
- Committee on the Executive Office and Budget (EOB) approved changes to investment strategy consistent with Council investment policy
- Congressional briefing held on "A Nation of Immigrants: Current Policy Debates Meet New Social Science Research" in April
- ASA provided comments in response to NIH proposal on "open access" to publications
- Gift accepted from family of William Goode, 63rd President of ASA, for dissertation grant
- Lewis Coser Award established by ASA Section on Theory
- Fund for the Advancement of the Discipline (FAD) awarded grant of $165,000 by NSF
- ASA computer systems and membership databases upgraded
- Integrating Data Analysis (IDA) project Capstone held in June

APPENDIX 2: ASA PRESIDENTS BY YEAR OF TERM

1906–1907	Lester F. Ward	1944	Rupert B. Vance
1908–1909	William G. Sumner	1945	Kimball Young
1910–1911	Franklin H. Giddings	1946	Carl C. Taylor
1912–1913	Albion W. Small	1947	Louis Wirth
1914–1915	Edward A. Ross	1948	E. Franklin Frazier
1916	George E. Vincent	1949	Talcott Parsons
1917	George E. Howard	1950	Leonard S. Cottrell, Jr.
1918	Charles H. Cooley	1951	Robert C. Angell
1919	Frank W. Blackmar	1952	Dorothy Swaine Thomas
1920	James Q. Dealey	1953	Samuel A. Stouffer
1921	Edward C. Hayes	1954	Florian Znaniecki
1922	James P. Lichtenberger	1955	Donald Young
1923	Ulysses G. Weatherly	1956	Herbert Blumer
1924	Charles A. Ellwood	1957	Robert K. Merton
1925	Robert E. Park	1958	Robin M. Williams, Jr.
1926	John L. Gillin	1959	Kingsley Davis
1927	William I. Thomas	1960	Howard Becker (died in office)
1928	John M. Gillette	1961	Robert E. L. Faris
1929	William F. Ogburn	1962	Paul F. Lazarsfeld
1930	Howard W. Odum	1963	Everett C. Hughes
1931	Emory S. Bogardus	1964	George C. Homans
1932	Luther L. Bernard	1965	Pitirim Sorokin
1933	Edward B. Reuter	1966	Wilbert E. Moore
1934	Ernest W. Burgess	1967	Charles P. Loomis
1935	F. Stuart Chapin	1968	Philip M. Hauser
1936	Henry P. Fairchild	1969	Arnold M. Rose (died in office)
1937	Ellsworth Faris	1969	Ralph Turner
1938	Frank H. Hankins	1970	Reinhard Bendix
1939	Edwin H. Sutherland	1971	William H. Sewell
1940	Robert M. MacIver	1972	William J. Goode
1941	Stuart A. Queen	1973	Mirra Komarovsky
1942	Dwight Sanderson	1974	Peter M. Blau
1943	George A. Lundberg	1975	Lewis A. Coser

1976	Alfred McClung Lee	1991	Stanley Lieberson
1977	J. Milton Yinger	1992	James S. Coleman
1978	Amos H. Hawley	1993	Seymour Martin Lipset
1979	Hubert M. Blalock, Jr.	1994	William A. Gamson
1980	Peter H. Rossi	1995	Amitai Etzioni
1981	William Foote Whyte	1996	Maureen T. Hallinan
1982	Erving Goffman	1997	Neil Smelser
1983	Alice S. Rossi	1998	Jill S. Quadagno
1984	James F. Short, Jr.	1999	Alejandro Portes
1985	Kai T. Erikson	2000	Joe R. Feagin
1986	Matilda White Riley	2001	Douglas S. Massey
1987	Melvin L. Kohn	2002	Barbara F. Reskin
1988	Herbert J. Gans	2003	William T. Bielby
1989	Joan Huber	2004	Michael Burawoy
1990	William Julius Wilson	2005	Troy Duster

APPENDIX 3: VICE PRESIDENTS OF THE ASA

Year		Name	Year		Name
1906	1st	William G. Sumner	1932	1st	C. J. Galpin
	2nd	Franklin H. Giddings		2nd	Neva R. Deardorff
1912	1st	Edward A. Ross	1933	1st	Ernest W. Burgess
	2nd	George E. Vincent		2nd	Floyd N. House
1913	1st	Edward A. Ross	1934	1st	H. P. Fairchild
	2nd	George E. Vincent		2nd	Stuart A. Queen
1914	1st	George E. Vincent	1935	1st	Arthur J. Todd
	2nd	George E. Howard		2nd	Clarence M. Case
1915	1st	George E. Vincent	1936	1st	Dwight Sanderson
	2nd	George E. Howard		2nd	J. H. Kolb
1916	1st	George E. Howard	1937	1st	Charles S. Johnson
	2nd	Charles H. Cooley		2nd	Carl C. Taylor
1917	1st	Charles H. Cooley	1938	1st	Warren S. Thompson
	2nd	Frank W. Blackmar		2nd	Warner E. Gettys
1918	1st	Frank W. Blackmar	1939	1st	Dorothy Swaine Thomas
	2nd	James Q. Dealey		2nd	Jesse F. Steiner
1919	1st	James Q. Dealey	1940	1st	Stuart A. Queen
	2nd	Edward C. Hayes		2nd	James H. S. Bossard
1920	1st	Edward C. Hayes	1941	1st	James H. S. Bossard
	2nd	J. P. Lichtenberger		2nd	Howard Becker
1921	1st	J. P. Lichtenberger	1942	1st	Harold A. Phelps
	2nd	Ulysses G. Weatherly		2nd	Katherine Jocher
1922	1st	Ulysses G. Weatherly	1943	1st	Kimball Young
	2nd	Charles A. Ellwood		2nd	Samuel A. Stouffer
1923	1st	Charles A. Ellwood	1944	1st	Read Bain
	2nd	Robert E. Park		2nd	Carl C. Taylor
1924	1st	Robert E. Park	1945	1st	Carl C. Taylor
	2nd	John L. Gillin		2nd	Leonard S. Cottrell, Jr.
1925	1st	John L. Gillin	1946	1st	Leonard S. Cottrell, Jr.
	2nd	Walter F. Willcox		2nd	E. Franklin Frazier
1926	1st	John M. Gillette	1947	1st	E. Franklin Frazier
	2nd	William I. Thomas		2nd	Robert C. Angell
1927	1st	William F. Ogburn	1948	1st	Robert C. Angell
	2nd	Emory S. Bogardus		2nd	Herbert Blumer
1928	1st	Frank H. Hankins	1949	1st	Dorothy Swaine Thomas
	2nd	Luther L. Bernard		2nd	Philip M. Hauser
1929	1st	Howard W. Odum	1950	1st	Robert K. Merton
	2nd	Edwin H. Sutherland		2nd	Margaret Jarman Hagood
1930	1st	Edwin H. Sutherland	1951	1st	Margaret Jarman Hagood
	2nd	Dwight Sanderson		2nd	Kingsley Davis
1931	1st	Ellsworth Faris	1952	1st	Clifford Kirkpatrick
	2nd	R. D. McKenzie		2nd	Joyce Hertzler

1953	1st	Herbert Blumer
	2nd	Jessie Bernard
1954	1st	Jessie Bernard
	2nd	Philip M. Hauser
1955	1st	Philip M. Hauser
	2nd	Robin M. Williams, Jr.
1956	1st	Robin M. Williams, Jr.
	2nd	Meyer F. Nimkoff
1957	1st	Kingsley Davis
	2nd	August B. Hollingshead
1958		Robert E. L. Faris
1959		Harry Alpert
1960		Wilbert E. Moore
1961		George C. Homans
1962		William H. Sewell
1963		Leonard Broom
1964		Reinhard Bendix
1965		Robert Bierstedt
1966		Arnold M. Rose
1967		Rudolf Heberle
1968		William J. Goode
1969		Ralph Turner
1970		Gerhard Lenski
1971		Morris Janowitz
1972		Mirra Komarovsky
1973		Raymond W. Mack
1974		Matilda White Riley
1975		Neil J. Smelser
1976		Alex Inkeles
1977		Suzanne Keller
1978		Alice S. Rossi
1979		Charles Y. Glock
1980		Helen MacGill Hughes
1981		Renee C. Fox
1982		Joan Huber
1983		Everett K. Wilson
1984		Edgar F. Borgatta
1985		Morris Rosenberg
1986		Rose Laub Coser
1987		Mayer N. Zald
1988		Richard J. Hill
1989		Glen H. Elder, Jr.
1990		Edna Bonacich
1991		Barbara F. Reskin
1992		Doris Y. Wilkinson
1993		Jill Quadagno
1994		Barrie Thorne
1995		Karen Cook
1996		Myra Marx Ferree
1997		Charles V. Willie
1998		Cora Bagley Marrett
1999		Patricia Roos
2000		Nan Lin
2001		Richard D. Alba
2002		Elijah Anderson
2003		Ivan Szelenyi
2004		Bernice Pescosolido
2005		Caroline Hodges Persell

APPENDIX 4: SECRETARIES OF THE ASA

1906–09	C. W. A. Veditz
1910–12	Alvan A. Tenney
1913–20	Scott E. W. Bedford
1921–30	Ernest W. Burgess
1931–35	Herbert Blumer
1936–41	Harold A. Phelps
1942–46	Conrad Taeuber
1947–48	Ernest Mowrer
1949	Irene Taeuber
1949–54	John W. Riley
1955–58	Wellman J. Warner
1959–60	Donald Young
1961–65	Talcott Parsons
1966–68	Robin M. Williams, Jr.
1969–71	Peter H. Rossi
1972–74	J. Milton Yinger
1975–77	William H. Form
1978–80	James F. Short, Jr.
1981–83	Herbert L. Costner
1984–86	Theodore Caplow
1987–89	Michael Aiken
1990–92	Beth B. Hess
1993–95	Arlene Kaplan Daniels
1996–98	Teresa A. Sullivan
1999–01	Florence B. Bonner
2002–04	Arne L. Kalleberg
2005–07	Franklin D. Wilson

APPENDIX 5: EXECUTIVE OFFICERS OF THE ASA

1949–60	Matilda White Riley
1960–61	Robert Bierstedt
1961–62	Robert O. Carlson
1963–66	Gresham Sykes
1966–70	Edmund H. Volkart
1971–72	N. J. Demerath III
1972–75	Otto N. Larsen
1975–77	Hans O. Mauksch
1977–82	Russell R. Dynes
1982–91	William V. D'Antonio
1991–2002	Felice J. Levine
2002–	Sally T. Hillsman

APPENDIX 6: EDITORS OF ASA PUBLICATIONS

[Note: All publications are listed under current names. For past names of journals, see Appendix 18]

American Sociological Review

1936–37	Frank H. Hankins
1938–42	Read Bain
1943	Joseph K. Folsom
1944–45	F. Stuart Chapin and George B. Vold
1946–48	Robert C. Angell
1949–51	Maurice R. Davie
1952–54	Robert E. L. Faris
1955–57	Leonard Broom
1958–60	Charles Page
1961–62	Harry Alpert
1963–65	Neil J. Smelser
1966–68	Norman B. Ryder
1969–71	Karl F. Schuessler
1972–74	James F. Short, Jr.
1975–77	Morris Zelditch
1978–80	Rita J. Simon
1981	William H. Form
1982–86	Sheldon Stryker
1987–89	William H. Form
1990–93	Gerald Marwell
1994–96	Paula England
1997–99	Glenn Firebaugh
2000–02	Charles Camic and Franklin D. Wilson
2004–06	Jerry A. Jacobs

Contemporary Sociology

1972–74	Dennis Wrong
1975–77	Bennett Berger
1978–80	Norval Glenn
1981–82	William D'Antonio
1983–84	Jerold Heiss
1985–86	Barbara Laslett
1987–91	Ida Harper Simpson
1992–94	Walter W. Powell

1995–97	Dan Clawson
1998–00	Donald Tomaskovic-Devey and Barbara Risman
2001–05	JoAnn Miller and Robert Perrucci

Contexts

2001–05	Claude Fischer
2005–07	Jeff Goodwin and James Jasper

Issues and Trends

1969–71	Amos H. Hawley
1974–76	Helen MacGill Hughes

Journal of Health and Social Behavior

1967–69	Eliot Freidson
1970–72	Howard E. Freeman
1973–75	Jacquelyne Jackson
1976–78	Mary E. W. Goss
1979–81	Howard B. Kaplan
1982–84	Leonard I. Pearlin
1985–89	Eugene B. Gallagher
1990–93	Mary L. Fennell
1994–97	Ronald J. Angel
1998–00	John Mirowsky
2001–04	Michael Hughes
2005–07	Peggy Thoits

Rose Monograph Series

1968–70	Albert J. Reiss
1971–73	Sheldon Stryker
1974–76	Ida Harper Simpson
1977–79	Robin M. Williams, Jr.
1980–82	Suzanne Keller
1983–87	Ernest Q. Campbell
1988–92	Teresa A. Sullivan
1993–94	Judith Blau

Rose Series in Sociology

1996–99	George Farkas
2000–05	Douglas Anderton, Dan Clawson, Naomi Gerstel, Randall Stokes, and Robert Zussman

Social Psychology Quarterly

1956–58	Leonard S. Cottrell, Jr.
1959–61	John A. Clausen
1962–64	Ralph H. Turner
1965–66	Melvin F. Seeman
1967–69	Sheldon Stryker
1970–72	Carl W. Backman
1973–76	Richard J. Hill
1977–79	Howard Schumann
1980–82	George Bohrnstedt
1983–87	Peter J. Burke
1988–92	Karen S. Cook
1993–96	Edward J. Lawler
1997–00	Linda Molm and Lynn Smith–Lovin
2001–03	Cecilia L. Ridgeway
2004–06	Spencer Cahill

Sociological Methodology

1968–70	Edgar F. Borgatta
1971–73	Herbert L. Costner
1974–76	David R. Heise
1977–79	Karl F. Schuessler
1980–84	Samuel Leinhardt
1985–86	Nancy Brandon Tuma
1987–90	Clifford C. Clogg
1991–95	Peter V. Marsden
1996–97	Adrian Raftery
1998–00	Michael E. Sobel and Mark P. Becker
2001–06	Ross M. Stolzenberg

Sociological Practice Review

1990–92	Robert A. Dentler

Sociological Theory

1981–83	Peter Berger, Randall Collins, and Irving Zeitlin
1984–85	Randall Collins
1986–89	Norbert Wiley
1990–94	Alan Sica
1995–99	Craig Calhoun

2000–04   Jonathan H. Turner

2005–07   Julia Adams, Jeffrey Alexander, Ron Eyerman, and Philip Gorski

Sociology of Education

1964–66   Leila Sussman

1967–68   Martin A. Trow

1969–72   Charles E. Bidwell

1973–75   John I. Kitsuse

1976–78   Doris Entwisle

1979–81   Alan C. Kerckhoff

1982–86   Maureen Hallinan

1987–91   Philip Wexler

1992–94   Julia Wrigley

1995–98   Pamela Barnhouse Walters

1999–02   Aaron Pallas

2003–05   Karl Alexander

Teaching Sociology

1986–90   Theodore C. Wagenaar

1991–93   Dean S. Dorn

1994–96   Kathleen McKinney

1997–99   Jeffrey Chin

2000–03   Helen Moore

2004–09   Elizabeth Grauerholz

The American Sociologist

1965–67   Talcott Parsons

1968–69   Raymond W. Mack

1970–72   Harold Pfautz

1973–75   Leon Mayhew

1976–79   Allen D. Grimshaw

1980–82   James L. McCartney

1983–85   Robert Perrucci

APPENDIX 7: ADMINISTRATIVE OFFICERS OF THE ASSOCIATION

1960–63	Janice S. Hopper
1963–64	Evelyn Stefansson
1966–79	Alice F. Myers
1979–81	Marjorie E. Miles
1981–84	Jo Ann Ruckel

APPENDIX 8: EXECUTIVE ASSOCIATES, SPECIALISTS, AND DEPUTY EXECUTIVE OFFICERS OF THE ASSOCIATION

Executive Associates and Specialists

1970–72	Kurt Finsterbusch, Executive Associate
1972–73	Maurice Jackson, Executive Specialist for Race and Minority Relations
1973–75	Joan R. Harris, Executive Specialist for Minorities and Women
1974–75	Lawrence J. Rhoades, Executive Associate
1975–77	Lucy W. Sells, Executive Specialist for Minorities and Women
1976–77	Sue Titus Reid, Executive Associate
1977–80	Doris Y. Wilkinson, Executive Associate for Careers, Minorities and Women
1977–81	Lawrence J. Rhoades, Executive Associate for Program and Teaching
1981	Grace G. Henderson, Executive Associate for Careers, Minorities and Women

Deputy Executive Officers

Paul R. Williams	Deputy Executive Officer (1981–85), Director of the ASA Minority Fellowship Program (1976–85) (Appendix 9)
Bettina J. Huber	Deputy Executive Officer (1984–87), Assistant Executive Officer (1981–83)
Lionel Maldonado	Deputy Executive Officer (1987–90), Assistant Executive Officer (1985–87); Director of the ASA Minority Fellowship Program (1985–90) (Appendix 9)
Carla Howery	Deputy Executive Officer (1990–); Director, Academic and Professional Affairs Program (1995–), Director, Research Program on the Profession (1992–95); Co-Director (with Executive Officer Felice J. Levine), the Sydney S. Spivack Program in Applied Social Research and Social Policy (1992–2002); Director of the Teaching Services Program (1982–93), Assistant Executive Officer (1982–91), Professional Associate (1981–82)
Phoebe Stevenson	Deputy Executive Officer, Finance, Administration, and Planning (1994–2002)

APPENDIX 9: DIRECTORS OF THE ASA MINORITY FELLOWSHIP PROGRAM

1974–75	Cheryl Leggon (Acting); William A. Anderson
1975–76	Phillip Carey
1976–85	Paul R. Williams
1985–90	Lionel Maldonado (also served as Interim Director in 1992 from California State University-San Marcos)
1991–92	Tahi Mottl
1993	Florence Bonner, Interim Director (served as MAP* Director from Howard University)
1993–95	Ramon Torrecilha (from 1994–95 served as MAP Director from the Social Science Research Council)
1995–97	Havidán Rodríguez (from 1997–98 served as MAP Director from the University of Puerto Rico-Mayagüez)
1998–2000	Edward Murguia
2000–2	Alfonso R. Latoni-Rodríguez
2002–3	Jean Shin (Acting)
2003–	Mercedes Rubio

Note: In 1992 the Minority Fellowship Program (MFP) became a part of the Minority Affairs Program (MAP).

APPENDIX 10: GOVERNING BODIES OF THE ASA

1st Year—1905 Executive Committee

Officers:
Lester F. Ward, President
William G. Sumner, First Vice President
Franklin H. Giddings, Second Vice President
C. W. A. Veditz, Secretary-Treasurer

Elected Members:
William Davenport
Samuel M. Lindsay
Edward A. Ross
Albion W. Small
David C. Wells
W. F. Willcox

25th Year—1930 Executive Committee

Officers:
Howard W. Odum, President
Edwin H. Sutherland, First Vice President
Dwight Sanderson, Second Vice President
Ernest W. Burgess, Secretary-Treasurer

Elected Members:
F. Stuart Chapin
Ethel Sturges (Mrs. W. F.) Dummer
Ellsworth Faris
Herbert A. Miller
Edward B. Reuter
Jesse F. Steiner

Past Presidents:
Franklin H. Giddings
Edward A. Ross
George E. Vincent
Frank W. Blackmar
James Q. Dealey
James P. Lichtenberger
Ulysses G. Weatherly
Charles A. Ellwood
Robert E. Park
John L. Gillin
William I. Thomas
John M. Gillette
William F. Ogburn

50th Year—1955 Council

Officers:
Donald Young, President
Herbert Blumer, President-Elect
Philip M. Hauser, First Vice President
Robin M. Williams, Jr., Second Vice President
Wellman J. Warner, Secretary
Leonard Broom, ASR Editor
Dorothy Swaine Thomas, Past President
Samuel A. Stouffer, Past President
Florian Znaniecki, Past President

Elected Members:
Gordon W. Blackwell
Kingsley Davis
Mabel A. Elliott
Margaret Jarman Hagood
Philip M. Hauser
Everett C. Hughes
Guy B. Johnson
Clifford Kirkpatrick
Harvey J. Loeke
Lowry Nelson
Calvin F. Schmid
Kimball Young

Representatives from Sociological Societies:
Ray E. Baber, Pacific
Howard W. Beers, Rural
William E. Cole, Southern
W. Fred Cottrell, Ohio Valley
Thomas D. Eliot, Society for the Study of Social Problems
Charles Hutchinson, District of Columbia
William L. Kolb, Southwestern
Alfred McClung Lee, Eastern
Stuart A. Queen, Midwest

75th Year—1980 Council

Officers:
Peter H. Rossi, President
Helen MacGill Hughes, Vice President
William Foote Whyte, President-Elect
Renee C. Fox, Vice President-Elect
James F. Short, Jr., Secretary
Herbert L. Costner, Secretary-Elect
Hubert M. Blalock, Jr., Past President
Russell R. Dynes, Executive Officer

Elected Members:
Pauline Bart
Norman Bimbaum
Ernest Q. Campbell
Arlene Kaplan Daniels
Irwin Deutscher
William A. Gamson
Helena Znaniecki Lopata
Thomas F. Pettigrew
Morris Rosenberg
Immanuel Wallerstein
Charles V. Willie
Maurice Zeitlin

100th Year—2005 Council

Officers:
Troy Duster, President
Caroline Hodges Persell, Vice President
Franklin D. Wilson, Secretary
Cynthia Fuchs Epstein, President-Elect
Lynn Smith-Lovin, Vice President-Elect
Michael Burawoy, Past President
Bernice Pescosolido, Past Vice President
Sally T. Hillsman, Executive Officer

Elected Members:
Rebecca Adams
Kathleen Blee
Eduardo Bonilla-Silva
Esther Ngan-Ling Chow
Jennifer Glass
Deborah K. King
Rhonda F. Levine
Nan Lin
Ann Shola Orloff
Diane Vaughan
Bruce Western
Min Zhou

APPENDIX 11: RECIPIENTS OF ASA AWARDS

MacIver Award

1956   E. Franklin Frazier, *The Black Bourgeoisie* (Free Press, 1957)

1957   no award given

1958   Reinhard Bendix, *Work and Authority in Industry* (Wiley, 1956)

1959   August B. Hollingshead and Frederick C. Redlich, *Social Class and Mental Illness: A Community Study* (Wiley, 1958)

1960   no award given

1961   Erving Goffman, *The Presentation of Self in Everyday Life* (Doubleday, 1959)

1962   Seymour Martin Lipset, *Political Man: The Social Bases of Politics* (Doubleday, 1960)

1963   Wilbert E. Moore, *The Conduct of the Corporation* (Random House, 1962)

1964   Shmuel N. Eisenstadt, *The Political Systems of Empires* (Free Press of Glencoe, 1963)

1965   William J. Goode, *World Revolution and Family Patterns* (Glencoe, 1963)

1966   John Porter, *The Vertical Mosaic: An Analysis of Social Class and Power in Canada* (University of Toronto, 1965)

1967   Kai T. Erikson, *Wayward Puritans* (Wiley, 1966)

1968   Barrington Moore, Jr., *Social Origins of Dictatorship and Democracy* (Beacon, 1966)

Sorokin Award

1968   Peter M. Blau, Otis Dudley Duncan, and Andrea Tyree, *The American Occupational Structure* (Wiley, 1967)

1969   William A. Gamson, *Power and Discontent* (Dorsey, 1968)

1970   Arthur L. Stinchcombe, *Constructing Social Theories* (Harcourt, Brace, & World, 1968)

1971   Robert W. Friedrichs, *A Sociology of Sociology*; and Harrison C. White, *Chains of Opportunity: Systems Models of Mobility in Organization* (Free Press, 1970)

1972   Eliot Freidson, *Profession of Medicine: A Study of the Sociology of Applied Knowledge* (Dodd, Mead, 1970)

1973   no award given

1974   Clifford Geertz, *The Interpretation of Cultures* (Basic, 1973); and Christopher Jencks, *Inequality* (Basic, 1972)

1975   Immanuel Wallerstein, *The Modern World System* (Academic Press, 1974)

1976   Jeffrey Paige, *Agrarian Revolution: Social Movements and Export Agriculture in the Underdeveloped World* (Free Press, 1975); and Robert Bellah, *The Broken Covenant: American Civil Religion in Time of Trial* (Seabury Press, 1975)

1977   Kai T. Erikson, *Everything In Its Path* (Simon & Schuster, 1976); and Perry Anderson, *Considerations on Western Marxism* (NLB, 1976)

1978   no award given

1979   Helen Fein, *Accounting for Genocide* (Free Press, 1979)

Distinguished Contribution to Scholarship Award

1980   Peter M. Blau, *Inequality and Heterogeneity* (Free Press, 1979); and Theda Skocpol, *States and Social Revolutions* (Cambridge University Press, 1979)

1981   E. Digby Baltzell, *Puritan Boston and Quaker Philadelphia* (Free Press, 1979); and Morris Rosenberg, *Conceiving the Self* (Basic Books, 1979)

1982   Stanley Lieberson, *A Piece of the Pie: Blacks and White Immigrants* (University of California Press, 1980)

1983   Orlando Patterson, *Slavery and Social Death* (Harvard, 1982)

1984   Marcia Guttentag and Paul F. Secord, *Too Many Women? The Sex Ratio Question* (Sage, 1983)

1985   Duncan Gallie, *Social Inequality and Class Radicalism in France and Britain* (Cambridge University Press, 1983)

Distinguished Scholarly Publication Award

1986   Aldon D. Morris, *Origins of the Civil Rights Movement: Black Communities Organizing for Change* (Free Press, 1984); and Lenore J. Weitzman, *The Divorce Revolution: The Unexpected Social and Economic Consequences for Women and Children in American* (Free Press, 1985)

1987   Andrew G. Walder, *Community Neo-Traditionalism: Work and Authority in Chinese Industry* (University of California Press, 1986)

1988   Michael Mann, *The Sources of Social Power, Volume 1* (Cambridge University Press, 1986)

1989   Charles Tilly, *The Contentious French* (Harvard University Press, 1986)

1990   John R. Logan and Harvey L. Molotch, *Urban Fortunes: The Political Economy of Place* (University of California Press, 1987)

Special Recognition to Kim Scheppele, *Legal Secrets: Equality and Efficiency in the Common Law* (University of Chicago Press, 1988)

1991   Andrew Abbott, *The System of Professions: An Essay on the Division of Expert Labor* (University of Chicago Press, 1988)

1992   James S. Coleman, *Foundations of Social Theory* (Harvard University Press, 1990)

1993   Jack Goldstone, *Revolution and Rebellion in the Early Modern World* (University of California Press, 1990)

1994   Mitchell Duneier, *Slim's Table* (University of Chicago Press, 1992)

1995   Nancy A. Denton and Douglas S. Massey, *American Apartheid* (Harvard University Press, 1993); and James B. McKee, *Sociology and the Race Problem* (University of Illinois Press, 1993)

1996   Murray Milner, Jr., *Status and Sacredness: A General Theory of Status Relations and an Analysis of Indian Culture* (Oxford University Press, 1994)

1997   Melvin L. Oliver and Thomas M. Shapiro, *Black Wealth/White Wealth: A New Perspective on Racial Inequality* (Routledge, 1995)

Honorable Mention: Diane Vaughan, *The Challenger Launch Decision: Risky Technology, Culture, and Deviance at NASA* (University of Chicago Press, 1996)

1998   John Markoff, *Abolition of Feudalism: Peasants, Lords and Legislators in the French Revolution* (Pennsylvania State University Press, 1996)

Honorable Mention: Kathryn Edin and Laura Lein, *Making Ends Meet* (Russell Sage Foundation, 1997); Sharon Hays, *The Cultural Contradictions of Motherhood* (Yale University Press, 1996); Erik Olin Wright, *Class Counts* (Cambridge University Press, 1997)

1999   Randall Collins, *The Sociology of Philosophies: A Global Theory of Intellectual Change* (Belknap Press/Harvard University Press, 1998)

2000   Charles Tilly, *Durable Inequality* (University of California Press, 1998)

2001   William P. Bridges and Robert L. Nelson, *Legalizing Gender Inequality: Courts, Markets, and Unequal Pay for Women in America* (Cambridge University Press, 1999)

2002   Alejandro Portes and Ruben G. Rumbaut, *Legacies: The Story of the Immigrant Second Generation* (University of California Press, 2001)

2003   Richard Lachmann, *Capitalists in Spite of Themselves: Elite Conflict and Economic Transitions in Early Modern Europe* (Oxford University Press, 2000)

2004   Mounira M. Charrad, for *States and Women's Rights: The Making of Postcolonial Tunisia, Algeria, and Morocco* (University of California Press, 2001)

2005   Beverly J. Silver, for *Forces of Labor: Workers' Movements and Globalization Since 1870* (Cambridge University Press, 2003)

Stouffer Award

1973   Hubert M. Blalock, Jr.; and special award to Paul F. Lazarsfeld

1974   Otis Dudley Duncan and Leo A. Goodman

1975   James S. Coleman and Harrison C. White

1976 no award given
1977 Otis Dudley Duncan

Career of Distinguished Scholarship Award
1980 Robert K. Merton
1981 Everett C. Hughes
1982 Kingsley Davis
1983 Herbert Blumer
1984 Morris Janowitz
1985 Reinhard Bendix
1986 Edward A. Shils
1987 Wilbert E. Moore
1988 George C. Homans
1989 Jessie Bernard
1990 Robin M. Williams, Jr.
1991 Mirra Komarovsky
1992 Daniel Bell
1993 Joan R. Acker
1994 Lewis A. Coser
1995 Leo Goodman
1996 Peter M. Blau
1997 William Hamilton Sewell
1998 Howard S. Becker
1999 Dorothy E. Smith
2000 Seymour Martin Lipset
2001 William Foote Whyte
2002 Gerhard E. Lenski
2003 Immanuel Walllerstein
2004 Arthur Stinchcombe
2005 Charles Tilly

DuBois-Johnson-Frazier Award
(1971–95, biennial award for work in the tradition of W.E.B. DuBois, Charles S. Johnson, and E. Franklin Frazier; 1996-present, annual)
1971 Oliver Cromwell Cox
1973 St. Clair Drake
1976 Hylan G. Lewis
1978 Ira DeAugustine Reid
1980 Joseph S. Himes
1982 Daniel C. Thompson
1984 Joyce A. Ladner
1986 James E. Blackwell
1988 Doris Y. Wilkinson
1990 William Julius Wilson
1992 Andrew Billingsley

1994	Charles V. Willie
1996	Edgar G. Epps
1997	G. Franklin Edwards
1998	Howard F. Taylor
1999	no award given
2000	Charles U. Smith
2001	Troy Duster
2002	Walter R. Allen
2003	John Moland, Jr.

Sydney Spivack Award

1977	Ernst Borinski James W. Loewen Richard A. Schermerhorn William Julius Wilson
1978	Reynolds Farley Leo Kuper Thomas F. Pettigrew Julian Samora
1979	James E. Blackwell Celia S. Heller Joan Moore Pierre van den Berghe

Jessie Bernard Award

(award given in recognition of scholarly work enlarging the horizons of sociology to encompass fully the role of women in society: 1977–94, biennial; 1995-present, annual)

1977	Mirra Komarovsky, career
1979	Valerie Kincaid Oppenheimer, *The Female Labor Force in the United States: Demographic and Economic Factors Governing Its Growth and Changing Composition* (University of California and Greenwood Press, 1976); Nancy Chodorow, *The Reproduction of Mothering: Psychoanalysis and the Sociology of Gender* (University of California Press, 1978); and honorable mention to Kristin Luker, *Taking Chances: Abortion and the Decision Not to Contracept* (University of California Press, 1975)
1981	Elise Boulding, career
1983	Alice S. Rossi, career
1985	Joan Huber, career; and Judith G. Stacey, *Patriarchy and the Socialist Revolution in China* (University of California, 1983)
1987	Sandra Harding, *The Science Question in Feminism* (Cornell University Press, 1986); and Judith Rollins, *Between Women: Domestics and Their Employers* (Temple University Press, 1986)
1989	Joan Acker, career; Samuel R. Cohn, *The Process of Occupational Sex Typing: The Feminization of Clerical Labor in Great Britain* (Temple University Press, 1985); and honorable mention to Karen Brodkin Sacks, *Caring by the Hour* (University of Illinois Press, 1988)
1991	Barbara Katz Rothman, *Recreating Motherhood: Ideology and Technology in a Patriarchical Society* (W. W. Norton & Co., 1989)
1993	Dorothy E. Smith, career; Memphis State University Center for Research on Women (Bonnie Thornton Dill, Elizabeth Higginbotham, Lynn Weber) for significant collective work; and Patricia Hill Collins, *Black Feminist Thought: Knowledge, Consciousness, and the Politics of Empowerment* (Unwin Hyman, 1990)

1995	Arlene Kaplan Daniels, career
	Ruth Frankenberg, *White Women, Race Matters: The Social Construction of Whiteness* (Minnesota, 1993); and Elizabeth Lapovsky Kennedy and Madeline D. Davis, *Boots of Leather, Slippers of Gold: The History of A Lesbian Community* (Routledge, 1993)
1996	Judith Lorber, career
	Diane L. Wolf, *Factory Daughters* (University of California Press, 1992)
1997	Nona Glazer, career
	Robbie Pfeufer Kahn, *Bearing Meaning: The Language of Birth* (University of Illinois Press, 1995)
	Honorable Mention: Pierrette Hondagneu-Sotelo, *Gendered Transitions: Mexican Experiences of Immigration* (University of California Press, 1994)
1998	Ruth A. Wallace, career
1999	Paula England, career
2000	Maxine Baca Zinn, career
2001	Barbara Laslett, career
2002	Barrie Thorne, career
2003	Cynthia Fuchs Epstein, career
2004	Myra Marx Ferree, career
2005	Evelyn Nakano Glenn, career

Distinguished Contributions to Teaching Award

1980	Everett K. Wilson
1981	Hans O. Mauksch
1982	John C. Pock
1983	David Riesman
1984	Joseph Bensman
1985	University of Kentucky Department of Sociology
1986	Sister Marie Augusta Neal
1987	William A. Gamson
1988	Sharon McPherron and Charles A. Goldsmid
1989	James A. Davis
1990	Southwest Texas State University Sociology Program
1991	no award given
1992	Theodore C. Wagenaar
1993	Memphis State University Center for Research on Women (Bonnie Thornton Dill, Elizabeth Higginbotham, Lynn Weber)
1994	Reece McGee
1995	Dean S. Dorn
1996	Vaneeta D'Andrea
1997	Robert R. Alford
1998	Sociology Major Program, Department of Anthropology and Sociology, Santa Clara University
1999	William G. Roy
2000	George Ritzer
2001	Indiana University's Department of Sociology
2002	John Macionis
2003	Michael Burawoy and Robert Hauser

2004 Jeanne Ballantine
2005 Caroline Hodges Persell

Distinguished Career Award for the Practice of Sociology
1986 Conrad Taeuber
1987 John W. Riley
1988 Paul C. Glick
1989 David L. Sills
1990 Elizabeth Briant Lee and Alfred McClung Lee
1991 Charles G. Gomillion
1992 Elliot Liebow and Matilda White Riley
1993 Grace M. Barnes
1994 Nelson Foote
1995 Albert D. Biderman
1996 Albert E. Gollin
1997 Irwin Deutscher
1998 Leonard I. Pearlin
1999 Peter H. Rossi
2000 Francis F. Pivan and Richard A. Cloward
2001 David Mechanic
2002 Lloyd H. Roger
2003 Lewis Yablonsky
2005 William Kornblum

Edward L. Bernays Foundation Radio-Television Award
1952 Mr. and Mrs. Kurt Lang, "The Unique Perspective of Television and Its Effects"

Award for Public Understanding of Sociology
1997 Charles Moskos
1998 William Julius Wilson
1999 Herbert J. Gans
2000 Arlie Hochschild
2001 Alan Wolfe
2002 no award given
2003 Frances Fox Piven
2004 Jerome Scott and Walda Katz Fishman
2005 Pepper Schwartz

Dissertation Award
1989 Richard Biernacki, "The Cultural Construction of Labor: A Comparison of Late Nineteenth Century German and British Textile Mills"
1990 Vedat Milor, "A Comparative Study of Planning and Economic Development in Turkey and France: Bringing the State Back In"
1991 Rogers Brubaker, "Citizenship and Nationhood in France and Germany"
1992 Elizabeth Mitchell, "The Interpenetration of Class and Ethnicity in the Perpetuation of Conflict in Northern Ireland"

1993	Ronen Shamir, "Managing Legal Uncertainty: Elite Lawyers in the New Deal"
1994	Steven Epstein, "Impure Science: AIDS, Activism, and the Politics of Knowledge"
1995	Wilma Dunaway, "The Incorporation of Southern Appalachia into the Capitalist World Economy, 1700–1860"
1996	Jeffrey Lee Manza, "Policy Experts and Political Change during the New Deal"
1997	Dalton Clark Conley, "Being Black, Living in the Red: Wealth and the Cycle of Racial Inequality"
1998	Douglas Guthrie, "Strategy and Structure in Chinese Firms: Organizational Action and Institutional Change in Industrial Shanghai"
1999	Sarah L. Babb, "The Evolution of Economic Expertise in a Developing Country: Mexican Economics, 1929–1998"
2000	Wan He, "Choice and Constraints: Explaining Chinese Americans' Low Fertility"
2001	Jeremy Freese, "What Should Sociology Do About Darwin?: Evaluating Some Potential Contributions of Sociobiology and Evolutionary Psychology to Sociology"
2002	Kieran Healy, "Exchange in Blood and Organs"
2003	Devah Pager, "The Mark of a Criminal Record"
2004	Brian Gifford, "States, Soldiers, and Social Welfare: Military Personnel and the Welfare State in the Advanced Industrial Democracies"; and Greta R. Krippner, "The Fictitious Economy: Financialization, the State, and Contemporary Capitalism"
2005	Ann S. Morning, "The Nature of Race: Teaching and Learning About Human Difference"; and Amélie Quesnel-Valée "Pathways from Status Attainment to Adult Health: The Contribution of Health Insurance to Socioeconomic Inequalities in Health in the United States"

APPENDIX 12: MEMBERSHIP BY YEAR

Year	Count	Year	Count	Year	Count
1906	115	1941	1,030	1974	14,654
1909	187	1942	1,055	1975	13,798
1910	256	1943	1,082	1976	13,958
1911	357	1944	1,242	1977	13,755
1912	403	1945	1,242	1978	13,561
1913	621	1946	1,651	1979	13,208
1914	597	1947	2,057	1980	12,868
1915	751	1948	2,450	1981	12,599
1916	808	1949	2,673	1982	12,439
1917	817	1950	3,582	1983	11,600
1918	810	1951	3,875	1984	11,223
1919	870	1952	3,960	1985	11,485
1920	1,021	1953	4,027	1986	11,965
1921	923	1954	4,350	1987	12,370
1922	1,031	1955	4,450	1988	12,382
1923	1,141	1956	4,682	1989	12,666
1924	1,193	1957	5,233	1990	12,841
1925	1,086	1958	5,675	1991	13,021
1926	1,107	1959	6,323	1992	13,072
1927	1,140	1960	6,875	1993	13,057
1928	1,352	1961	7,306	1994	13,048
1929	1,530	1962	7,368	1995	13,254
1930	1,558	1963	7,542	1996	13,136
1931	1,567	1964	7,789	1997	13,109
1932	1,340	1965	8,892	1998	13,273
1933	1,149	1966	10,069	1999	13,056
1934	1,202	1967	11,445	2000	12,854
1935	1,141	1968	12,567	2001	12,368
1936	1,002	1969	13,485	2002	12,666
1937	1,006	1970	14,156	2003	13,167
1938	1,025	1971	14,827	2004	13,700
1939	999	1972	14,934		
1940	1,034	1973	14,398		

APPENDIX 13: CHARACTERISTICS OF MEMBERSHIP AND MEMBERSHIP PARTICIPATION IN ASA: 1982, 1992, 2001

Table 1. Distribution of ASA Membership by Gender and Race/Ethnicity, 1982*

	Sex		Ethnicity					N
	Male	Female	White	Black	Nat. Amer.	Asian	Hispanic	
Member**	70.5	29.5	92.3	2.8	0.5	3.3	1.1	8,329
Associate	63.9	36.1	92.5	3.7	1.1	1.8	0.9	1,063
Intl.***	83.5	16.5	78.2	1.7	0.2	18.0	1.9	808
Student	44.7	55.3	85.9	3.4	1.1	7.5	2.1	1,559
TOTAL	67.4	32.6	90.5	2.9	0.6	4.7	1.3	11,759

*Source: Table is reproduced from "Minorities and Women in Sociology: An Update," by Paul R. Williams, Footnotes, December 1982:6 (Table 1). The nonresponse rate was reported as: no information on sex: 114 (1.0%); no information on race/ethnicity: 1,916 (16.3%).

**Includes regular, emeritus, and life members. (Membership categories are those used prior to changes in membership requirements which became effective in the 1983 membership year.)

***Includes international members and international associates.

Table 2. Distribution of ASA Membership by Gender and Race/Ethnicity, 1992*

	Sex		N	Ethnicity					N
	Male	Female		White	Black	Nat. Amer.	Asian	Hispanic	
Member**	6,609	4,513	11,122	8,657	389	62	761	243	10,112
%	59.4	40.6	100.0	85.6	3.9	0.6	7.5	2.4	100.0
unknown			541						1,551

*Source: Data were collected ASA on members in 1990–91 and are presented in the "August Biennial Report on the Participation of Women and Minorities in ASA for 1990 and 1991," August 1992.

Table 3. Distribution of ASA Membership by Gender and Race/Ethnicity, 2001

Gender	Membership Type		All Regular and Student Members
	Regular	Student	
Men	53.5%	34.9%	48.1%
Women	46.5	65.1	51.9
Total	100.0	100.0	100.0
(N)	(6,588)	(2,704)	(9,292)
Race/Ethnicity			
White	81.5%	72.6%	79.6%
African American	5.6	7.9	6.0
Asian American, Pacific Islander	6.3	6.5	6.3
Hispanic or Latina/o	3.3	7.6	4.3
Native American/Alaskan, American Indian	0.6	1.1	0.7
Other	2.6	4.4	3.2
Total	100.0	100.0	100.0
(N)	(5,984)	(2,246)	(8,230)

Table is reproduced from data tables prepared by the ASA Research Program on the Discipline and the Profession. The data were obtained from the 2001 Membership Application/Renewal forms, and were extracted and compiled into the ASA Membership Database, 1999–2003.

Table 4. Distribution of Dues Categories Among Regular ASA Members by Race/Ethnicity and Gender, 2001

	Regular Membership							
Gender	A $20,000 or less	B $20,000 to $29,999	C $30,000 to $39,999	D $40,000 to $54,999	E $55,000 to $69,999	F $70,000 or more	Total	(N)
Men	5.5%	7.8%	12.8%	24.3%	16.3%	33.3%	100.0%	(3,526)
Women	8.9	10.5	14.9	30.3	16.2	19.2	100.0	(3,062)
Total	7.1	9.0	13.8	27.1	16.3	26.8	100.0	(6,588)
Race/Ethnicity								
White	5.8%	7.8%	12.6%	27.4%	16.3%	30.0%	100.0%	(4,877)
African American	7.4	5.3	10.9	28.1	19.8	28.4	100.0	(338)
Asian American	11.3	12.9	20.6	27.4	15.3	12.4	100.0	(379)
Hispanic or Latina/o	7.5	9.5	17.1	29.1	19.1	17.6	100.0	(199)
Native American/ Alaskan, American Indian	2.9	14.7	20.6	26.5	17.6	17.6	100.0	(34)
Other	16.6	13.4	16.6	22.3	13.4	17.8	100.0	(157)
All Members	6.6	8.3	13.3	27.4	16.4	28.0	100.0	(5,984)

Table is reproduced from data tables prepared by the ASA Research Program on the Discipline and the Profession. The data were obtained from the 2001 Membership Application/Renewal forms, and were extracted and compiled into the ASA Membership Database, 1999–2003.

Table 5. Participation of Women and Minorities in ASA Governance and Activities: 1982, 1992, 2002

	Elected Officers & Council		Constitutional (Elected Committees)*		Council/ Presidential Appointments		Editorial Boards		Elected Section Officers	
Year	Women	Minorities	Women	Minorities	Women	Minorities	Women	Minorities	Women	Minorities
1982	50.0 (18)	6.0 (18)	43.0 (30)	0.0 (30)	43.0 (186)	20.0 (186)	28.0 (164)	6.0 (164)	34.0 (184)	6.0 (184)
1992	.60 (20)	.25 (20)	50.5 (99)	21.2 (99)	45.4 (324)	20.9 (324)	39.1 (189)	7.4 (189)	46.7 (240)	12.9 (240)
2002	36.8 (19)	31.6 (19)	54.9 (82)	35.4 (82)	47.1 (276)	30.8 (276)	48.4 (312)	23.4 (312)	52.8 (362)	18.0 (362)

Note: The numbers in parenthesis represent the total number of available positions: For example, in 2002, out of 276 Presidential/Council appointments, women had 47.1 percent of the positions and minorities had 30.8 percent of these positions. (Because the unit of analysis is the position rather than the person, an individual who serves on two committees/positions is counted twice.)

*This category includes the "Constitutional Committees" (see Appendix 15), which prior to the 1998 reorganization of the committee structure were elected. Since the 1998 reorganization, several of these committees are appointed by the President with the approval of Council, but are included in this category for consistency.

Sources:

(a) Data for 1982 are derived from Table 7 in "Minorities and Women in Sociology: An Update," by Paul R. Williams, Footnotes, December 1982:7.

(b) With the exception of editorial boards, data for 1992 were compiled and tabulated by Katherine Rosich in January 2005 from NOAH records. Rate of response on race/ethnicity was 93 percent or higher. In addition there were no records in NOAH for 12 people across all categories. Data for editorial boards for 1992 are from an internal ASA report, "August Biennial Report on the Participation of Women and Minorities in ASA for 1990 and 1991," August 1992.

(c) Data for 2002 are based on information submitted by the members of ASA from the NOAH database. Data on participation by women and minorities on editorial boards are routinely compiled by the Publications Department of ASA from this source. Tabulations on other categories were performed by Katherine Rosich in December 2004. Overall, the response rate on ethnicity was 95 percent or higher across categories. Also, the minority category includes a few cases where individuals identified themselves in the "other" minority race/ethnicity category.

APPENDIX 14: ASA SECTION MEMBERSHIP: SELECTED YEARS 1975–2004

#	Section	1975	1980	1985	1990	1995	2000	2001	2004
1	Teaching and Learning	390	562	419	420	433	397	384	587
2	Methodology	574	487	365	400	410	407	386	382
3	Medical Sociology	928	1,018	993	1,080	980	1,019	1,007	1,014
4	Crime, Law, and Deviance	550	558	381	520	632	623	563	657
5	Sociology of Education	511	417	337	431	519	602	563	719
6	Sociology of the Family	515	474	410	565	774	736	726	719
7	Organizations, Occupations, and Work	692	699	649	832	936	1,005	950	947
8	Theory	515	450	416	615	749	653	618	678
9	Sociology of Sex and Gender	538	425	536	977	1,317	1,031	1,054	1,045
10	Community and Urban Sociology	500	446	341	412	538	576	575	695
11	Social Psychology	695	590	440	555	619	651	609	615
12	Peace, War, and Social Conflict	129	290	202	211	216	266	248	317
13	Environment and Technology		295	276	329	423	431	411	377
14	Marxist Sociology		488	360	401	406	307	282	412
15	Sociological Practice		277	337	400	358	250	219	216
16	Sociology of Population		354	330	438	457	417	412	440
17	Political Economy of the World System		261	254	356	410	390	378	419
18	Aging and the Life Course		449	450	510	560	570	480	484
19	Sociology of Mental Health					421	412	377	416
20	Collective Behavior and Social Movements		243	320	413	549	568	536	643
21	Racial and Ethnic Minorities		223	400	610	865	646	632	691
22	Comparative Historical Sociology			377	434	538	538	528	625
23	Political Sociology			534	487	554	612	584	656
24	Asia and Asian America			214	276	330	325	312	321
25	Sociology of Emotions				304	308	279	270	259
26	Sociology of Culture				606	865	878	810	974
27	Science, Knowledge, and Technology				350	407	416	381	413
28	Communication and Information Technologies				331	278	208	199	252
29	Latino/a Sociology					249	236	226	311
30	Sociology of Alcohol, Drugs and Tobacco					271	221	210	303
31	Sociology of Children and Youth					378	310	316	334
32	Sociology of Law					305	299	288	338
33	Rationality and Society					205	202	186	170
34	Sociology of Religion					433	502	481	540
35	International Migration					326	312	318	401
36	Race, Gender, and Class						777	731	803
37	Mathematical Sociology						204	198	179
38	Sociology of Sexualities						289	266	367
39	History of Sociology						241	195	179
40	Economic Sociology						417	439	614
41	Labor and Labor Movements							327	341
42	Animals and Society							102	198
43	Ethnomethodology and Conversational Analysis								308
	# of Section Memberships -->	6,537	9,006	9,341	13,263	18,019	19,223	18,777	21,366
	Year -->	1975	1980	1985	1990	1995	2000	2001	2004
	# of ASA Members -->	13,798	12,868	11,485	12,841	13,254	12,854	12,368	13,715
	# of Sections -->	12	20	23	27	35	40	42	43

APPENDIX 15: CHANGES IN THE ASA CONSTITUTION AND BYLAWS

From 1980 to 2003, ASA Council approved a number of changes to the Constitution and Bylaws of the Association, which were subsequently approved by the membership through a mail ballot. These changes, published in Council Minutes or in *Footnotes* articles, are summarized below. Also included are dates when the membership referendum results were formally announced.

A. Changes in the ASA Constitution and Bylaws: 1980–1990

- On January 23, 1981, Council approved an amendment to Article VI, Section 1 of the Bylaws by changing the minimum number of members required to establish a new section from 200 to 250, and keeping the existing limit to retain section status at 200 members (*Footnotes*, May 1981:7). The members approved this change in the spring of 1981 (*Footnotes*, August, 1981:20).

- The 1982 Council made two important modifications to membership practices, by changing the (a) definition of Association membership, and (b) dues structure. The objective of the membership change was to "shift the focus of the membership qualifications away from 'status' or 'credentials' criteria to commitment to the purposes of the Association." (*Footnotes*, March 1982:1). Membership in the Association was defined as follows, "Persons subscribing to the objectives of the Association may become Members. Those subscribing to the objectives of the Association, but desiring fewer services may become Associate Members. Students enrolled in undergraduate or graduate institutions can become Student Members . . ." (*Footnotes*, August 1982:13–14)

  Also according to this resolution, Council, as the elected representatives of the members, would have the authority to set dues for the membership up to cost of living adjustments. Increases in dues above cost of living adjustments required the approval of members through a mail ballot.

  These measures were approved by the membership in spring 1982 (*Footnotes*, August, 1982:1).

- In January 1983, Council approved emeritus membership for persons 70 years of age or older, who on application for membership became entitled to all rights of active membership except journals, without further payment of annual dues, provided that at the time of application, they were dues paying members of the Association for the preceding 10 years (*Footnotes*, February 1984:10). Members voted to reinstate emeritus membership in spring 1983 (*Footnotes*, August, 1983:3).

- On September 1, 1984, Council approved changes to the structure of the Program Committee to increase its membership by two persons, because of the increased diversity of the membership of the Association, and the increased length and complexity of the Program. Article V, Section 3 of the Bylaws was amended to: "the Program Committee shall consist of nine to 11 persons: The President Elect, serving as Chair, the Vice President Elect, the Secretary, and six to eight other members of the Association selected as follows: Each year the Council will appoint four to six members from a list presented by the President-Elect. Two of the members shall be appointed for two-year terms and others for one-year terms . . ." (*Footnotes*, March 1985:15). Members approved this measure in the spring ballot of 1985 (*Footnotes*, August, 1985:1).

- On August 22, 1987, Council amended the ASA Constitution by adding the current President and Past President as voting members of the Committee on the Executive Office and Budget (EOB). Members of Council could be appointed as members of the EOB to the three positions having staggered three-year terms. Other minor working changes and deletions that updated the Constitution as part of the referendum (i.e., to make these changes) were also adopted (*Footnotes*, November 1987:15). These changes, which affected Article V. Section 5, Article 1.Section 5 and Article V.Section 4, and Article VII.Section 3 of the Constitution and Bylaws were approved by the members in spring 1988 (*Footnotes*, August, 1988:5).

- Two referenda were placed on the spring 1989 ballot for membership approval: (1) On August 27, 1988, Council voted to change policies with respect to emeritus membership, so that emeritus members would be affixed dues of $15 (with a low income waiver on request), and would include free Annual Meeting registration in addition to preexisting benefits. (2) In January 1989, Council voted to adopt the eight-district proposal for revising the ASA election system. The Subcommittee on Redistricting recommended models for redistricting using criteria "such as regional social networks, as well as a nearly equal distribution of population among districts." (*Footnotes*, April 1989:14) (A December 1988 *Footnotes* article focused on a discussion of a five- versus eight- district model.) Both measures (on emeritus benefits and fees and on redistricting) were approved by the membership in the referendum of spring 1989 (*Footnotes*, August, 1989:1).

- The 1990 Council adjusted the qualifications for the emeritus category: "Persons are eligible for emeritus membership at retirement, providing that they have been members of ASA for ten years." (*Footnotes*, December 1989:15). By removing the existing restrictions of age 70 and consecutive ten-year membership prior to that age, emeritus membership became much more accessible. This measure was approved by the members in spring 1990 (*Footnotes*, August 1990:1).

- In January 1991, Council passed a resolution giving students the right to vote and hold office (*Footnotes*, May 1991:15). This referendum on changing the status of student membership was approved by the members in spring 1991 (*Footnotes*, August 1991:1).

B. Changes in the ASA Constitution and Bylaws: 1991-2002

The following changes to the ASA Constitution and Bylaws were enacted from 1991 to 2002:

- In February 1992, Council made changes to the *Organizer's Manual* aimed at promoting diversity in nominating Program Committee members. A Council subcommittee was also appointed to revise language in the ASA Bylaws and *Organizer's Manual* to correct for minor inconsistencies that emerged during this process "so that formal policies and current practices would be in greater conformity" (*Footnotes*, May 1992:22). The referendum on changes in appointing the Program Committee passed in spring 1992 (*Footnotes*, August 1992:1).

- In January 1996, Council voted to eliminate the emeritus membership category and to incorporate those members in the regular income categories (*Footnotes*, July/August 1996:18-19). This measure was approved in the spring 1996 ballot (*Footnotes*, July/August 1996:1,3). (The membership voted on the change to the Bylaws on the elimination of the emeritus category in spring 1997.)

- In January 1997, Council approved a number of changes in the ASA Bylaws based on suggestions from the Committee on Professional Ethics (COPE), the Executive Office, and ASA legal counsel. These changes included: "(1) the elimination of the Emeritus Membership category and clearer definition of conditions of membership, including the requirement to comply with the provisions of the Code of Ethics; (2) clarification of the nomination process played by at-large members of Council and the need to ensure the anonymity of individual voters; (3) clarification of the role of the Vice President on the Nominations Committee and the inclusion of the Committee on Professional Ethics as a constitutional committee; and (4) clarification of guidelines for section formation and operations." (*Footnotes*, July/August 1997:15). Members approved changes in the Bylaws in spring 1997 (*Footnotes*, July/August 1997:1).

- In January 1998, in changing the ASA Committee structure, Council approved a number of amendments to the ASA Constitution and Bylaws. Council action on the committee restructuring is in *Footnotes*, May/June, 1998:10-11; a summary of results from the vote by the membership on the amendments is summarized in *Footnotes*, July/August, 1998:5), and is presented below:

  - ***Amendment 1:*** (approved) To amend Article V of the ASA Bylaws to add the Committee on Sections.

  - ***Amendment 2:*** (approved) To amend Article V of the ASA Bylaws to add the Committee on Awards,

  - ***Amendment 3:*** (approved) To amend Article V, Section 7 (c) of the ASA Bylaws so that the ASA President recommends members to serve on the Committee on Professional Ethics (COPE).

  - ***Amendment 4:*** (approved) To amend Article V, Section 4 of the ASA Bylaws so that the ASA Secretary recommends members to serve on the Committee on the Executive Office and Budget (EOB).

  - ***Amendment 5:*** (approved) To amend Article II, Section 2 (d) and Article V, Section 2 of the ASA Bylaws to reduce the Committee on Nominations to 11 members and eliminate elections by districts

  - ***Amendment 6:*** (approved) To amend Article V, Section 1 (a) of the ASA Bylaws to remove ASA journal editors as members of the Committee on Publications.

  - ***Amendment 8:*** (approved) To amend Article V of the ASA Bylaws to remove Section 6, in its entirety, regarding the Membership Committee.

  - ***Amendment 9:*** (approved) To amend Article II and Article V of the ASA Bylaws to remove the Committee on Committees.

[Only one Amendment (Amendment 7) was not approved: To amend Article II and Article V, Section 1 (a) of the ASA Bylaws so that the Committee on Publications is appointed by Council on recommendations of the President rather than elected by the voting members of the Association.]

- On August 25, 1998, after a survey of lapsed emeritus members, Council voted to reinstate the emeritus membership category for persons who have been ASA members for at least ten years and are retired from their primary employment, with such members receiving *Footnotes* but no journals as part of this membership (*Footnotes*, January 1999:10). In February 1999, Council moved to amend the ASA Bylaws through a referendum in the 1999 ballot to permit reintroducing the emeritus membership category (*Footnotes*, July/August:13). The measure to reinstate the emeritus membership was approved by the members in spring 1999, and became effective in the 2000 membership year (*Footnotes*, July/August 1999:1).

- In January 2000, Council approved a change to the Committee on Sections, requiring a revision in the Bylaws to Article V. Committees, Section 5: "The Committee on Sections shall consist of nine members. Six members shall be appointed by Council for three-year terms based on the recommendation of the President. Three of these members shall be appointed from among the Association membership and three shall be appointed from among the Council members-at-large. Three members shall also be elected for three-year terms by current section chairs from among current section chairs according to section membership size. All terms will be staggered" (*Footnotes*, September/October 2000:15). This amendment was approved by the membership in spring 2000 (*Footnotes*, July/August 2000:1).

- In February 2001, Council voted to establish a new Committee on Committees with the composition and scope recommended by the Task Force on the Reexamination of the Committee on Committees and the Committee on Nominations, and to seek approval of this in a referendum after the Annual Meeting.

In a special referendum held in October 2001, ASA members voted on whether to support the reestablishment of the Committee on Committees (COC) as recommended by Council in February 2001, and to modify the ASA Bylaws (Article V.Committees. Section 8.Committee on Committees) as follows:

(a) The Committee on Committees shall be responsible for making ranked recommendations to Council for appointments to all Award Selection Committees and Status Committees. Additionally, the Committee on Committees shall make ranked recommendations to Council for appointments to the Awards Committee, the Committee on Professional Ethics, and the at-large portion of the Committee on Sections. The Committee on Nominations will have the responsibility of nominating the candidates for the Committee on Committees.

(b) The Committee on Committees shall to be composed of eight members each serving two-year terms. Four are to be elected at-large and four in seats reserved for specific institutional constituencies (one seat each for members employed by PhD granting institutions; by MA and four-year institutions; by 2-year schools; and by non-teaching institutions and in self-employment), with two at-large and two reserved seats up for election each year. (*Footnotes*, July/August:22 as presented on the Special Referendum Ballot).

The membership overwhelmingly endorsed the reestablishment of the Committee on Committees in the referendum (*Footnotes*, November 2001:1).

C. Changes in the ASA Bylaws: 2003

In February 2003, Council voted to make changes to the Bylaws in order to clarify certain articles, or to resolve inconsistencies and other technical problems that had been detected in a thorough review of the Constitution and Bylaws by ASA legal counsel. For each proposed change, ASA legal counsel provided recommendations for specific word changes for Council consideration. Council approved the following changes (subsequently approved by the membership in the spring of 2003). The changes to the Bylaws, which are summarized below, appear in full in the Official Reports and Proceedings (*Footnotes*, May 2003:28–29).

- *Formal Council Actions Between Meetings:* A conflict existed between the ASA Constitution Article IV, Section 5 and Bylaws Article III, Section 6, and both were in conflict with the District of Columbia laws under which ASA operates as a corporation. Council voted to permit Council actions between face-to-face meetings either by teleconference or by unanimous written vote after requests for actions are submitted by mail, electronic mail, fax or by other means.

- *Nominations of Members to Award Selection Committees:* Inconsistencies existed between Sections 7(a) and 8(a) of Article V of the Bylaws after the responsibility for nominating members to the Awards Selection Committees shifted back to the Committee on Committees. Council voted to change Bylaws Article V Section 7(a) to place responsibility for nominating members to the Awards Selection Committees with the Committee on Committees, and to amend Bylaws Article V Section 7(b) to remove the word "President" and replace it with "Committee on Committees."

- *Method of Annual Election:* At the August 20, 2002 meeting, Council voted to offer members the option of voting by electronic means as well as by paper ballot in the 2003 election. Due to changing means of communication, Council also asked legal counsel to propose amendments to the Bylaws to make the method of voting more flexible. Council voted to change the Bylaws suggested by removing all references to a specific method of membership voting (mailed ballots) and give Council the authority to determine the procedures to be followed provided that such procedures protect the privacy of members and ensure an accurate and fair count.

- *When the President-Elect Assumes the Presidency:* Article II, Section (1) required an adjustment due to the shift to a four-day Annual Meeting. Council voted to amend the Bylaws to begin the term of office for officers on the last day of the Annual Meeting in the year during which they are elected.

- *Clarification of Emeritus Membership Status:* Council unanimously voted to make persons eligible for emeritus membership at retirement from their primary employment as sociologists, providing that they have been full voting members of the Association for at least ten years.

- *Publication of Annual Financial Audit:* Legal counsel recommended that Bylaws should be general and not restrict an association to only one particular method of communication (e.g., in this case the Bylaws specifically direct that audits be published in *Footnotes*). Council voted to make the report of the audit, and the reporting of members' resolutions, available in an appropriate Association publication or by other means as deemed necessary by the Council.

- *Publication of Council Meeting Minutes:* Council discussed how to disseminate the Council Minutes most effectively. Council voted unanimously to authorize the Executive Office to place a copy of the full, approved Minutes of Council meetings on the ASA website, and to place a summary of selected actions and discussions in *Footnotes*.

The membership approved the seven proposed amendments in spring 2003 (*Footnotes*, July/August 2003:6).

APPENDIX 16: ASA COMMITTEES AND TASK FORCES

A. ASA Committees in 1990

The following list of Committees, taken from the ASA Council Agenda Book of August 14, 1990, includes the Constitutional Committees, Standing Committees, Subcommittees of Council, Task Forces, and Ad Hoc Committees, which existed at the time. The organizations to which Council sent an official representative in 1990 are also listed below.

Constitutional Committees

- Committees
- Executive Office and Budget
- Membership
- Nominations
- Program
- Publications

Standing Committees

- ASA/AAAS Relations
- Awards Policy

Awards Selection Committees:

- Career of Distinguished Scholarship Award
- Dissertation Award
- Distinguished Career Award for the Practice of Sociology
- Distinguished Contribution to Teaching Award
- Distinguished Scholarly Publication Award
- Dubois-Johnson-Frazier Award
- Jesse Bernard Award

- Certification Program, Evaluation of
- Certification, Oversight

Certification Committees

- Certification in Demography
- Certification in Law and Social Control
- Certification in Medical Sociology
- Certification in Organizational Analysis
- Certification in Social Policy and Evaluation Research
- Certification in Social Psychology

- Employment
- Freedom of Research and Teaching
- Masters Level Certification Program
- Minority Fellowship Program

- Minority Opportunity Summer Training (MOST) Program
- National Statistics
- Professional Ethics
- Public Information
- Research on the Profession
- Regulation of Research
- Sections
- Society and Persons with Disabilities
- Sociological Practice
- Sociologists in Government
- Status of Homosexuals in Society
- Status of Racial and Ethnic Minorities in Sociology
- Status of Women in Sociology
- Teaching
- U.S. Dept. of Agriculture Sociology History Project Oversight
- World Sociology

Subcommittees of Council

- Annual Meeting Session Format
- ASA and the Needs of the Poor and Dispossessed
- Blue Ribbon Subcommittee
- Emory University Proposal
- Exchanges with Foreign Scholars
- Legal Briefs
- ASA Honors Program (Standing Council Subcommittee Advisory Board)
- Problems of the Discipline (Standing Council Subcommittee Advisory Board)
- Teaching Services Advisory Board
- Warren Weaver Fellows Program
- Work Distribution/Participation
- Sociology at Washington University and Rochester University

Ad Hoc Committees

- Annual Meeting Childcare Review
- ASA Archives
- Cornerhouse Proposal
- Electronic Sociological Networks
- Professional Development Program, Evaluation of
- Representativeness in ASA Governance

Task Forces

- Association of American Colleges (AAC) Task Force on the Sociology Major
- Graduate Education in the Year 2000
- Sociology in Elementary and Secondary Schools

Official Representation

- American Association for the Advancement of Science
- American Council of Learned Societies (ACLS)
- Federal Statistics User's Conference
- International Sociological Association (ISA), Council
- Social Science Research Council (SSRC), Directors
- U.S. National Commission for UNESCO
- Journal of Consumer Research, Policy Board
- Council of Professional Associations on Federal Statistics (COPAFS)
- Committee on Problems of Drug Dependence
- American Association for the Advancement of Slavic Studies (AAASS)
- Coalition for the Advancement of Foreign Languages and International Studies (CAFLIS)

B. ASA Committees and Task Forces: 1998–2004

In January 1998, Council approved a major restructuring of ASA Committees. The following lists provide a summary of the outcomes of Council actions in 1998 as well as the changes that have occurred with respect to Task Forces up to 2004.

1. **Committees and Task Forces: 1998–99:** With one exception, the Committees in the following list were approved by Council in January 1998 and subsequently by the membership in a Spring1998 referendum. (The exception is the Committee on Committees, which was eliminated in 1998 and reinstated in 2001). After a period of input by the membership, the first Task Forces were approved by Council in February 1999. Committees and Task Forces include:

    (1) *Constitutional Committees.* Constitutional committees are committees central to the governance operations and functions of the Association. They include: Awards, Ethics, Executive Office and Budget, Nominations, Program, Publications, Sections, and Committees.

    (2) *Awards Selection Committees.* Awards selection committees select ASA award winners. These committees include: Career of Distinguished Scholarship Award, Dissertation Award, Distinguished Career Award for the Practice of Sociology, Distinguished Contribution to Teaching Award, Distinguished Scholarly Publication Award, DuBois-Johnson-Frazier Award, Jessie Bernard Award, and Public Understanding of Sociology Award.

    (3) *Status Committees.* The status committees advise and guide the Association on the status in the discipline and profession of those groups that have experienced a pattern of discrimination in society. The four status committees are: Status of Women in Sociology; Status of Racial and Ethnic Minorities in Sociology; Society of Persons with Disabilities; and Status of Gay, Lesbian, Bisexual, and Transgender Persons in Sociology.

    (4) *Advisory Panels.* Those committees that provide advice to Executive Office programs and related activities are advisory panels. In 1998 Council authorized the Executive Officer with establishing advisory panels as needed to provide such advice and guidance. The following committees are advisory panels: Spivack Program in Applied Social Research and Social Policy, Minority Fellowship Program Advisory Committee, and Fund for the Advancement of the Discipline (FAD).

(5) Task Forces. The most significant change in the Committee reorganization of 1998 took place with respect to the task forces. Task forces are established and appointed by Council for specific tasks and fixed terms (generally no more than two years) based on advice from the membership, sections, officers, staff, or Council itself. The first task forces were established in February, 1999, and included:

- **Task Force on the Implications of the Evaluation of Faculty Productivity and Teaching Effectiveness:** (Final Report, August 19, 2003).

- **Task Force on the Articulation of Sociology in Two-Year and Four-Year Sociology Programs:** (Final Report, August 19, 2002).

- **Task Force on Current Knowledge on Hate/Bias Acts on College and University Campuses:** (Final Report, January 2002).

- **Task Force on the International Focus of American Sociology:** (Final Report, August 19, 2003. Council voted to charge the existing Council Subcommittee on International Collaborations to handle international issues for two years, at which time the Subcommittee will issue a report on how to proceed in this area.)

- **Task Force on ASA/AAAS Relations:** (Final Report, August 2001).

2. **Task Forces Established by Council 1999–2004:** Since the original restructuring in 1998–99, the following Task Forces have been added:

    - **Task Force on the Reexamination of the Committee on Committees and the Committee on Nominations:** (Established August 1999; Mandate completed in February 2001).

    - **Task Force on the Statement on Race:** (Established January 2000; Final Report, August 2002).

    - **Task Force on the Advanced Placement Course in Sociology for High Schools:** (Established January 2000 and August 15, 2000; Final Report, August 18, 2004).

    - **Task Force on ASA Journal Diversity:** (Established: January 2000; Final Report, August 19, 2003).

    - **Task Force on Opportunities Beyond Graduate Education: Post Doctoral Training and Career Trajectories:** (Established: February 2001; disbanded with no report).

    - **Task Force on Contingent Employment in the Academic Workplace** (Established February 2001; Final Report, August 17, 2004).

    - **Task Force on Undergraduate Sociology Curriculum:** (Established February 2001; Final Report, August 18, 2004).

    - **Task Force on the Assessment of the Undergraduate Major:** (Established February 2003; Final Report, August 18, 2004).

    - **Task Force to Revise the ASA Areas of Specialty:** (Established: February 2003).

    - **Institutionalization of Public Sociology:** Originally created as the Task Force on Bridges to the Real World in February 2003, it became part of the new Task Force on Institutionalization of Public Sociology in January 2004.

APPENDIX 17: ASA SECTION FORMATION HISTORY

Section #	Section Name (As of August 2004)*	Year Attained Full Section Status**
1	Teaching and Learning	1973
2	Methodology	1961
3	Medical Sociology	1962
4	Crime, Law, and Deviance	1966
5	Sociology of Education	1967
6	Sociology of the Family	1967
7	Organizations, Occupations, and Work	1970
8	Theory	1968
9	Sociology of Sex and Gender	1973
10	Community and Urban Sociology	1973
11	Social Psychology	1961
12	Peace, War, and Social Conflict	1978
13	Environment and Technology	1977
14	Marxist Sociology	1977
15	Sociological Practice	1979
16	Sociology of Population	1978
17	Political Economy of the World System	1981
18	Aging and the Life Course	1980
19	Sociology of Mental Health	1993
20	Collective Behavior and Social Movements	1981
21	Racial and Ethnic Minorities	1981
22	Comparative Historical Sociology	1983
23	Political Sociology	1985
24	Asia and Asian America	1986
25	Sociology of Emotions	1988
26	Sociology of Culture	1988
27	Science, Knowledge, and Technology	1990
28	Communication and Information Technologies	1990
29	Latino/a Sociology	1994
30	Sociology of Alcohol, Drugs, and Tobacco	1993
31	Sociology of Children and Youth	1994
32	Sociology of Law	1994
33	Rationality and Society	1995
34	Sociology of Religion	1994
35	International Migration	1995
36	Race, Gender, and Class	1997
37	Mathematical Sociology	1997
38	Sociology of Sexualities	1997
39	History of Sociology	1999
40	Economic Sociology	2000
41	Labor and Labor Movements	2002
42	Animals and Society	2002
43	Ethnomethodology and Conversational Analysis	2004
44	Evolution in Sociology	SIF 2004

.**Year section began functioning, particularly election of its officers.

*Name changes:

Section 1: Undergraduate Education became Teaching and Learning (2001).

Section 4: Criminology became, Crime, Law, and Deviance (1988).

Section 7: Organizations and Occupations became Organizations, Occupations, and Work (1996).

Section 8: Theoretical Sociology became Theory (1994).

Section 10: Community became Community and Urban Sociology (1988).

Section 12: World Conflicts became Sociology of World Conflicts (1983) became Sociology of Peace and War (1985) became Peace, War, and Social Conflict (1998).

Section 13: Sociology of Environment became Environment and Technology (1987).

Section 18: Aging became Sociology of Aging (1982) became Aging and the Life Course (1998).

Section 21: Racial and Cultural Minorities became Racial and Ethnic Minorities (1981).

Section 28: Sociology of Microcomputing (1988) became Sociology and Computers (1995) became Communication and Information Technologies (2002).

Section 30: Alcohol and Drugs became Sociology of Alcohol, Drugs, and Tobacco (2003).

Section 31: Sociology of Children became Sociology of Children and Youth (2000).

Section 33: Rational Choice became Rationality and Society (2001).

Note on Section 19: Visual Sociology attempted to form as a Section in approximately 1980. They were assigned Section number 19. They failed to reach the required 200-minimum and thus disbanded. After Visual Sociology disbanded the number 19 was reassigned to the Section on Mental Health.

APPENDIX 18: MAJOR PUBLICATIONS OF THE ASA

1980–2004

A. Journals (dates reflect years of ASA publication of journal)
- *The American Sociologist* (*TAS*) (1965–1982)
- *American Sociological Review* (*ASR*) (1936–)
- *Contemporary Sociology* (*CS*) (1972–)
- *Journal of Health and Social Behavior* (*JHSB*) (1960–)[1]
- *Social Psychology Quarterly* (*SPQ*) (1956–)[2]
- *Sociology of Education* (*SOE*) (1963–)[3]
- *Teaching Sociology* (*TS*) (1986–)[4]
- *Sociological Methodology* (*SM*) (1969–)[5]
- *Sociological Theory* (*ST*) (1985–)[6]
- *Sociological Practice Review* (*SPR*) (1990–1992)
- *Employment Bulletin* (*EB*)
- *Contexts* (2002–)
- *City and Community* (2002–)[7]

B. Directories, Reference Materials
- *Guide to Graduate Departments* (annually, beginning 1965)
- *Directory of Departments* (bi-annually beginning 1978, ceased publication in 1999)
- *Directory of Members* (published either as a directory or as a biographical directory annually from 1963–82, bi-annually from 1984-present)
- *Employment Bulletin* (monthly, 1976-present).
- *Style Guide* (1st edition-1997, 2nd edition-1999).
- *Footnotes* (published monthly or bi-monthly in at least eight issues each year, beginning 1973).

C. The ASA *Rose Series in Sociology*

Established in 1967 through a bequest to the ASA from Arnold and Caroline Rose, the *Rose Series* aims to bring the best of sociology to wide audiences in the social sciences. (The Series was known as the *ASA Rose Monograph Series* up to 1995; since 1995, as the *ASA Rose Series in Sociology*.)

1996-Current—Published for the ASA by Russell Sage
- ***America's Newcomers and the Dynamics of Diversity***, by Frank D. Bean and Gillian Stevens (2003).
- ***Beyond College for All: Career Paths for the Forgotten Half***, by James E. Rosenbaum (2001).
- ***Making Hate a Crime: From Social Movement to Law Enforcement***, by Valerie Jenness and Ryken Grattet (2001).
- ***Trust in Schools: A Core Resource for Improvement***, by Anthony S. Bryk and Barbara Schneider (2002).

---

[1] Published by ASA as *Journal of Health and Human Behavior* 1960–1966, as *JHSB* 1967–present.

[2] Published as *Sociometry* by Beacon House, 1937–55, by ASA under the same name 1956–77, as *Social Psychology* in 1978, and as *SPQ* 1979-present.

[3] Published as *Journal of Educational Sociology* by American Viewpoint Society, Inc. 1927–63, by ASA under title *Sociology of Education* 1963-present.

[4] Published by Sage Publications 1973–85. ASA purchased in 1985, published first full volume in 1986.

[5] 1969–1985, published by Jossey-Bass. Began as an official ASA-published journal in 1986.

[6] 1983–84, published by Jossey-Bass. Began as an official ASA-published journal in 1985.

[7] An ASA section-published journal, published by ASA Section #10, Section on Community and Urban Sociology.

1991–1995—Published for the ASA by Rutgers University Press

- *Buying for Armageddon: Society, Economy, and the State Since the Cuban Missile Crisis*, by John L. Boise (1994).
- *Educating for Freedom: The Paradox of Pedagogy*, by Donald L. Finkle and William Ray Arney (1995).
- *Flesh Peddlers and Warm Bodies: The Temporary Help Industry and Its Workers*, by Robert E. Parker (1994).
- *Gender Differences in Science Careers: The Project Access Study*, by Gerhard Sonnert with Gerald Holton (1995).
- *Identity Designs: The Sights and Sounds of a Nation*, by Karen A. Cerulo (1995).
- *Organizing for Equality: The Evolution of Women's and Racial-Ethnic Organizations in America, 1955–1985,* by Debra C. Minkoff (1995).
- *Macrodynamics: Toward a Theory on the Organization of Human Populations*, by Jonathan H. Turner (1995).
- *Relations Into Rhetorics: Local Elite Structure in Norfolk, England, 1540–1640,* by Peter S. Bearman (1993).
- *The Social Control of Religious Zeal: A Study of Organizational Contradictions*, by Jon Miller (1994).
- *Supermarkets Transformed*, by John P. Walsh (1993).
- *A Weberian Theory of Human Society: Structure and Evolution*, by Walter L. Wallace (1994).

1977–1990—Published for the ASA by Cambridge University Press

- *Age, Class, Politics, and the Welfare State*, by Fred C. Pampel and John B. Williamson (1989).
- *Charisma and Control in Rajneeshpuram: The Role of Shared Values in the Creation of a Community*, by Lewis F. Carter (1990).
- *Cities with Little Crime: The Case of Switzerland*, by Marshall B. Clinard (1978).
- *Continuity and Change: A Study of Two Ethnic Communities*, by Rita J. Simon (1978).
- *The Cooperative Workplace: Potentials and Dilemmas of Organizational Democracy and Participation*, by Joyce Rothschild and J. Allen Whitt (1986).
- *The Cost of Regime Survival: Racial Mobilization, Elite Domination, and Control of the State in Guyana and Trinidad*, by Perry C. Hintzen (1989).
- *Different Worlds: A Sociological Study of Taste, Choice, and Success in Art*, by Liah Greenfeld (1989).
- *Education, Employment, and Migration: Israel in Comparative Perspective*, by Paul Ritterband (1978).
- *Ego Defenses and the Legitimation of Behavior*, by Guy E. Swanson (1988).
- *The Field of Social Investment*, by Severyn T. Bruyn (1987).
- *From Student to Nurse: A Longitudinal Study of Socialization*, by Ida Harper Simpson (1979).
- *Historical Role Analysis in the Study of Religious Change: Mass Educational Development in Norway, 1740–1891,* by John T. Flint (1990).
- *Juvenile Delinquency and Its Origins*, by Richard E. Johnson (1979).
- *Manufacturing Green Gold*, by William H. Friedland, Amy E. Barton, and Robert J. Thomas (1981).
- *The Meaning of General Theoretical Sociology: Tradition and Formalization*, by Thomas J. Fararo (1989).
- *The Methodology of Herbert Blumer*, by Kenneth Baugh, Jr. (1990).
- *Middle Start: An Experiment in the Educational Enrichment of Young Adolescents,* by J. Milton Yinger, Kiyoshi Ikeda, Frank Laycock, and Stephen J. Cutler (1977).
- *Opening and Closing: Strategies of Information Adaptation in Society*, by Orrin E. Klapp (1978).
- *Pathways in the Workplace: The Effects of Race and Gender on Access to Organizational Resources*, by Jon Miller (1986).
- *Paradoxical Harvest*, by Richard Adams (1982).
- *Protest and Participation: The New Working Class in Italy*, by John R. Low-Beer (1982).
- *Religion and Fertility*, by Joseph Chamie (1981).
- *The Shape of Culture*, by Judith R. Blau (1989).

- *Situations and Strategies in American Land-Use Planning*, by Thomas K. Rudel (1989).
- *Society and Identity: Toward a Sociological Psychology*, by Andrew J. Weigert, J. Smith Teitge, and Dennis W. Teitge (1986).
- *Sociological Explanation as Translation*, by Stephen Turner (1980).
- *Sociology, Ethnomethodology, and Experience*, by Mary K. Rogers (1983).
- *The Strategy and Tactics of Dynamic Functionalism*, by Michael Faia (1986).
- *Tasks and Social Relationships in Classrooms*, by Stephen T. Bossert (1979).
- *Theory of Societal Constitutionalism: Foundations of a Non-Marxist Critical Theory*, by David Sciulli (1992).
- *Trafficking in Drug Users*, by James R. Beniger (1983).
- *Undocumented Mexicans in the United States*, by David M. Heer (1990).
- *Understanding Events: Affect and the Construction of Social Action*, by David R. Heise (1979).
- *We Shall Live Again: The 1870 and 1890 Ghost Dance Movements in Demographic Revitalization*, by Russell Thornton (1986).

1970–1976—Published by the American Sociological Association

- *Ambition and Attainment: A Study of Four Samples of American Boys*, by Alan C. Kerckhoff (1974).
- *Attitudes and Facilitation in the Attainment of Status*, by Ruth M. Gasson, Archibald O. Haller, and William Sewell (1972).
- *Black and White Self-Esteem: The Urban School Child*, by Morris Rosenberg and Roberta G. Simmons (1972).
- *Black Students in Protest: A Study of the Origins of the Black Student Movement*, by Anthony M. Orum (1972).
- *Deviance, Selves and Others*, by Michael Schwartz and Sheldon Stryker (1971).
- *Ethnic Stratification in Penisular Malaysia*, by Charles Hirschman (1975).
- *The Greek Peasant*, by Scott McNall (1974).
- *Interorganizational Activation in Urban Communities: Deductions from the Concept of System*, by Herman Turk (1973).
- *Looking Ahead: Self-Conceptions, Race and Family as Determinants of Adolescent Orientation to Achievement*, by Chad Gordon (1972).
- *Patterns of Contact with Relatives*, by Sheila R. Klatzky (1972).
- *Patterns of Scientific Research: A Comparative Analysis of Research in Three Scientific Fields*, by Lowell Hargens (1975).
- *Socioeconomic Background and Educational Performance*, by Robert M. Hauser (1972).
- *The Study of Political Commitment*, by John DeLamater (1973).

APPENDIX 19: THE PRESIDENTIAL SERIES

The *Presidential Series* consists of volumes produced by presidents of the Association drawn primarily from the Thematic and Plenary Sessions of their Annual Meetings. Launched in 1975, the *Presidential Series* consists of the following volumes:

- ***Approaches to the Study of Social Structure***, edited by Peter M. Blau. New York: The Free Press (1975).
- ***The Uses of Controversy in Sociology***, edited by Lewis A. Coser and Otto N. Larsen. Newbury Park, CA: Sage Publications (1976).
- ***Societal Growth: Processes and Implications***, edited by Amos H. Hawley. New York: The Free Press (1979).
- ***Sociological Theory and Research: A Critical Approach***, edited by Hubert M. Blalock. New York: The Free Press (1980).
- ***Gender and the Life Course***, edited by Alice S. Rossi. New York: Aldine Publishing Company (1985).
- ***The Social Fabric: Dimensions and Issues***, edited by James Short Jr. Newbury Park, CA: Sage Publications (1986).
- ***Social Structures and Human Lives: Social Change and the Life Course, Vol. 1***, edited by Matilda White Riley in association with Bettina J. Huber and Beth B. Hess. Newbury Park, CA: Sage Publications (1988).
- ***Sociological Lives: Social Change and the Life Course, Vol. 2***, edited by Matilda White Riley. Newbury Park, CA: Sage Publications (1988).
- ***Cross-National Research in Sociology***, edited by Melvin L. Kohn. Newbury Park, CA: Sage Publications (1989).
- ***The Nature of Work: Sociological Perspectives***, edited by Kai Erikson and Peter Vallas. Yale University Press (1990).
- ***Sociology in America***, edited by Herbert J. Gans. Newbury Park, CA: Sage Publications (1990).
- ***Macro-Micro Linkages in Sociology***, edited by Joan Huber. Newbury Park, CA: Sage Publications (1991).
- ***The Social Context of AIDS***, edited by Joan Huber and Beth E. Schneider. Newbury Park, CA: Sage Publications (1991).

APPENDIX 20: TEACHING SERVICES PROGRAM (TSP)

A. Teaching Resource Center (TRC) Materials (1980-1990)

CLASSROOM TECHNIQUES

- *Ideology and Controversy in the Classroom: A Special Issue of The Journal of Ideology*, edited by Richard Wright.
- *Directory of Teaching Innovations in Sociology*, edited by L. R. Meeth and Dean S. Gregory, a cooperative publication of Studies in Higher Education and the ASA (1981).
- *Discussion in the College Classroom: Applications for Sociology Instruction*, by William Ewens and Vaneeta D'Andrea (1989).
- *Handbook of Outcome Assessment*, by Stephen Sharkey (1990).
- *Innovative Techniques for Teaching Sociology: Essays from the Teaching Newsletter, 1982–1985,* edited by Norman Layne, Jr. and Patrick Fontane (1986).
- *Learning Group Exercises for Political Sociology*, edited by William A. Gamson, in cooperation with the ASA Section an Political Sociology (1989).
- *Methods of Evaluating Student Performance*, edited by Theresa G. Turk (1982).
- *Passing on Sociology: The Teaching of a Discipline*, Charles A. Goldsmid and Everett K. Wilson (Published in 1980 by Wadsworth Publishing; reprinted by ASA in 1985).
- *A Sociologist's Song*, produced by Michel Richard (45-rpm record with copy of lyrics).
- *Songware: Using Popular Music in Teaching Sociology*, edited by David Walczak, Janet Merrill Alger, and Monica Reuter (1989).
- *Students with Reading and Writing Problems (revision)*, by Ashakant Nimbark, (1990).
- *Teaching the Mass Class*, compiled and edited by Reece McGee (1986).
- *Using Humor In Teaching Sociology (revision)*, edited by David S. Adams (1988).
- *Techniques for Teaching Sociological Concepts*, edited by Roger C. Barnes and Edgar W. Mills (1985).
- *Using Films In Sociology Courses; Guidelines and Reviews* **(Third Edition).** Contains reviews by Sally Rogers and an essay on using films by Robert Wolensky (1987).
- *The Undergraduate Sociology Curriculum*, by Jess Enns and John Seem (1990).
- *Writing for Social Scientists: Subtitled "How to Start and Finish Your Thesis, Book, or Article,"* by Howard S. Becker with a chapter by Pamela Richards. Chicago, IL: University of Chicago Press (1986).

CURRICULUM AND DEPARTMENTAL MANAGEMENT

- *Academic Leadership: The Role of the Department Chair*, by Lee H. Bowker with the assistance of Hans O. Mauksch (1986).
- *Constraints and Opportunities for Sociology Curricula*, edited by Frederick L. Campbell. A Special Issue of The American Sociologist 15:1(February 1980).
- *Curriculum Materials for Sociology of the Future*, edited by Nancy Wendlandt Stein (1990).
- *Curriculum Materials in Visual Sociology*, edited by Delores Wunder (1990).
- *33 Suggestions For Increasing Sociology Enrollments*, by Dean S. Dorn and Bryce Johnson (1985).
- *Guidelines and Resources for Assessing Your Sociology Program*, edited by Charles S. Green III (1986).
- *Guidelines for Initial Appointments in Sociology*, prepared by the ASA Committee on Freedom of Research and Teaching (COFRAT).
- *The Internship Handbook. Development and Administration of Internship Programs in Sociology*, edited by Richard Salem and Barbara Altman (1990).
- *Nurturing Excellence in Teaching Sociology: Essays from the Teaching Newsletter, 1982-1985,* edited by Norman Layne, Jr. and Patrick Fontane (1986).
- *Process and Structure: The Institutional Context of Teaching Sociology*, edited by Lee Bowker (1980).

- *Simulation and Gaming and the Teaching of Sociology* **(Fifth Edition),** by Richard L Dukes and Sandra Matthews (Previous Editions: 1975, 1980,1983,1986).
- *Sociology and the Liberal Arts*, by Raymond G. DeVries (1987).
- *Sociology and the Small College Environment*, by Rodger A. Bates and John J. Crowden (1986).
- *Strategies for Effective Undergraduate Advising in Sociology*, by Martha McMillian and Kathleen McKinney (1986).
- *Suggestions for Improving the Departmental Procedures for Hiring Teachers of Sociology*, by the ASA Committee on Freedom of Research and Teaching (1976).
- *Teaching Applied Sociology: A Resource Book*, edited by Carla B. Howery (1983).
- *Teaching Sociology: The Quest for Excellence*, edited by Frederick L. Campbell, Hubert M. Blalock, Jr., and Reece McGee (1984).
- *Teaching Sociology on the Branch Campus*, by Juliet Saltman.
- *Training Teaching Assistants*, edited by Edward Kain and Shelley Immel (1989).

SYLLABI SETS

- *A Basic Bibliography in Political Sociology*, compiled by Frederick D. Weil and Betty Dobratz; in cooperation with the ASA Section on Political Sociology (1984).
- *The Sociology of AIDS: A Set of Syllabi and Related Materials*, edited by Rose Weitz; a cooperative project with the Sociologists' AIDS Network (1988).
- *Applied Sociology: A Resource Book (revision)*, by Carla B. Howery, American Sociological Association (1990).
- *The Clinical Sociology Resource Book*, edited by Jan M. Fritz and Elizabeth J. Clark for the Sociological Practice Association (formerly the Clinical Sociology Association) (1986).
- *Comparative Historical Sociology: Teaching Materials and Bibliography*, compiled by William G. Roy with the assistance of Rachel R. Parker (1987).
- *Crime and Control. Syllabi and Instructional Materials for Criminology and Criminal Justice (1989 Revision)*, edited by Richard A. Wright, Max Ewalt and Linda Deutschmann (previous edition: 1984)
- *Course Syllabi, Resources, and Instructional Materials on the Sociology of Culture*, edited by Roseanne Martoreila; in cooperation with the ASA Section on Sociology of Culture.
- *Internationalizing the Sociology Curriculum (revision)*, by J. Michael Armer (1990).
- *Resources, Instructional Materials, and Syllabi for Courses on the Sociology of Death and Dying*, by Gerry R. Cox and Ronald J. Fundis (1986).
- *Environmental Sociology: A Collection of Course Syllabi*, edited by Monica A. Seff, Riley E. Dunlap, and Arthur St. George in cooperation with the ASA Section on Environmental Sociology (1985).
- *The Humanist Sociology Resource Book*, edited by Martin D. Schwartz. A joint project with the Association for Humanist Sociology (1987).
- *An Inclusive Curriculum: Race, Class & Gender*, edited by Patricia Hill Collins and Margaret Andersen. A joint project of the ASA Teaching Services Program and the ASA Sections on Sex and Gender, and Racial and Ethnic Minorities (1988).
- *Syllabi and Resources for Internationalizing Courses in Sociology*, edited by J. Michael Armer for the ASA Committee on World Sociology (1983).
- *Syllabi and Instructional Materials for Chicano Studies In Sociology*, edited by Mary Romero in cooperation with the National Association for Chicano Studies (1985).
- *Syllabi and Instructional Materials in Collective Behavior*, edited by Stephen Barkan and Debra Friedman; in cooperation with the Section on Collective Behavior and Social Movements (1990).
- *Syllabi and Instructional Materials in Complex Organizations*, by Howard M. Kaplan (1990).
- *Syllabi and Instructional Materials for Courses in Demography* **(Second Edition, 1989),** edited by Brian Pendleton (Previous Edition: 1984).

- *Syllabi and Instructional Materials for Courses on Deviance and Social Control*, edited by Robert J. Lavizzo-Mourey (1985).
- *Syllabi and Instructional Materials for the Sociology of Emotions*, edited by David Franks and Shelley Ottenbrite; In cooperation with the ASA Section on Sociology of Emotions (1989).
- *Syllabi and Instructional Materials for Courses in Juvenile Delinquency*, edited by John Broderick (1984).
- *Syllabi and Instructional Materials for Juvenile Delinquency (revision)*, by Maureen Kelleher (1990).
- *Syllabi and Instructional Materials for Sociology of Law*, edited by Ronald J. Berger (1985).
- *Syllabi and Instructional Materials for Latino Studies Courses in Sociology (revision)*, by Mary Romero (1990).
- *Syllabi and Instructional Materials for Courses in Political Sociology*, edited by Frederick D. Weil and Betty Dobratz in cooperation with the ASA Section on Political Sociology (1984).
- *Syllabi and Instructional Materials for Courses in Race and Ethnic Relations (revision)*, by Donald Cunnigen (1990).
- *Syllabi and Instructional Materials for Science and Technology*, by Thomas Gieryn (1990).
- *Syllabi and Instructional Materials for Sociology of Religion*, edited by Madeleine Adriance and Dallas Blanchard. A joint project with the Association for the Sociology of Religion (1987).
- *Syllabi and Instructional Materials for Social Problems Courses*, by J. Michael Brooks and Richard J. Hurzeler (1990).
- *Syllabi and Instructional Materials for Courses in Social Statistics*, by Louis Gaydosh (1990).
- *Syllabi and Instructional Materials for Courses on Sociology of Sport*, edited by William C. Whit (1985).
- *Syllabi and Instructional Materials for Sociology of Sport (revision)*, by Gai Berlage (1990).
- *Syllabi and Instructional Materials for Sex and Gender (revision)*, by Virginia Powell (1990).
- *Syllabi and Instructional Material for World Conflicts*, by Margaret Herrman, (1990).
- *Marriage and the Family Courses: Print and Visual Resources*, edited by LeRoy A. Furr with Carla B. Howery, Corinne A. Bordieri, and Edward Kain (1986).
- *Syllabi Set for Medical Sociology (revision)*, edited by Kathy Charmaz, Nan Chico, Adele Clarke, and Sheryl F. Ruzek in cooperation with the ASA Section on Medical Sociology (1985).
- *Preparing Graduate Students to Teach: Syllabi and Related Materials from Graduate Courses on the Teaching of Sociology*, edited by Thomas L. Van Valey (1984).
- *The Profession of Sociology: Syllabi and Selective Bibliography (1989 revision)*, by James K. Skipper and David F. Mitchell (previous editions: 1980, 1984).
- *Qualitative Research Methods: Syllabi and Instructional Materials*, edited by Kenneth Stoddart (1986).
- *Research Methods Courses: Syllabi, Assignments, and Projects* **(Second Edition),** edited by Russell K. Schutt, Theodore C. Wagenaar, and Kevin Mulvey (1987).
- *The Sociology of Sex and Gender: Syllabi and Teaching Materials*, edited by Barrie Thorne, Mary McCormack, Virginia Powell, and Delores Wunder; A project of the ASA Section on Sex and Gender (revision) (1985).
- *The Sociology of Sexuality and Homosexuality: Syllabi and Teaching Materials*, edited by Martin P. Levine and Meredith Gould. A joint project with the Lesbian and Gay Caucus (1987).
- *Social Stratification Courses: A Set of Syllabi and Instructional Materials* **(Second Edition),** edited by Carol J. Auster (1988).
- *Resource Book for Teaching Sociological Theory (1989 Revision)*, edited by Richard W. Moodey; in cooperation with the ASA Section on Sociological Theory (previous edition: 1984).
- *Teaching Sociology. A Bibliography* **(Fourth Edition),** compiled by Wilhelmina Perry (1988).
- *Teaching Sociology of Aging*, edited by Diana K. Harris, Erdman B. Palmore, and Sandra C. Stanley in cooperation with the ASA Section on Aging (revision of earlier set) (1986).
- *Teaching About Families: A Collection of Syllabi*, edited by Ginger Macheski (1989).
- *Teaching Introductory Sociology: A Resource Book (revision)*, edited by Kathleen McKinney and James Sikora (1990).

- *Teaching Introductory Sociology: A Resource Manual (revision of 1977 syllabi set)*, edited by Charlene Black and Norma Seerley in cooperation with the ASA Section on Undergraduate Education (1983).
- *Teaching Rural Sociology: A Resource Manual*, edited by Eric O. Hoiberg with the assistance of Donald Crider, Joseph Donnermeyer, George Ohlendorf, Irving Spaulding, and Alton Thompson. A joint project with the Rural Sociological Society (1987).
- *Teaching Social Change: Course Designs, Syllabi and Instructional Materials* (**Second Edition**), edited by Rosalie Cohen (1988).
- *Teaching Sociology of Education: Syllabi and Instructional Materials* (**Third Edition, 1989**), edited by Jeanne Ballantine, Floyd Hammack, Edith King, Caroline Persell, and Theodore Wagenaar; in cooperation with the ASA Section on Sociology of Education (previous editions: 1980, 1984).
- *Teaching Sociology from a Marxist Perspective*, edited by Rhonda Levine (1990).
- *Teaching the Sociology of Work and Occupations: Syllabi, Course Materials, and Bibliographies*, edited by Jane C. Hood and David Booth in cooperation with the ASA Section on Organizations and Occupations (1985).
- *Teaching Undergraduate Social Psychology* (**Second Edition**), edited by Jeffrey Chin and Judith Little; in cooperation with the ASA Section on Social Psychology (Previous Edition: 1984).
- *Teaching War as a Social Problem: A Report on Soc 101 at Indiana University*, by Allen D. Grimshaw (1984).
- *Urban Sociology: A Resource Book*, by Philip Olson, Karen Whetsell, and Gary Glunt. A joint project with the ASA Section on Community (1988).
- *The Welfare State Revisited* (**Second Edition,1989**), edited by Bernice Pescosolido (previous edition 1984).

B. Teaching Services Program Workshops 1980–91

Teaching Services Program workshops drew on the membership of the Teaching Resources Group (TRG) as well as other faculty as staff. The workshops were also a training venue for staff. A Lilly grant paid expenses so that one experienced and one less experienced person from TRG formed a team to lead a session. Workshops were held on the following topics:

1980-82

- *Workshop on Course and Curriculum Planning*, Pittsburgh, PA; November 6–8, 1980.
- *Workshop on the Evaluation of Students and Teachers*, Colorado State University, Fort Collins CO; November 20–22, 1980.
- *Workshop at two levels (basic and advanced; the advanced package consisted of topical areas such as Research Methods, the Family Course, The First Course, and the Theory Course)*, held simultaneously in five locations (Boston, MA; Chicago, IL; Reno, NV; Phoenix, AZ; and New Orleans, LA; May 14-17, 1981.
- *Workshops at the 1982 Annual Meeting on "Teaching Introductory Sociology," "Teaching Social Problems," "Teaching Marriage and the Family," and "Teaching Research Methods"*; September 8, 1982.
- *"Teaching Techniques and Practice,"* New York City, Dallas, and Los Angeles; March 25–27, 1982.
- *"Teaching Applied Sociology,"* University of Wisconsin-Whitewater, WI; June 23–27, 1982.

1983

- *"Functioning as a Departmental Chair and Fostering Teaching,"* St. Louis, MO: April 21–23, 1983.
- *"Preparing Teaching Units for Lower Division Courses,"* Atlanta, GA; April 21–23, 1983.
- "*Working Laboratory on Teaching Styles and Teaching Techniques,"* Denver, CO; May 5–7, 1983.

1984

- *"Applied Sociology Programs and Curricula: Career Opportunities for BA, MA, and PhD Students,"* Sacramento, CA; February 9–12, 1984.
- *"Techniques and Resources for Evaluating Sociology Programs and Faculty Effectiveness,"* College of DuPage, Glen Ellyn, IL; March 8–11, 1984.

- *"Issues of Sexism and Racism in Teaching Sociology,"* American University, Washington, DC; March 30–April 1, 1984.
- *"Academic Leadership: Helping Sociologists to be Effective Chairpersons and Deans,"* Milwaukee, WI; June 7–9, 1984.
- *"Using the Computer in Teaching Sociology,"* Georgetown University, Washington, DC; June 20–23, 1984.
- *"Using the Computer in Teaching Sociology,"* Ball State University, Muncie, IN; July 19–22, 1984.
- *"Sociology's Service Mission: Strengthening the Lower Division and Introductory Courses,"* Furman University, Greenville, SC; October 24–27, 1984.

1985

- *"Basic Skills: Teaching Reading, Writing and Sociology to Non-Majors,"* Kennesaw College, Atlanta, GA: February 28–March 2, 1985.
- *"Teaching Sociology of Sex and Gender"* and *"Teaching Sociology of War and Peace"* (at the Eastern Sociological Society Meeting), Philadelphia, PA; March 15–17, 1985.
- *"Teaching Sociology of War and Peace"* and *"Teaching Sociology in the High Schools"* (at the Midwest Sociological Society Meeting), St Louis, MO; April 10–12, 1985.
- *"Evaluating Students, Teachers, and Sociology Programs,"* College of DuPage, Glen Ellyn, IL; May 16–18, 1985.
- *"Strengthening Graduate Education in Sociology,"* University of Indiana-Bloomington. IN; May 30–June 1, 1985.
- *"Using the Computer in Teaching Sociology,"* Hamline University; June 20–23, 1985 and Drexel University, July 23–26, 1985.
- *"Designing Computer-based Instruction,"* University of Minnesota; June 23–24, 1985.
- *"Teaching Applied and Clinical Sociology,"* University of Texas-Dallas; November 14–16, 1985.

1986

- *"Vivifying the Classroom: Teaching Sociology Using Media, Visuals, Simulations, and Other Methods,"* Pleasant Valley Community College, St. Louis, MO; March 13–15, 1986.
- *"Improving Sociology Programs: Changing the Sociology Curriculum to Better Meet the Needs of a Changing Generation of Students,"* University of Central Florida, Orlando, FL; March 23–25, 1986.
- *"Teaching the Sociology of Law,"* Cosponsored with the American Bar Association Advisory Committee on Non-Professional Legal Studies and the Eastern Sociological Society, New York City; April 4, 1986.
- *"Two Year/Four Year Articulation and the Improvement of Undergraduate Education in Sociology,"* University of Washington, Seattle; April 24–25, 1986.
- *"The Computer as a Basic Sociology Teaching Tool,"* California State University, Sacramento, CA; June 9–13, 1986.
- *"Using the Computer in Qualitative Research,"* Macalester College, St. Paul, MN; June 14–16, 1986.
- *"Instructional Computer Simulations and Games,"* Skidmore College, Saratoga Springs, NY; June 26–28, 1986.
- *"Field Experience and Teaching: Learning Through Participatory Research,"* with Paulo Freire and William Foote Whyte at UCLA; July 31–August 1, 1986.

1987

- *"Establishing Local College and University Research Centers,"* co-sponsored with Anne Arundel Community College at Annapolis, MD; March 19–20, 1987.
- *"Changing the Sociology Curriculum to Better Meet Changing Student Needs,"* Orlando, FL; April 6–8, 1987.
- *"Teaching Sociological Practice,"* University of Maine; May 21–23, 1987.
- *"Integrating Computers into the Sociology Curriculum,"* College of DuPage, Glen Ellyn, IL; June 10–13, 1987.

- *"Sociology and Experiential, Community-Based Learning,"* Knoxville, TN; June 16–19, 1987.
- *"Sociology and Critical Thinking,"* Whittier College; June 25–27, 1987.

1988

- *"The Integration of Computers into the Sociology Curriculum,"* University of Texas, San Antonio; March 30–April 3, 1988.
- *"Establishing College and University Local Research Centers,"* co-sponsored with Anne Arundel Community College at Annapolis, MD; April 6–8, 1988.
- *"Teaching the Sociology of Family Violence,"* Northeastern University, Boston; May 12–14, 1988.
- *"Using Computers in Teaching Sociology for Personal Empowerment and Social Change,"* Northern Illinois University; June 2–4, 1988.
- *"Participatory Research and Community-Based Education,"* At the Oglala Lakota College, Kyle SD; June 15–18, 1988.
- *"Introducing Cross-Cultural Materials into the Sociology Curriculum,"* University of Hawaii; June 23–25, 1988.
- *"Integrating the New Scholarship on Women into the Sociology Curriculum,"* cosponsored with Sociologists for Women in Society (SWS) at San Francisco State University; July 7-9, 1988.
- *"Visual Resources for Teaching Sociology,"* cosponsored with International Visual Sociology Association at Rochester, NY; July 15-17, 1988.

1989

- *"Outcome Assessment: The Role of Sociologists and Selected Teaching Issues,"* Louisville, KY; March 2-4, 1989.
- *"Teaching About the Sociology of Family Crises,"* Fort Worth, TX; April 20–22, 1989.
- *"Teaching About Substance Abuse and Prevention Efforts,"* cosponsored with the National Institute on Drug Abuse (NIDA), Rockville, MD; October 9–21, 1989.

1990

- *"Establishing College and University Local Research Centers,"* Chapman College, Orange, CA; January 25–27, 1990.
- *"Using Writing to Improve Undergraduate Courses and Student Performance,"* Florissant Valley, Community College, St. Louis, MO: February 22–24, 1990.
- *"Introducing Multi-Cultural and International Content and Experiences into Sociology Courses and Curricula,"* University of New Orleans, New Orleans, LA; March 15–17, 1990.
- *"Introducing Computers to Teaching: The Integration of Computers into the Sociology Curriculum,"* Tennessee State University, Nashville, TN; May 10–12, 1990.
- *"Enhancing Undergraduate Sociology Programs: Creating Courses and Activities to Attract Better Students,"* Wright State University, Dayton, OH; May 17–19, 1990.
- *"Integrating Internships and Experimental Education into Sociology Curricula,"* cosponsored with NSIEE), North Carolina A&T State University, Greensboro, NC; October 4–6, 1990.
- *"Teaching About Substance Abuse and Prevention Efforts,"* Lexington, KY: May 17–19, 1991.
- *"Teaching Critical Thinking Skills,"* Macomb Community College, Detroit, MI; May 23–25, 1991.

APPENDIX 21: PROFESSIONAL DEVELOPMENT PROGRAM (PDP)

A. Career Information (in collaboration with the Teaching Services Program) (1980–91)

The following is a sample of materials on careers produced jointly by the Teaching Services Program (TSP) and the Professional Development Program (PDP):

- *Career Possibilities for Sociology Graduates*, by Bettina J. Huber.
- *Careers in Sociology* (A booklet on the multiple career options in sociology).
- *Embarking Upon a Career with an Undergraduate Sociology Major*, by Bettina J. Huber (1982).
- *Controlling the Ascent through Sociology, Teacher Manual*, revised by Susan Takata (originally written by Jeanne Curran and Carol Telesky) (1987).
- *The Internship Handbook. Development and Administration of Internship Programs in Sociology*, edited by Richard Salem and Barbara Altman (1990).
- *The Industrial Sociologist as Teacher and Practitioner. A Career Bulletin for Graduate Students*, edited by Delbert C. Miller (1988).
- *Majoring in Sociology: A Guide for Students*.
- *Mastering the Job Market: Using Graduate Training in Sociology for Careers in Applied Settings*, by Bettina J. Huber (1982).
- *Preparing for Teaching: Suggestions for Graduate Students of Sociology*, by William Ewens (1976).

Other Publications:

- "*Sociological Practitioners: Their Characteristics and Role in the Profession,*" by Bettina Huber, *Footnotes*, May 1983.
- "How to Join the Federal Workforce and Advance Your Career."
- "*Career Possibilities for Sociology Graduates,*" by Bettina Huber, *Footnotes*, December 1984.
- **Brochure to promote sociology to corporate employers**, by Wayne Baker, University of Chicago, 1989.

B. Sociological Practice: Seminars and Outreach (1981–85)

- "**Directions in Applied Sociology,**" at George Washington University; sponsored by ASA Committee on Professional Opportunities in Applied Sociology; December 4–6, 1981.
- "**Employment Opportunities in Applied Settings for Sociologists,**" Washington, DC; May 28–29, 1983 (repeated on June 2–3).
- "**Consulting Skills for the Sociologist,**" Washington, DC; May 30–June 1, 1983.
- **Job Clinic conducted by Richard Irish at the 1984 Annual Meeting,** (August 25–26, 1984) at the Annual Meeting.
- **Three Workshops from March 21–24, 1985 in Washington DC:**
  - "**Getting a Job in the Federal Government,**" with Lawrence J. Rhoades, NIMH (March 21);
  - "**The Ins and Outs of Grants and Contracts,**" with David Myers, Decision Resources Corporation; and Sandra Hofferth, NICHD (March 22); and
  - "**Writing Skills for Sociologists,**" with Carolyn Mullins, Virginia Polytechnic Institute and State University (March 23–24).
- **Job Clinic conducted by Richard Irish and Workshop on "Effective Federal Job Hunting,"** with David Waelde, Federal Research Service, Inc. at the 1985 Annual Meeting; August 24–25, 1985.
- "**Careers in Advertising and Marketing,**" with Deborah David (October 5–6, 1985).
- "**Effective Writing for Lay Audiences and the Mass Media,**" with Jan Yager (October 7–8, 1985).

APPENDIX 22: ACADEMIC AND PROFESSIONAL AFFAIRS PROGRAM (APAP)

Products from the Teaching Resources Center (TRC) (retrieved from the ASA homepage, Summer 2005)

Products Currently Under Development (2005), including name of person(s) leading the project:

- *Aging and the Life Course: Teaching the Sociology of Aging and the Life Course*, Diane Zablotsky.
- *Applying to and Surviving Graduate School*, Victoria Hougham.
- *The Capstone Course in Sociology* **(Fourth Edition)**, Theodore Wagenaar.
- *Community College: Teaching Sociology in a Community College*, Carol A. Jenkins.
- *Criminology: Teaching Criminology: Resources and Issues*, Andrew Austin.
- *Disseminating Computational Modeling in the Social Sciences*, James A. Kitts.
- *Emotions: Sociology of Emotions: Syllabi & Instructional Materials*, Ann Branaman, Leslie Irvine, and Kathryn Lively.
- **HIV/AIDS-Teaching the Sociology of HIV/AIDs: Syllabi, Lectures & Other Resources for Instructors and Students (Third Edition)**, Eric R. Wright.
- *Internationalizing: Internationalizing Sociology in the Age of Globalization*, Alan Brown-Hart.
- *Innovative Techniques for Teaching Sociological Concepts* **(Fourth Edition)**, Edward L. Kain and Sandi Nenga.
- *The Internship Handbook*, edited by Richard Salem (2005; previous edition in 1999).
- *Law: Syllabi and Instructional Materials for Sociology of Law*, Lloyd Klein.
- *Mental Health: Teaching Materials for the Sociology of Mental Health and Illness*, Teresa Scheid.
- *Preparing Graduate Students to Teach: Preparing Graduate Students to Teach—Syllabi and Related Material from Graduate Courses on the Teaching of Sociology*, Marilyn Krogh.
- *Recruiting and Retaining Quality Majors*, Susan L. Caulfield, Edward L. Kain, Sarah S. Willie, and Esther I. Wilder.
- *Research Methods Courses: Syllabi, Assignments and Projects* **(Sixth Edition)**, Kevin Mulvey and Augusto Diana
- *The Role of the Department Chair*, Katherine O'Donnell and Tom Van Valey.
- *Social Statistics-Syllabi and Instructional Materials for Social Statistics*, Rhoda Estep Macdonald.
- *Software and Sociology: Software and Sociology*, Kevin D. Henson.
- *Theory: Resource Book for Teaching Sociological Theory*, (editor to be determined).
- *Theory—Integrating Women into Theory Courses*, Jan E. Thomas.
- *Welfare: The Welfare State Revisited*, Robin Roth.
- *When you are What you Teach: Experiences of Women of Color Professors at Historically White Colleges and Universities*, Marcia Hernandez.

Curriculum Development and Department Leadership

Assessment

- *Assessing Student Learning in Sociology*, edited by Charles S. Hohm and William S. Johnson (revised 2001).
- *Creating an Effective Sociology Assessment Plan*, Janet Huber Lowry and the Task Force on Assessing the Undergraduate Sociology Major.

Curriculum Development

- *Directory of Programs in Applied Sociology and Sociological Practice*, edited by Jeffrey Breese and copy edited by Sarah H. Grzesik (2000).
- *The Capstone Course in Sociology* **(Third Edition)**, edited by Theodore C. Wagenaar and updated by Meghan Rich (2001).
- *Classroom Research: Implementing the Scholarship of Teaching*, by K. Patricia Cross and Mimi Harris Steadman. Published by Jossey-Bass (1996).
- *Community-based Research*, edited by Sam Marullo and Kerry Strand (2004).

- *Constraints and Opportunities for Sociology Curricula*, edited by Frederick L. Campbell. Special issue of *The American Sociologist* 15:1 (Feb.1980).
- *Cultivating the Sociological Imagination: Concepts and Models For Service-Learning in Sociology*, edited by James Ostrow, Gary Hesser, and Sandra Enos. Published by the American Association for Higher Education in cooperation with the American Sociological Association (1999).
- *Distance and Cross-Campus Learning*, edited by Meredith Redlin and Susan Hilal (2003).
- *Included in Sociology: Learning Climates that Cultivate Racial and Ethnic Diversity*, edited by Jeffrey Chin, Catherine White Berhide, and Dennis Rome. Published by the American Association for Higher Education in cooperation with the American Sociological Association (2002).
- *Liberal Learning and the Sociology Major.* A cooperative project with the Association of American Colleges (1991).
- *Service Learning and Undergraduate Sociology: Syllabi and Instructional Materials* **(Second Edition)**, edited by JoAnn DeFiore, Morten G. Ender, and Brenda Marsteller Kowalewski, (revised 2005).
- *Teaching Introduction to Sociology as a Hybrid Course*, edited by Lynn H. Ritchey (2005).

Department Leadership
- *Chairing the Multidisciplinary Department*, edited by Beth Rushing (2003).
- *Preparing Future Faculty in the Humanities and Social Sciences: A Guide for Change*, by Jerry Gaff, Anne S. Pruitt-Logan, Leslie B. Sims, and PFF program participants (2003).
- *The Role of the Department Chair* (out of print), by Lee H. Bowker, Hans O. Mauksch, Barbara Keating, and Dennis R. McSeveney (1997).
- *The Social World of Higher Education*, edited by Bernice A Pescosolido and Ronald Aminzade (1999).
- *Teaching Sociology at Small Institutions*, edited by Eric P. Godfrey (1998).
- *The Sociology Student Club Tool Kit*, created by Steve Hoffman (1999).
- *Teaching Sociology in the Community College*, edited by Maria I. Bryant (1995).
- *Teaching Sociology: The Quest for Excellence*, edited by Frederick L. Campbell, Hubert M. Blalock Jr., and Reece McGee (1984).

Graduate Education
- *Preparing Graduate Students to Teach* **(Third Edition)**, edited by Kimberly Mahaffy (2000).
- *Graduate Student Instructor and Teaching Assistant Program Development: Materials for the Selection and Preparation of Teaching Assistants in Sociology Courses* **(Third Edition)**, edited by Melinda Messineo (revised 2001).

Guidelines
- *Applying for a Faculty Position in a Teaching-Oriented Institution*, by Kathleen Piker-King, Edward L. Kain, Keith A. Roberts, and Gregory L. Weiss (2001).
- *Employment of Part-Time Faculty in Departments of Sociology, Guidelines,* approved by ASA Council 1986 (1986).
- *Equity Issues for Women Faculty in Sociology Departments*, prepared by the ASA Committee on the Status of Women (1988).
- *Initial Appointments in Sociology, Guidelines for*, prepared by the ASA Committee on Freedom of Research and Teaching (1978).
- *New Faculty Discuss Academic Job Searching*, by Shelia R. Cotten, Jammie Price, Shirley Keeton, Russell P.D. Burton, and Janice E. Clifford Wittekind.
- *New Faculty Discuss the First Year as an Assistant Professor*, by Jammie Price, Shelia R. Cotten, Shirley Keeton, Russell P. D. Burton, and Janice E. Clifford Wittekind.
- *Preparing for Promotion & Tenure Review: A Faculty Guide*, by Robert M. Diamond. Published by Anker Publishing Company (1995).

- *Serving on Promotion, Tenure, and Faculty Review Committees: A Faculty Guide*, by Robert M. Diamond (2002).

Teaching Resource Guides
- **Aging**—*Teaching Sociology of Aging and the Life Course* **(Fifth Edition)**, edited by Diana K. Harris (2000).
- **Alcohol and Drugs**—*The Sociology of Alcohol and Drugs: Syllabi and Teaching Materials*, edited by Carrie B. Oser, Richard Dembo, and Paul M. Roman (2005).
- **Animals and Society**—*Teaching About Animals and Society: A Collection of Syllabi, Projects, Assignments, Web Sites, Articles and Bibliographies*, edited by Janet M. Alger, Tracey Smith-Harris, Shawn McEntee, and Kim W. Smallwood.
- **Appalachian Studies**—*Appalachian Studies: Syllabus Guide and Teaching Materials* **(Second Edition)**, edited by Chris Baker (2000).
- **Applied Sociology**—*Teaching Applied Sociology*, edited by Duane Dukes, James Petersen, and Tom VanValey (2003).
- **Chicano/Latino Studies**—*Chicano and Latino Studies in Sociology: Syllabi and Instructional Materials* **(Fifth Edition)**, edited by Jose Calderon and Gilda Ochoa (2002).
- **Children**—*Sociology of Children/Childhood* **(Second Edition)**, edited by Sue Marie Wright (2003).
- **Clinical Sociology**—*The Clinical Sociology Resource Book* **(Fifth Edition)**, edited by Jan Marie Fritz. In cooperation with the Sociological Practice Association (2001).
- **Comparative & Historical**—*Syllabi & Instructional Materials for Teaching Comparative & Historical Sociology*, edited by Linda B. Deutschmann (2001).
- **Consumption**—*Syllabi & Teaching Resources for Teaching the Sociology of Consumption*, edited by George Ritzer, Todd Stillman, and Meghan Rich (2002).
- **Criminology**—*Teaching Criminology: Resources and Issues*, edited by Richard A. Wright (2000).
- **Culture**—*Course Syllabi on the Sociology of Culture* **(Third Edition)**, edited by William G. Holt III (2005).
- **Death and Dying**—*Death, Dying & Bioethics: A Teaching Resource Manual for Courses on the Sociology of Death*, edited by Gerry R. Cox and Timothy B. Gongaware (2005).
- **Demography**—*Syllabi and Instructional Material in Demography* **(Fourth Edition)**, edited by Loretta E. Bass and Rebecca Nees (2003).
- **Development**—*Syllabi and Teaching Resources for the Sociology of Development and Women in Development*, compiled and edited by Basil Kardaras (2005).
- **Deviance/Social Control**—*Teaching the Sociology of Deviance*, edited by Marty Schwartz and Michael Maume (2003).
- **Disabilities**—*Instructional Materials for Teaching Sociology and Disability Studies* **(Second Edition)**, edited by Lynn Schlesinger and Diane E. Taub. Sponsored by the ASA Committee on the Status of Persons with Disabilities (2004).
- **Economic**—*Economic Sociology: Syllabi & Instructional Materials* **(Second Edition)**, edited by Gary P. Green and David Myhre (2002).
- **Education**—*Teaching the Sociology of Education: A Resource Manual* **(Sixth Edition)**, edited by Jeanne Ballantine, Richard Arum, Floyd Morgan Hammack, Edith King, Caroline Hodges Persell, and Theodore C. Wagenaar (2004).
- **Emotions**—*Sociology of Emotions: Syllabi and Instructional Materials*, edited by Catherine G. Valentine, Steve Derné, and Beverly Cuthbertson Johnson (revised 1999).
- **Environmental**—*Syllabi and Instructional Material in Environmental Sociology* **(Fifth Edition)**, edited by Rik Scarce and Michael Mascarenhas (2003).
- **Families**—*Teaching About Families: A Collection of Essays, Syllabi, Projects, and Assignments, Websites, and Bibliographies*, edited by Ginger Macheski, Kathleen Lowney, Michael Capece, Kate Warner, and Martha Laughlin (2004).
- *Food: Sociology of Food*, edited by Denise A. Copelton and Betsy Lucal (2005).

- *Teaching About Family Violence: A Collection of Instructional Materials* (Third Edition), edited by Barbara Keating and Amy Skatter (2003).
- *Gender—The Sociology of Gender: Syllabi & Other Instructional Materials* (Fifth Edition), edited by Amy Blackstone and Betsy Lucal (2002).
- *Genocide/Holocaust—The Sociology of the Holocaust and Genocide: A Teaching and Learning*, edited by Jack Nusan Porter and Steve Hoffman (1999).
- *Teaching About Genocide: A Guidebook for College and University Teachers* (Third Edition), edited by Joyce Apsel and Helen Fein (2002).
- *Hate Crimes—Teaching About Ethnoviolence and Hate Crimes* (Second Edition), compiled by Howard J. Ehrlich and Regina Fidazzo (2000).
- *HIV/AIDS—Teaching the Sociology of HIV/AIDS: Syllabi, Lectures & Other Resources for Instructors and Students* (Second Edition), edited by Eric R. Wright (revised 2001).
- *Human Rights: Teaching about Human Rights*, edited by Joyce Apsel (2005).
- *Humanist—'Professing' Humanist Sociology*, edited by Glenn A. Goodwin and Martin D. Schwartz (2000).
- *Humanist Sociology: 'Professing' Humanist Sociology*, edited by Marty Schwartz and Glenn Goodwin (2005).
- *Immigration—Issues in U.S. Immigration: Resources and Suggestions for High School Teachers and College Instructors*, edited by Nadeja Chapkina, Charles Jaret, Guangya Liu, and Angela Pollock (2004).
- *International—Internationalizing Sociology in the Age of Globalization*, edited by Nathan Rouseau for ASA Committee on International Sociology (1999) (under revision).
- *Introduction—Introductory Sociology Resource Manual* (Sixth Edition), compiled by James Sikora and Njeri Mbugua (2004)
- *Jewry—The Sociology of Jewry: A Curriculum Guide*, edited by Jack Nusan Porter with Steve Hoffman (1998).
- *Juvenile Delinquency—Syllabi and Instructional Materials for Courses in Juvenile Delinquency*, edited by Michael O. Maume and Rick A. Matthews (revised 2001).
- *Law Syllabi and Instructional Materials for Sociology of Law* (Second Edition), edited by Lloyd Klein (2000).
- *Life Course—The Life Course: A Handbook of Syllabi and Instructional Materials*, edited by Danielle Fettes, Fang Gong, Sigrun Olafsdottir, and Eliza K. Pavalko (2002).
- *Mass Media—Teaching about Mass Media in the Classroom*, edited by Heather Laube and Sarah J. Sobieraj (2005).
- *Marxist—Teaching Sociology from a Marxist Perspective* (Second Edition), edited by Martha E. Gimenez and Brian V. Klocke, in cooperation with the ASA Section on Marxist Sociology (2002).
- *Medical—A Handbook for Teaching Medical Sociology* (Fourth Edition), edited by Robin D. Moremen (2001).
- *Mental Health—Teaching Materials for the Sociology of Mental Health and Illness*, edited by Teresa Scheid and William Magee (2000).
- *Organizations—Organizational Sociology: A Handbook of Syllabi and other Teaching Resources*, edited by Donna C. Bird (2002).
- *Peace/War—Teaching the Sociology of Peace and War: A Curriculum Guide* (Fourth Edition), edited by John McDougall and Morten G. Ender (2003).
- *Political—Political Sociology: Syllabi and Instructional Materials* (Fifth Edition), compiled and edited by Sarah Sobieraj (2005).
- *Proseminars—Proseminars in Sociology: Graduate and Undergraduate Programs* (Second Edition), edited by Jean Beaman (2004).
- *Race and Ethnic Relations—Teaching Race and Ethnic Relations: Syllabi and Instructional Materials* (Fourth Edition), edited by Donald Cunnigen (revised 2001).
- *Race, Gender, & Class—Race, Gender, and Class in Sociology: Toward an Inclusive Curriculum* (Fifth Edition), edited by BarBara Scott, Joya Misra, and Marcia Segal (2003).
- *Religion—Teaching the Sociology of Religion* (Fourth Edition), edited by Lutz Kaelber and Douglas E. Cowan (2004).

- **Research**—*Qualitative Research Methods: Syllabi and Instructional Materials* **(Third Edition)**, edited by James David Ballard (2001) (out of print; under revision).
- **Research Methods Courses:** *Syllabi, Assignments and Projects* **(Fifth Edition)**, edited by Kevin P. Mulvey (2000) (under revision).
- **Rural**—*Rural Sociology: Teaching About the Complexities and Diversities of American Rural Life*, compiled by Carol A. Jenkins and Cathy Rakowski (2000).
- **Science/Technology**—*Syllabi & Instructional Materials for the Sociology of Science, Knowledge, & Technology* **(Fourth Edition)**, edited by Jennifer Croissant (2003).
- **Sexuality**—*The Sociology of Sexuality & Sexual Orientation: Syllabi & Teaching Materials* **(Fourth Edition)**, edited by Tracy Ore (revised 2002).
- **Social Movements**—*Social Movements and Collective Action: Syllabi and Instructional Materials* **(Third Edition)**, edited by Bob Edwards, Marieke Van Willigen, and Tisha Yelverton (2003).
- **Social Problems**—*Instructor's Resource Manual on Social Problems* **(Third Edition)**, edited by Lutz Kaelber and Walter Carroll (2001).
- **Social Psychology**—*Teaching Social Psychology* **(Second Edition)**, edited by Robert Kettlitz (2003).
- **Social Statistics**—*Syllabi and Instructional Materials for Social Statistics*, edited by Cynthia Line (2000).
- **Social Stratification**—*Social Stratification Courses: Syllabi & Instructional Materials* **(Fifth Edition)**, edited by Scott Sernau and Johnnie Griffin (2004).
- **Sport**—*The Sociology of Sport*, edited by James Steele (2003).
- **Theory**—*Resource Book for Teaching Sociological Theory* **(Fourth Edition)**, edited by Terri LeMoyne (revised 2001).
- **Utopias**—*Utopian Thinking in Sociology: Creating the Good Society*, edited by Arthur B. Shostak (2001).
- **Violence**—*Violence in American Society: A Curriculum Guide*, edited by Suzanne Goodney-Lea (2002).
- **Welfare**—*The Welfare State Revisited: A Review of Research, an Annotated Bibliography, & A Set of Course Syllabi* **(Second Edition)**, edited by Bernice Pescosolido and Norman Furniss (1996) (under revision).
- **Work and Occupations**—*The Sociology of Gender and Work: Syllabi and Teaching Materials* **(Second Edition)**, edited by Carrie Yang Costello (2002).
- *Sociology of Work and Occupations* **(Fifth Edition)**, edited by Carol Auster (2004).

Teaching Techniques
- **Passing On Sociology: The Teaching of a Discipline**, by Charles Goldsmid and Everett K. Wilson (1985).

Classroom Techniques
- *The Courage to Teach: Exploring the Inner Landscape of a Teacher's Life*, by Parker J. Palmer (1998).
- *Critical Pedagogy in the Classroom*, edited by Peter Kaufman (2002).
- *Critical Thinking in the Sociology Classroom*, edited by Agnes Caldwell (2004).
- *Data Analysis: Integrating Data Analysis into the Undergraduate Curriculum*, edited by Susan Hilal and Julie Chiders (2005).
- *Discussion in the College Classroom* **(Second Edition)**, edited by Jay Howard (2004).
- *Gender: Teaching Sociological Concepts and the Sociology of Gender*, edited by Marybeth Stalp (2005).
- *Innovative Techniques for Teaching Sociological Concepts* **(Third Edition)**, edited by Edward L. Kain and Robin Neas (1993) (under revision).
- *Managing Hostility in the Classroom: A Book of Resources for Teaching*, edited by Rebecca Bach and Betsy Lucal (2002).
- *Research Methods in Cyberspace: Internet Exercises for Social Science Research Courses*, by Norah D. Peters-Davis and Susan G. Lehmann (2002).
- *Simulation and Gaming and the Teaching of Sociology* **(Ninth Edition)**, compiled by Richard L. Dukes (2004).

- *Software and Sociology: An Annotated Bibliography of Programs, Journals, and Articles* **(Second Edition)**, by Dan Cover (revised in 1998).
- *Teaching and Learning in Large Classes*, compiled by George S. Bridges and Scott A. Desmond (2000).
- *Teaching Sociological Concepts and the Sociology of Gender*, edited by Marybeth C. Stalp and Julie Childers (2005).
- *Voices from the Classroom: Interviews with Thirty-Six Sociologists About Teaching*, compiled by Dean S. Dorn (1996).

Videos/Films
- *Visual Sociology: Teaching with Film/Video, Photography, and Visual Media* **(Fifth Edition)**, edited by Diana Papademas (2002).

Writing
- *Handbook of the Mechanics of Paper, Thesis and Dissertation Preparation*, compiled by Joan Krenzin and James Kanan (1997).
- *Writing in the Undergraduate Sociology Curriculum: A Guide for Teachers* **(Second Edition)**, edited by Kay Stokes, Keith Roberts, and Marjory Kinney (2002).

Reference Materials
- *Teaching Sociology: Twenty-Seven Year Index*, compiled by Tara Burgess, Pauline Pavlakos, and Jeffrey Chin (2000).
- *Teaching Sociology: Twenty-Seven Year Index* (MAC or DOS version of index).

APPENDIX 23: MINORITY FELLOWSHIP PROGRAM AWARDS

By Year, Race/Ethnicity, and Gender, 1974–2002

Year	African American		Latino/a		Asian American		Native American		Other		New Awards	Total Awards
	M	F	M	F	M	F	M	F	M	F		
1974–75	5	5	5	1	0	2	3	0	0	0	21	21
1975–76	4	12	6	3	2	0	2	0	0	0	29	49
1976–77	13	15	9	0	2	1	1	1	0	0	42	82
1977–78	7	9	5	6	3	4	0	0	0	0	34	80
1978–79	2	3	7	1	2	0	3	0	0	0	18	69
1979–80	1	5	3	2	0	3	0	0	0	0	14	67
1980–81	2	2	2	0	2	0	2	0	0	0	10	69
1981–82	2	3	3	0	1	1	0	1	0	0	11	62
1982–83	2	3	2	1	1	0	0	2	0	0	11	56
1983–84	3	4	1	2	2	2	0	3	0	0	17	45
1984–85	3	2	2	4	0	0	1	0	0	0	12	44
1985–86	0	2	1	0	0	2	0	0	0	0	5	36
1986–87	3	3	1	2	0	3	0	0	0	0	12	23
1987–88	2	2	1	2	2	2	0	2	0	0	13	23
1988–89	3	4	2	3	0	3	0	0	0	0	15	32
1989–90	0	3	1	1	1	1	0	0	1	1	9	28
1990–91	2	9	1	1	1	2	0	2	0	1	19	34
1991–92	3	3	1	2	1	4	0	0	0	0	14	34
1992–93	1	1	1	2	0	1	0	0	0	0	6	30
1993–94	3	7	2	1	0	2	0	0	0	0	15	28
1994–95	1	8	2	1	0	5	1	0	0	0	18	39
1995–96	2	2	2	1	1	1	0	0	0	0	9	33
1996–97	3	1	2	2	0	2	0	0	0	0	10	33
1997–98	1	4	2	2	0	1	0	0	0	0	10	31
1998–99	2	4	2	1	1	0	0	0	0	0	10	29
1999–00	1	3	0	1	2	3	0	1	0	0	11	31
2000–01	0	4	2	0	0	4	0	0	0	0	10	29
2001–02	3	5	1	1	1	3	0	2	0	0	16	31
2002–03	0	4	1	1	0	2	0	0	0	0	8	30
2003–04	3	1	1	0	1	0	1	0	0	0	7	31
2004–05	3	3	3	2	1	0	0	0	0	0	12	28
TOTAL	80	136	74	46	27	54	14	14	1	2	448*	1257

*It is important to note that this total includes eighteen (18) Fellows who have been funded by ASA with non-NIMH funds (i.e., from contributions received by ASA members and sister and regional associations).

NOTE: This table is compiled from ASA records on awards.

APPENDIX 24: OTHER ASA PUBLICATIONS

Major publications of the American Sociological Association are listed in Appendix 18. Publications from the Academic and Professional Affairs Program (APAP) are listed in Appendix 22, and those from the Spivack Program are included in Appendix 25. The following list includes all other major publications of the ASA, including from the Research Program on the Discipline and the Profession.

A. The Research Program on the Discipline and the Profession

The ASA's Research Program on the Discipline and Profession was renamed the ASA Research and Development Department in 2004. Publications and resources produced by the Program/Department include the following:

- "After the Fall: The Growth Rate of Sociology BAs Outstrips Other Disciplines Indicating an Improved Market for Sociologists," by staff of the Research Program on the Discipline and Profession, *Data Brief* (1998).
- "After the Fall: The Growth Trends Continue," by staff of the Research Program on the Discipline and Profession, *Data Brief Update* (1999).
- "BA Growth Trend: Sociology Overtakes Economics," by Roberta Spalter-Roth (with graphics by Andrew Sutter), *Data Brief Update* (2000).
- "New Doctorates in Sociology: Professions Inside and Outside the Academy," by Roberta Spalter-Roth, Jan Thomas, and Felice J. Levine, *Research Brief*, Vol.1, No.1 (2000).
- "Gender in the Early Stages of the Sociological Career," by Roberta Spalter-Roth and Sunhwa Lee (graphics prepared by Andrew Sutter), *Research Brief*, Vol.1, No.2 (2000).
- "Use of Adjunct and Part-time Faculty in Sociology," by Roberta Spalter-Roth and Andrew Sutter, *Data Brief* (2001).
- "Profile of the 2001 ASA Membership," by Stacey S. Merola and Roberta Spalter-Roth *Data Brief* (2001).
- "The Pipeline for Faculty of Color in Sociology," by Roberta Spalter-Roth, Felice J. Levine, and Andrew Sutter, *Data Brief* (2001).
- "Minorities at Three Stages in the Sociology Pipeline," by Roberta Spalter-Roth, Sunhwa Lee, and Felice J. Levine, *Research Brief* Vol.2, No.1 (2001).
- "Graduate Department Vitality: Changes Continue in the Right Direction," by Roberta Spalter-Roth and Andrew Sutter, *Data Brief* (2001).
- "Sociology Holds the Line as Faculty Salaries Feel the Pinch in the Economic Downturn," by Stacey S. Merola and Roberta Spalter-Roth, *Data Brief* (2002).
- "How Does Your Department Compare: A Peer Analysis From the 2000–2001 Survey of Baccalaureate and Graduate Programs in Sociology," by Roberta Spalter-Roth and William Erskine, *Report* (2003).
- "Departures and Replacements: Are Sociology Departments Downsizing in a Period of State Budget Shortfalls?" by Roberta Spalter-Roth and William Erskine, *Data Brief* (2004).
- "Have Faculty Salaries Peaked? Sociology Wage Growth Flat in Constant Dollars," by Roberta Spalter-Roth and William Erskine, *Information Brief* (2004).
- "Academic Relations: The Use of Supplementary Faculty," by Roberta Spalter-Roth and William Erskine, *Research Brief* (2004).
- "The Best Time to Have a Baby: Institutional Resources and Family Strategies Among Early Career Sociologists," by Roberta Spalter-Roth and William Erskine, *Research Brief* (2004).
- "The State of Sociology," by Roberta Spalter-Roth and William Erskine, *Report* (2004 on CD-Rom).
- "Need Today's Data Yesterday? Trend Data on the Profession," by staff of the ASA Research and Development Department (2005). Retrieved March 15, 2005 http://www.asanet.org/research/faqintro2002].

B. Other ASA Publications: 1980–2004

Promoting Diversity and Excellence in Higher Education Through Department Change, by Felice J. Levine, Havidán Rodríguez, Carla B. Howery, and Alfonso R. Latoni-Rodríguez (2002).

A History of the American Sociological Association: 1905-1980, by Lawrence J. Rhoades (1981).

C. ASA Committee Reports: 2001–4

Task Force Reports

(published on the American Sociological Association homepage: www.asanet.org/governance/reports.htm)

Task Force on ASA/AAAS Relations, *Final Report* (August 2001).

Final Report of the Task Force on the Articulation of Sociology in Two-Year and Four-Year Sociology Programs (2002).

Task Force on the Implications of the Evaluation of Faculty Productivity and Teaching Effectiveness, *Final Report* (July 28, 2003).

Report of the Task Force on Journal Diversity (January 2003).

Liberal Learning and the Sociology Major Updated: Meeting the Challenge of Teaching Sociology in the Twenty-First Century, by Kathleen McKinney, Carla B. Howery, Kerry Strand, Edward L. Kain, and Catherine White Berheide (2004).

The Importance of Collecting Data and Doing Social Scientific Research on Race (2003).

Status Committee Reports

Report on the Status of Gay, Lesbian, Bisexual, and Transgender Persons in Sociology (July 16, 2002).

2004 Report of the American Sociological Association's Committee on the Status of Women in Sociology, Final Report (October 22, 2004).

Report of the ASA Committee on the Status of Persons with Disabilities (PWD) in Sociology, (February 2005).

APPENDIX 25: THE SPIVACK PROGRAM: POLICY BRIEFINGS, ISSUE SERIES, AND SPECIAL INITIATIVES

Appendices 25–27 provide detailed information on several components of the Sydney S. Spivack Program in Applied Social Research and Social Policy.

A. Policy Briefings

Policy briefings target key Congressional staff, Administration officials, representatives of non-profit associations, and the media.

- **Work and Family, December 10, 1992 and February 1, 1993:** Two briefings linking work and family research to current issues of family care arrangements, and family and medical leave. Congressional Briefing on Work-Family Linkages on December 10, 1992 featured Phyllis Moen, Cynthia Deitch, Roberta Spalter-Roth, and Judith Auerbach. A media briefing complementing the Congressional Briefing was held on February 1, 1993 at the National Press Club, and featured Carla Howery and Catherine White Berheide as panelists, with Felice J. Levine as moderator.

- **Social Dimensions of AIDS, May 3, 1993:** An overview of key insights sociology and other social sciences have provided on AIDS prevention and transmission. Panelists were Gary L. Albrecht, Karen J. Peterson, and Edward O. Laumann.

- **Revitalizing Public Education—The Relationship Between Resources and Learning, May 12, 1994:** With a backdrop of discussion on the Elementary and Secondary Education Act, Peter Cookson, Amy Stuart Wells, and Jomills Braddock shared their research on factors limiting or enhancing a world-class education for all U.S. children.

- **Highlights of Sexual Behavior Survey, December 12, 1994:** Presentation of key findings from the comprehensive study of sexual habits of American adults. Featured Edward O Laumann, John H. Gagnon, and Stuart Michaels. ASA co-sponsored with other organizations.

- **The Myth of the Entitlement Crisis, March 9, 1995:** A Congressional symposium featuring Jill Quadagno, who challenged the notion that the Social Security System was in need of a total overhaul.

- **Basic Science and Transforming the United States Economy, February 22, 1996:** Lynne Zucker and Michael Darby informed policy makers at two ASA-sponsored events argued that basic science played a key role in the financial success of the United States biotechnology industry.

- **Sociological Perspectives on Promoting Safe Schools, June 11, 1996:** Joan Spade, Joan McCord, and Richard J. Gelles summarized research on school climate, social organization of schools, research on youth and delinquency, with policy recommendations on safe schools, for an audience of school administrators and community leaders in the Washington, DC area.

- **Welfare to Work—Opportunities and Pitfalls, March 10, 1997:** Kathryn Edin, Kathleen Mullan Harris, and Gary Sandefur presented findings on the employment patterns and opportunities of welfare recipients, and addressed the impact of new legislation, focusing on which groups might thrive or suffer difficulties under its provisions.

- **Youth Violence—Children at Risk, June 17, 1997:** Three sociologists (Delbert Elliott, John Hagan, and Joan McCord) who had researched the demography of youth crime, effective and less effective interventions, youth development trajectories and points of intervention summarized findings about how to curtail the incidence of youth violence, and the use of deadly force.

- **Immigrant Families and Children, June 4, 1998:** Lisandro Peréz, Richard D. Alba, Douglas S. Massey, and Rubén G. Rumbaut made policy recommendations and suggested necessary changes in social services for immigrants. Their recommendations were based on recent research findings on contemporary patterns of immigration, variations of experience by country of origin, and impact of the immigrant experience on children across generations.

- **Hate Crime in America—What Do We Know? October 21, 1999:** Abby L. Ferber, Ryken Grattet, and Valerie Jenness presented research on the history of hate crime in America, data on victims and perpetrators of hate-motivated crimes, the social and economic factors associated with hate crimes, and legal responses to hate crime.

- **How Neighborhoods Matter—The Value of Investing at the Local Level, September 25, 2000:** Robert J. Sampson, Gregory D. Squires, and Min Zhou—experts on community relations, discrimination, and criminology—reported findings on neighborhood characteristics and further community or policy needs.

- **Reactions to Terrorism—Attitudes and Anxieties, June 18, 2002:** As a part of the multidisciplinary Decade of Behavior initiative, Mansoor Moaddel, Michael Traugott, and Len Lecci presented the divergent world views of Americans and Islamic terrorists.

- **Racial and Ethnic Data—Why We Collect it; How We Use It in Public Policy, May 28, 2003:** Co-sponsored by the California Institute for Federal Policy Research, the Council of Professional Associations on Federal Statistics, and the Population Resource Center. Hon. Thomas C. Sawyer, Troy Duster, Brian Smedley, and Gerald Sanders explained the value of racial/ethnic data and research for policymaking. The briefing was held to publicize ASA's official statement on race, and to counter a 2003 California ballot measure that would have prohibited state and local governments from classifying current or prospective students, contractors, or employees by race, ethnicity, color or national origin.

- **The Human Dimensions of Disasters—How Social Science Research Can Improve Preparedness, Response, and Recovery, October 27, 2003:** Co-sponsored with the Institute for Crisis, Disaster and Risk Management at George Washington University. William Anderson, Lee Clarke, John Harrald, Eric Klinenberg, and Kathleen Tierney presented research findings on social factors of disasters.

- **A Nation of Immigrants—Current Policy Debates Meet New Social Science Research, April 19, 2004:** Douglas S. Massey, Rogelio Saenz, and Victor Nee discussed research on immigrants in America, including immigrant settlement patterns, the social and economic role of immigrant workers, assimilation processes, and policy connections.

B. The Issue Series In Social Research And Social Policy

The Issue Series in Social Research and Social Policy is published by the American Sociological Association to link social science research to social policy. The *Series* is intended to make accessible to wide audiences the substantive contributions of ASA Congressional seminars, workshops, media briefings, and related events. The *Series* presents timely research and draws the connections to current policy discussions and debates. Each volume in the Issue Series includes edited presentations, dialogue and commentary, fact sheets, expert resource lists, and reference materials.

- *How Neighborhoods Matter: The Value of Investing at the Local Level*, by Robert J. Sampson, Gregory D. Squires, and Min Zhou (2001).

- *Hate Crime in America: What Do We Know?* by Abby L. Ferber, Ryken Grattet, Valerie Jenness (1999).

- *The Immigration Experience for Families and Children*, by Richard D. Alba, Douglas S. Massey, and Rubén G. Rumbaut (1998).

- *Families, Youth, and Children's Well Being*, by Linda Burton, Donald Hernandez, and Sandra Hofferth (1997).

- *Welfare to Work: Opportunities and Pitfalls*, by Kathryn Edin, Kathleen Mullan Harris, and Gary Sandefur (1997).

- *Youth Violence: Children at Risk,* by Delbert Elliott, John Hagan, and Joan McCord (1997).

C. Special Initiatives

ASA seeks to integrate basic research and public policy through educational fora:

- **Invitational workshop "Research Challenges on the Social Causes of Violence," June 19–20, 1993:** A report based on the workshop outlines a strategic agenda for violence research. This report was timely, as the Clinton Administration gave high profile to the reduction of violence in communities and schools and as the federal government reexamined science policy and R & D investments in violence. *Social Causes of Violence: Crafting a Science Agenda* by Felice J. Levine and Katherine J. Rosich (1996) was published from workshop proceedings.

- **Invitational workshop "Initiative on Genocide and Human Rights," November 13-14, 1993:** An initiative to develop strategies for the social science community to identify research and social science knowledge that could be used to respond to and prevent genocide.

- **Invitational workshop "Rethinking the Urban Agenda," May 20–24, 1994:** A group of urbanists challenged the view that cities are economic dinosaurs, and argued that cities continue to play a central role in metropolitan areas.

- **Invitational workshop "Prevention of HIV and Hatred," June 3–5, 1994:** An initiative to bring sociological work to bear on HIV/AIDS, community care, and the reduction of hatred.

- **Conference on Implementing Recent Federal Legislation on Education, January 8-10, 1995:** This conference was co-sponsored with the University of South Florida and the Department of Education Office of Educational Research and Improvement. The commissioned papers and rejoinders form a book published by Ablex.

- **Invitational workshop "Social Science Perspectives on Affirmative Action in Employment," June 27–29, 1996:** The workshop assembled research literature on affirmative action policies and practices, organizational responses, conditions under which such initiatives are effective or less effective. *The Realities of Affirmative Action in Employment* by Barbara F. Reskin (1998) was published from workshop proceedings.

- **Invitational workshop on the President's Initiative on Race, April 26, 1998:** The symposium summarized social science research on race and ethnicity, prejudice and discrimination, and racial identity.

APPENDIX 26: THE SPIVACK PROGRAM: CONGRESSIONAL FELLOWS

The Congressional Fellowship Program, a component of the Sydney S. Spivack Program in Applied Social Research and Social Policy, included the following Fellows:

- Catherine White Berheide (Skidmore College), Office of Senator Patty Murray (D-WA) (1992)
- Peter Cookson (Adelphi University), Senate Subcommittee on Education, Labor, and Human Relations (1993)
- Jill Quadagno (Florida State University), the President's Bipartisan Commission on Entitlement and Tax Reform (1994)
- Richard J. Gelles (University of Rhode Island), House Subcommittee on Human Resources and the Senate Subcommittee on Youth Violence (1996)
- Nora Jacobson (Johns Hopkins University), Senate Subcommittee on Labor, Human Relations, and Education (1997)
- Lois Monteiro (Brown University), House Committee on Veteran's Affairs (1998)
- Susan Rachel Gragg (University of Washington), Office of Sen. Paul Wellstone (D-MN) (1999)
- George Dowdall (St. Joseph's University), Office of Sen. Joseph Biden (D-DE) (2000)
- Larry Burmeister (University of Kentucky), Office of Sen. Kent Conrad (D-ND) (2001)
- Joyce Iutcovich (Keystone University Research Corp.), Office of Sen. Jack Reed (D-RI)
- Susan Dimock (University of California-San Diego), Office of Sen. Jack Reed (D-RI) (2002)
- Marjorie Schaafsma (University of Chicago), Senate Democratic Policy Committee (2003-4)
- Tomás Jiménez (Harvard University), Office of Rep. Mike Honda (D-CA) (2005)

[Note: Through the Fund for the Advancement of the Discipline (FAD), ASA also supported three Congressional Fellows in 1983–84: Carol Weiss (Harvard University) and William R. Freudenburg (Washington State University) were appointed Congressional Fellows in 1983, and Raymond Russell received a fellowship in 1984 at the General Accounting Office (GAO).]

APPENDIX 27: THE SPIVACK PROGRAM: AAAS/ASA MASS MEDIA SCIENCE FELLOWSHIP

The American Association for the Advancement of Science (AAAS) and the ASA cosponsored a Mass Media Science Fellowship from 1997–2003. Discontinued in 2003, the Program at ASA was a component of the Sydney S. Spivack Program in Applied Social Research and Social Policy. The AAAS/ASA Fellows and their assignments were:

- Anne Boyle, Yale University, at the *Albuquerque Tribune* (the first fellow in 1997)
- Sara Eichberg, University of Pennsylvania, at the *Detroit Free Press* (1998)
- Daniel Harrison, Florida State University, at the *Richmond Times Dispatch* (1999)
- Rachel Rinaldo, University of Chicago, at the *Raleigh News Observer* (2000)
- Quynh-Giang H. Tran, Pennsylvania State University, at the *Chicago Tribune* (2001)
- Linda Waldron, Syracuse University, at the Voice of America (2001)
- Marcia Gossard, Washington State University, at *Newsweek* (2002)
- Vinita Mehta, Columbia University-Teachers College, at Dateline NBC in New York City (2003)

APPENDIX 28: ASA'S ORGANIZATIONAL AFFILIATIONS AND COLLABORATIONS: JANUARY 1, 2005

The ASA has a long history of nurturing collaborative efforts with scientific, publishing, advocacy, and social science aligned organizations and of developing a strong working relationship with regional, state, and other sociological associations.

The following are organizations with which ASA has had collaborative ties over recent years. (This list excludes federal agencies with which ASA works to promote the interests of members and to advance the discipline of sociology.)

Social Science Associations
- Academy of Management (AOM)
- American Anthropological Association (AAA)
- American Association for Higher Education (AAHE)
- American Association for the Advancement of Science (AAAS)
- American Association for Public Opinion Research (AAPOR)
- American Council of Learned Societies (ACLS)
- American Economic Association (AEA)
- American Educational Research Association (AERA)
- American Evaluation Association (AEA)
- American Historical Association (AHA)
- American Political Science Association (APSA)
- American Psychological Association (APA)
- American Society of Criminology (ASC)
- American Statistical Association (ASA)
- Association of American Colleges and Universities (AAC&U)
- Association of American Geographers (AAG)
- Association of American Law Schools (AALS)
- Association for Gerontology in Higher Education (AGHE)
- Consortium of Social Science Associations (COSSA)
- Council of Professional Associations on Federal Statistics (COPAFS)
- Law and Society Association (LSA)
- Linguistic Society of America (LSA)
- National Council on Family Relations (NCFR)
- National Council for Social Studies (NCSS)
- National Humanities Alliance (NHA)
- Popular Culture Association
- Population Association of American (PAA)
- Religious Research Association (RRA)
- Social Science Research Council (SSRC)
- Social Science History Association (SSHA)
- Society for the Advancement of Socio-Economics (SASE)
- Society for Research in Child Development (SRCD)
- Society for the Scientific Study of Religion (SSSR)
- Society for Social Studies of Science (4S)
- Society for the Study of Social Problems (SSSP)

- Society for the Study of Symbolic Interaction (SSSI)
- Southern Demographic Association (SDA)

General Sociological Associations
- Alpha Kappa Delta (AKD)
- Anabaptist Sociological and Anthropological Association (ASAA)
- Association for Humanist Sociology (AHS)
- Association for the Sociology of Religion (ASR)
- Association of Black Sociologists (ABS)
- Association of Christians Teaching Sociology (ACTS)
- Chicago Sociological Practice Association
- The Christian Sociological Society (CSS)
- Mid-West Sociologists for Women in Society
- North American Chinese Sociologists Association
- North American Society for the Sociology of Sport (NASSS)
- Rural Sociological Society (RRS)
- Society for Applied Sociology (SAS)
- Sociological Practice Association (SPA)
- Sociologists' AIDS Network (SAN)
- Sociologists' Lesbian, Gay, Bisexual, and Transgender Caucus (SLGBTC)
- Sociologists for Women in Society (SWS)
- Sociology of Education Association (SEA)

Regional Sociological Associations
- Eastern Sociological Association (ESS)
- Mid-South Sociological Association (MSSA)
- Mid-West Sociological Society (MSS)
- New England Sociological Association (NESA)
- North Central Sociological Association (NCSA)
- Pacific Sociological Association (PSA)
- Southern Sociological Society
- Southwestern Sociological Association (SSA)

State Sociological Associations
- District of Columbia Sociological Society (DCSS)
- National Council on State Sociological Associations (NCSSA)
- Alabama-Mississippi Sociological Association (AMSA)
- California Sociological Association (CSA)
- Great Plains Sociological Association (North and South Dakota)
- Illinois Sociological Association (ISA)
- Anthropologists and Sociologists of Kentucky (ASK)
- Michigan Sociological Association (MSA)
- Sociologists of Minnesota (SOM)
- Missouri Sociological Association (MSA)
- New York Sociological Association

- North Carolina Sociological Association (NCSA)
- Pennsylvania Sociological Association
- Virginia State Science Association (VSSA)
- Wisconsin Sociological Association (WSA)

International Sociological Associations
- Asia Pacific Sociological Association (APSA)
- Australian Sociological Association (TASA)
- British Sociological Association
- Canadian Sociology and Anthropology Association
- European Society for Rural Sociology (ESRS)
- European Sociological Association (ESA)
- International Network for Social Network Analysis
- International Society for the Sociology of Religion
- International Sociological Association (ISA)
- International Visual Sociology Association (IVSA)
- Sociologists Without Borders
- Sociological Association of Aotearoa (New Zealand) (SAANZ)

Commissions
- Commission on Applied and Clinical Sociology

Public Outreach and Advocacy Organization

ASA maintains close ties or has representation on these public outreach organizations and advocacy coalitions (January 1, 2005):
- Behavioral and Social Science Research Coordinating Committee (BSSR-CC) at the National Institutes of Health (NIH)
- Coalition for the Advancement of Health Through Behavioral and Social Science Research (CAHT-BSSR)
- Coalition for Health Funding (CHF)
- Coalition for National Science Funding (CNSF)
- Consortium of Social Science Associations – Behavioral and Social Science Representatives (COSSA-BSSR), coordinated by the White House Office of Science and Technology Policy (OSTP)
- Decade of Behavior (DoB)

APPENDIX 29: ASA DEPARTMENTS AND PROGRAMS: JANUARY 1, 2005

In 2005, the Executive Office of the American Sociological Association included the following Departments and Programs (staff members who fill these positions as of January 1, 2005 are listed in Appendix 30):

ASA Departments

- **Operations and Meeting Services Department**

  The primary objective of the Meeting Services function is to plan and support meetings sponsored by the Association, which are intended to serve sociologists in their work. The major meeting activity is the national Annual Meeting held in August of each year. The Department also coordinates other ASA events, which are usually small meetings of ASA committees/boards or educational seminars of ASA programs.

  Janet Astner, Director of the Meeting Services Department also directs the Office Administration Department, which has the function of coordinating general office operations and human resources functions in the Executive Office.

- **Publications and Membership Department**

  The primary mission of ASA publications is to provide information on and about the discipline of sociology to ASA members and subscribers, and a growing number of outside audiences (e.g., media, government) with an interest in sociological information and research. The Publications Department is responsible for the oversight and production of ASA's publications.

  Karen Gray Edwards, Director of the ASA Publications Department, also directs the ASA Membership/Customer Services/Subscription Department, which is responsible for member customer service, subscription fulfillment, data entry, and Annual Meeting registration.

- **Governance, Sections, and Archives Department**

  The Department of Governance, Sections and Archives is responsible for ensuring Association compliance with the ASA Constitution and Bylaws. This department is responsible for staffing five of the seven constitutionally mandated components, management of annual association nominations and elections, coordination of appointment of members to ASA components, administration of eight Association awards, management of all aspects of special-interest sections and their more than 20,000 members, and preservation of Association records and history. Michael Murphy, Director of the Governance and Sections Department, is also ASA Archivist.

- **Research and Development Department**

  The ASA Research Program on the Profession and the Discipline is responsible for developing and disseminating knowledge on sociology both as a discipline and a profession. This responsibility is carried out by collecting primary and secondary data, building and maintaining databases, and disseminating research findings through a variety of media and a series of venues. ASA's goal is for a wide array of members of the profession to benefit from the availability of these findings and to use them for research, policy, and planning purposes. Roberta Spalter-Roth, Director of the Research and Development Department, also directs the Fund for the Advancement of the Discipline (FAD) Program. (Appendix 24 contains a list of all datasets, documents, and publications produced by the Research Program.)

- **Public Affairs and Public Information Department**

  Public Affairs Departmental activities encompass those undertaken by the Association, or others acting on its behalf, to educate about and advocate for sociology especially at the national level. This objective is accomplished in various ways, including by speaking on behalf of sociology in different arenas (such as at the Congressional, federal agency, and other governmental levels), collaborating with other scientific and learned societies on joint ventures to advance the social sciences, and increasing awareness of sociology and sociological issues among the wider public through the media.

  Influencing the media's portrayal of sociology and sociological research is achieved by the Public Information Program which seeks (1) to respond to media inquiries with timely and relevant information, including referrals to experts on specific issues, and (2) to initiate press briefings and other actions that inform and educate about sociology. Topics emanating from the substantive programs such as the Spivack Program are viewed as particularly appropriate for nurturing media interest in sociological issues.

- **Information Services and Technology Department:**
  The Information Services and Technology Department manages the ASA Information Technology (IT) systems and infrastructure.

  The following outline provides the technical specifications for the computer system that operates the system following the upgrade in 2004:

  - Five servers running Microsoft Windows 2000 Server. Two of the five are new HP/Compaq servers. Three of the pre-upgrade servers were reused and upgraded to Windows 2000 Server.
  - One Dell server running Linux operating system. The old Unix-based server was replaced with this new Dell and runs the Listserv software.
  - Several application upgrades:
    - The email application was upgraded from Microsoft Exchange 5.5 to Microsoft Exchange 2003.
    - The Document Management System was migrated from Hummingbird's DOCS Open version 3.9 to Hummingbird's DM version 5.2.
    - The databases now run on one database platform – Microsoft SQL 2000
    - The NOAH database and application were upgraded to the current (at the time) version of 9.3b.
  - The tape backup hardware was replaced with two high-speed, high volume tape backup units.

ASA Programs:

- **The Academic and Professional Affairs Program (APAP)**
  APAP advances the place of sociology in colleges and universities; strengthens departments and their programs; engenders effective communication and collaboration with sociology departments; and encourages the best practices in education, training, and teaching. The Department seeks to provide services for those engaged in the teaching and practice of sociology. Its major components include the Department Affiliates Program, Chair and Director of Graduate Study Conferences, the Teaching Resources Center (TRC), and the Departmental Resources Group (DRG). (Appendix 22 contains a detailed listing of teaching, career and professional publications and resource materials produced by APAP as of July 2005.)

- **The Minority Affairs Program (MAP)**
  MAP encompasses the core Minority Fellowship Program (MFP), as well as other programs that provide support to students and minorities, or those that relate to health issues more broadly. Funded by the National Institute of Mental Health (NIMH), the MFP supports the development and training of predoctoral minority sociologists in mental health. The ASA provides the MFP with national coordination for minority students participating in the program, and in various ways offers support (e.g., through workshops, travel support to conferences, a structure for building networks, and so forth) that "extends the professional development provided by Fellows' home departments." (See Appendix 23 for a summary of MFP awards). Mercedes Rubio, Director of MAP, also directs the ASA Honors Program, the Student Forum, and other student-related activities of the ASA.

- **The Sydney S. Spivack Program in Applied Social Research and Social Policy**
  The Spivack Program is a multifaceted effort to advance the uses and contributions of sociology to social policy. The Program links sociological knowledge to social policy, promotes social policy based on sound sociology, and provides relevant social research through policy briefings, special research workshops, community initiatives, and fellowship opportunities. The Spivack Advisory Committee, appointed by Council sets priorities for the Program and guides its activities. (Appendices 25–27 contain a detailed list of all Spivack Program activities.)

APPENDIX 30: ASA EXECUTIVE OFFICE STAFF: JANUARY 1, 2005

Executive Officer
Sally T. Hillsman

Deputy Executive Officer
Carla B. Howery

Business Office
Controller: Les Briggs
Accounting Manager: Girma Efa

Departments:

Operations and Meeting Services Department
Director: Janet L. Astner

Meeting Services
Meeting Services Manager: Kareem Jenkins
Meeting Services Assistant: Kendra Eastman

Office Administration
Office Coordinator: Donya Williams
Receptionist: Sarah Frazier
Office Assistant: Jamie Panzarella
Office Assistant and Mail Room: David Mathews

Publications and Membership Department
Director: Karen Gray Edwards

Publications
Production Manager: Redante Asuncion-Reed

Membership, Customer Services, Subscriptions
Membership Manager: Craig Schaar
Customer Service Representatives:
Glen Grant and Shannon Lymore

Governance, Sections, and Archives
Director: Michael Murphy
Governance Assistant: Jessica Spickard
Archivist: Michael Murphy

Research and Development Department
Director: Roberta Spalter-Roth
Research Associate: William Erskine
Fund for the Advancement of the Discipline Program Director: Roberta Spalter-Roth

Information Services and Technology Department
Director: Kevin Darrow Brown

Public Affairs and Public Information Department
Director: K. Lee Herring
Public Information Officer: Johanna Ebner

Programs:

Academic and Professional Affairs Program (APAP)
Director: Carla B. Howery
Program Assistant: Victoria Hougham

Minority Affairs Program (MAP)
Director: Mercedes Rubio
Program Assistant: Felicia Evans

Spivack Program in Applied Social Research and Social Policy
Coordinators: Carla Howery, Roberta Spalter-Roth, K. Lee Herring
Program Assistant: Johanna Ebner

References and Index

References

The primary sources of information used for these analyses were those published in *Footnotes*, particularly minutes of Council meetings and reports by elected and appointed officers of the Association. In addition, Council and Committee on the Executive Office and Budget (EOB) agenda books, EOB minutes, Annual Meeting Programs, program records in the files, committee reports to Council, and ASA Journals and other publications were also used as sources. Extant literature on relevant topics was also reviewed in some areas.

References in the text refer to:

Official Proceedings and Publications

- Minutes of the ASA Council (as published in *Footnotes*)
- Minutes of the Committee on the Executive Office and Budget (EOB)
- *Footnotes* (Volumes 1 to 33), including:
    - Reports of the Secretaries and Executive Officers, "Reflections of the Presidents," feature articles by Executive Officers ("Inter Nos" by Russell Dynes, "Observing" by William D'Antonio, "Open Window" by Felice Levine, and "Vantage Point" by Sally Hillsman)
    - Other official records (e.g., election results)
- ASA homepage (website) (www.asanet.org)

Reports and Memoranda

American Sociological Association. 1992. August Biennial Report on the Participation of Women and Minorities in ASA for 1990 and 1991, August 1992. Unpublished report.

———. 1991. Proposal for the Sydney S. Spivack Program in Applied Social Research and Social Policy, January 1991.

———. 1993. The Committee on Freedom of Research and Teaching (COFRAT), December 15, 1993. Unpublished report.

———. 2001. Report by the Alba Subcommittee to ASA Council, Council Agenda Book, February 2001.

———. 2003. Report of the Task Force on Journal Diversity, January 2003. Retrieved January 15, 2005 (http://www.asanet.org/governance/reports.htm).

———. 2003. Task Force on the International Focus of American Sociology (TFIFAS), *Final Report*, August 2003. Unpublished report.

———. 2004. 2004 Report of the American Sociological Association's Committee on the Status of Women in Sociology, *Final Report:* October 22, 2004. Retrieved January 15, 2005 (http://www.asanet.org/governance/reports.htm).

Hallowell, Lyle. 1985. "The Outcome of the Brajuha Case: Legal Implications for Sociologists." *Footnotes*, December, 1985:1,13.

Kennedy, John. M. 1994. "Committee to Review ASA Certification Program." *Footnotes*, November 1994:4.

Levine, Felice J., Havidan Rodriguez, Carla B. Howery, and Alfonso R. Latoni-Rodriguez. 2002. *Promoting Diversity and Excellence in Higher Education Through Department Change*. (Washington, DC: American Sociological Association).

Parsons, Talcott. 1966. "The Editor's Column." *The American Sociologist*, February 1966:70.

Rossi, Alice. 1982. Report to Council on Fund for the Advancement of Discipline (FAD). American Sociological Association. Unpublished report.

Name Index

A

Abbott, Andrew, 100
Abu-Lughod, Janet, 79
Aiken, Michael, 5–7, 21, 24, 27, 92
Alba, Richard D., 50–51, 81
Aldous, Joan, 12
Allen, Ivan, 87
Allen, Walter, 64
Andersen, Margaret L., 27, 57
Anderson, William, 7
Anthony, Richard, 11
Astner, Janet L., 8, 33, 41
Avison, William R., 55

B

Babbie, Earl, 44
Baldwin, Wendy L., 11, 19, 49, 70
Ballantine, Jeanne H., 22, 65
Barnes, Steven, 11
Becker, Howard S., 44
Berg, Ivar, 18, 19, 70
Berheide, Catherine White, 24, 67
Bernard, Jessie, 26, 51, 82
Bielby, William T., 86, 95
Biernacki, Richard G., 12
Bills, David B., 83
Billson, Janet Mancini, 42, 65
Blackwell, James E., 20, 27, 60, 61
Blalock, Jr., Hubert M., 29, 30
Bonacich, Edna, 2, 18, 21
Bonilla-Silva, Eduardo, 64
Bonjean, Charles M., 27, 59
Bonner, Florence B., 40, 43
Borgatta, Edgar F., 26
Boulding, Elsie M., 32
Boyer, Ernest, 23, 67
Boyle, Ann, 77
Brajuha, Mario, 10, 49, 75
Brent, Edward, 8, 78
Bressler, Marvin, 18
Briggs, Les, 92
Brooks, J. Michael, 22
Brown, Diane R., 87
Brown, Ronald Hon., 73
Brown, William R., 29

Buff, Stephen A., 25
Burawoy, Michael, 64, 86, 91, 93
Burton, Linda, 29, 77

C

Calhoun, Craig J., 31, 81, 99, 100
Camic, Charles, 64
Campbell, James D., 8
Caplow, Theodore, 7, 14
Carey, Jane Quellmalz, 62
Carley, Kathleen M., 44
Chavetz, Janet, 83
Clarke, Lee, 97
Clawson, Dan, 44
Coleman, James S., 79, 80
Collins, Patricia Hill, 56, 101
Collins, Randall, 14
Cortese, Anthony J., 48
Coser, Lewis A., 92–93
Costello, Cynthia B., 42, 48, 72
Costner, Herbert L., 6
Craig, Fran, 43
Crittenden, Kathleen S., 24
Crutchfield, Robert D., 95, 100

D

D'Antonio, William V., 4, 6–8, 11–13, 16–17, 19, 22–24, 29, 31–33, 42, 48, 70, 74, 80
Daniels, Arlene Kaplan, 35
Darrow, William W., 25
Davis, James, 29–30
Davis, Robert, 24
Deegan, Mary Jo, 81
DeFleur, Lois B., 24, 92
DeMartini, Joseph, 23
Demerath, N.J. III (Jay), 15
Dentler, Robert A., 19, 20
Dickerson, Bette J., 87
Dill, Bonnie Thornton, 27, 64
DiMaggio, Paul J., 92
Dorn, Dean S., 23
Dukes, Duane, 83
Duster, Troy, 18, 87–88, 100–102
Dynes, Russell R., 6–7, 16, 24, 32

E

Eberts, Paul R., 24
Ebner, Johanna, 77
Edwards, Karen Gray, 8, 19, 41
England, Paula, 56, 63
Erikson, Kai T., 10, 17
Erskine, William, 72
Etzioni, Amitai, 18, 63
Everett, Robert W., 40
Ewens, William, 22
Eweson, Dorothy, 18–19

F

Farkas, George, 61
Farley, Reynolds, 19
Feagin, Joe R., 41, 46, 63–64
Featherman, David L., 37, 40, 67
Feree, Myra Marx, 12, 49, 67
Fischer, Claude S., 26, 61
Form, William H., 1
Freeman, Howard E., 24
Freudenburg, William R., 25
Frey, William H., 66

G

Gamson, William A., 11, 32, 57, 67, 81
Gamson, Zelda, 24
Gans, Herbert J., 14, 17
Gilkes, Cheryl Townsend, 48, 53
Glock, Charles Y., 18
Goering, John M., 82
Goode, William J., 92
Goodman, Louis W., 31
Gragg, Rachel, 77
Gray, Paul S., 8, 19, 23
Greeley, Andrew, 15
Grutter, Barbara, 89

H

Hallinan, Maureen T., 21, 44
Hallowell, Lyle A., 11
Halpern, Sydney A., 82
Hampton, Keith N., 77
Harris, Joan R., 5
Hatcher, Edward, 42, 77
Hawkins, Augustus Hon., 16
Heimer, Carol, 95
Hernandez, Donald J., 77
Herring, Lee, 42, 77

Hess, Beth B., 15, 40
Heyns, Barbara, 24
Hill, Michael R., 81–82
Hill, Robert, 96
Hillsman, Sally T., 42, 85–88, 90–92, 94–97, 99, 101, 104
Hiltz, Roxanne Starr, 44
Hofferth, Sandra L., 77
Hoffman, William S., 70
Hope, Richard O., 27
Hoppe, Sue K., 48
Horowitz, Irving, 20
Hout, Michael, 55, 64
Howery, Carla B., 4, 6, 22–24, 26, 28, 42, 60, 65–67, 70, 72, 83
Huber, Bettina J., 6, 24–25
Huber, Joan, 21, 24, 67
Husch, Jerri A., 11

I

Ibrahim, Saad Eddin, 81, 99
Iutcovich, Joyce Miller, 48

J

Jacobs, Jerry A., 100
Jeffords, James Hon., 16

K

Kain, Edward L., 65, 67
Kalleberg, Arne L., 87, 91–92, 95, 99
Kasarda, John D., 25
Kennedy, John M., 26, 43, 48, 57
Kincaid, A. Douglas, 99, 101
King, Deborah K., 87
Kirchner, Corinne, 96
Kling, Rob E., 44
Kohn, Melvin L., 31, 79
Kornblum, William, 16

L

Land, Kenneth C., 24, 46
Largey, Gale, 101
Larsen, Otto N., 26
Laslett, Barbara, 100
Latoni-Rodríguez, Alfonso R., 43, 60, 70
Laue, James H., 32
Lee, Sharon M., 87
Lee, Sunhwa, 43
Leggon, Cheryl B., 27, 70

Levine, Felice J., 6, 11–12, 17, 19, 28, 35, 37, 40–42, 44, 48–49, 55, 57–58, 60–63, 65–66, 68, 70, 73–76, 78, 82–83, 86–87
Lieberson, Stanley, 24, 32, 49
Lin, Nan, 32, 64
Lindsay, Paul, 23
Lipset, Seymour Martin, 79, 83
Lo, Clarence Y. H., 27
Lofland, John, 11
Love, Ruth L., 25

M

Maldonado, Lionel A., 27–29, 42
Mandela, Nelson, 33, 83
Marconi, Katherine, 26
Marrett, Cora B., 18
Martin, William C., 26
Marx, Gary T., 29
Massey, Douglas S., 64, 81
Mauksch, Hans O., 22–23
Maynard, Douglas W., 21
McCarthy, John, 14, 57
McCartney, James L., 78
McKinney, Kathleen, 67
Meiksins, Peter, 57
Melber, Barbara Desow, 48
Merola, Stacey S., 43
Meyer, Marshall W., 14
Micklin, Michael, 78
Milavsky, J. Ron, 26
Miles, Marjorie (Midge), 6
Miller, Eleanor M., 48
Miller, JoAnne, 17
Miller Roberta, 16–17
Moaddel, Mansoor, 97
Model, Suzanne, 87
Moen, Phyllis, 70
Moore, Helen A., 48
Mortimer, Jeylan T., 21
Mottl, Tahi, 42
Murguia, Edward, 43

N

Nee, Victor, 100

O

Ofshe, Richard, 11
Oliver, Pamela E., 14
Olsen, Marvin, 19, 70
Omi, Michael, 87
Oppenheimer, Valerie K., 27, 40
Orum, Anthony M., 61

P

Pager, Devah, 96
Parish, William, 32
Patel, Sujata, 101
Pearson Jr., Willie, 87
Persell, Caroline Hodges, 66, 101
Pescosolido, Bernice A., 48, 95
Pettigrew, Thomas F., 32
Portes, Alejandro, 31, 41, 64
Presser, Harriet B., 70
Puente, Manuel de la, 70, 87

Q

Quadagno, Jill S., 12, 18, 19, 67, 101
Quellmalz, Henry, 62
Quellmalz, Marion, 62

R

Rafferty, Adrian, 44
Rakowski, Cathy A., 78
Rayman, Paula M., 16
Reskin, Barbara F., 12, 60, 71, 77, 83, 87, 89
Rhoades, Lawrence J., 6, 22, 26
Richardson, Herbert, 11
Riley, Jack, 15
Riley, Matilda White, 16-17, 19, 29, 33, 62,104
Rodríguez, Havidán, 43, 60, 70
Rogler, Lloyd H., 27
Roos, Patricia A., 50, 64
Roshco, Bernard, 26
Rosich, Katherine J., 42, 60, 77
Rossi, Alice S., 1, 30, 32
Rossi, Peter H., 24
Rubio, Mercedes, 43
Ruckel, Jo Ann, 6
Russell, Raymond, 25
Rutledge, Essie M., 57

S

Sanders, Gerard R., 88
Sassen, Saskia, 78
Sawyer, Thomas C., 88
Scarce, Richard (Rik), 49, 75
Schnabel, John F., 4
Schram, Rosalie, 26
Schwartz, Michael, 60
Scimecca, Joseph A., 7
Scott, W. Richard, 17, 83
Sewell, William H., 15, 27

Shalala, Donna, 75
Shaomin, Li, 81
Shapiro, Clara, 18
Shaw, Nancy Stoller, 14
Shea, Brent, 78
Shin, Jean H., 43
Shope, John H., 29
Short, Jr., James F., 6
Sica, Alan, 100
Sills, David L., 15, 17
Simon, Paul Hon., 16
Simpson, Ida Harper, 48–49
Singer, Margaret, 11
Smedley, Brian, 88
Smelser, Neil J., 40, 48, 52–53, 79, 100
Smith, Marc A., 44, 77
Smith-Lovin, Lynn, 93
Snipp, C. Matthew, 87
Snow, David A., 53
Snyder, Douglas S., 23
Somers, Margaret R., 100
Sorokin, Pitirim, 91, 92, 101
Spalter-Roth, Roberta, 38, 42, 72, 78, 87, 100
Sproull, Lee, 44
Stanfield, John H., 82
Starr, Jerold M., 23
Stevenson, Phoebe H., 40, 42–45
Stewman, Shelby, 32
Strand, Kerry J., 67, 83
Sullivan, Louis, 74–75
Sullivan, Teresa, 21, 40, 43
Sutter, Andrew, 78

T

Taeuber, Conrad, 12, 25
Taylor, Howard F., 27
Taylor, Rosemary C. R., 25
Telles, Edward E., 87
Thomas, Jan E., 43
Thorne, Barrie, 49, 57
Tierney, Kathleen J., 97
Torrecilha, Ramon, 43
Tucker, James, 90
Tumin, Melvin, 18
Turner, Jonathan H., 14
Turner, Stephen, 81–82

U

Useem, Michael, 26

V

Vera, Hernan, 87

W

Wagenaar, Theodore C., 22, 24
Waite, Linda J., 52, 54
Waldron, Joan, 18
Wallerstein, Immanuel, 99
Walsh, John P., 44
Walters, Pamela Barnhouse, 55, 100
Ward, Lester, 101
Waring, Joan, 19, 70
Warren, Hal, 45
Weber, Lynn, 87
Weinstein, Jack B., 10
Weiss, Carol H., 25
Wellman, Barry, 32, 44, 62, 77
Wellman, David, 87
Wendel, Donna L., 23
Western, Bruce, 96
White, Patricia E., 43, 74
Whyte, William Foote, 10, 24, 29
Wiley, David, 78
Wilkinson, Doris, 67
Williams, Barbara R., 26
Williams, David, 87, 96
Williams, Paul R., 4–6, 27, 39
Willie, Charles V., 15, 27, 48, 56, 87
Wilson, Franklin D., 64, 83, 87, 92
Wilson, William J., 19, 24, 59
Woodstock, Gail, 23
Woody, Bette, 48
Wright, Burton, 22, 29

Y

Yinger, J. Milton, 87

Z

Zald, Mayer N., 24, 26
Zhan, Gao, 81
Zucker, Lynne G., 82
Zuiches, James J., 17

Subject Index

A

Academic and Professional Affairs Program (APAP), 23, 36, 42, 61–62, 65–68, 94, 97–98
Accrediting Council for Continuing Education and Training (ACCET), 46
Advanced Placement (AP), 66–67, 98
Advisory Panels (see Committees)
Affirmative Action, see Grutter v. Bollinger
AIDS, 2, 12, 25
Alpha Kappa Delta (AKD), 28, 69
American Association for the Advancement of Science (AAAS), 17, 23, 53, 71, 77, 80, 99
American Association for Higher Education (AAHE), 66
American Association of Colleges for Teacher Education (AACTE), 46
American Association of State Colleges and Universities (AASCU), 46
American Association of University Professors (AAUP), 38
American Communities Survey, 96
American Council of Learned Societies (ACLS), 16, 63, 73
American Journal of Sociology (*AJS*), 20, 22
American Political Science Association (APSA), 21–22
American Political Science Review (*APSR*), 21–22
American Psychological Association (APA), 11, 45, 56, 76
American Public Health Association, 38
American Sociological Foundation (ASF), 13–15, 28, 51, 59, 71, 99
American Sociological Fund, 59, 92, 99
American Sociological Review (*ASR*), 19–22, 41, 44, 60, 62–65, 77, 95, 100
American Teenage Study (see also peer review), 37, 74–75
Amicus curiae briefs, 9–12, 48–49, 86, 87, 89–90
Annual Meeting, ASA, 1–2, 12–13, 17, 19–20, 26–27, 29–36, 38, 41, 44–46, 48–51, 53–55, 61, 64–65, 68–70, 72, 77–79, 82–86, 91, 98–102
Apartheid, 5, 31–33, 41
Applied Social Research and Social Policy Program (see Cornerhouse Fund, Spivack Program)
Applied sociology, 1, 24–26
Applied Sociology (1983), 24
Archiving, ASA Project on, 81–82
Association Links, 43, 45
Association of American Colleges and Universities (AAC&U), 24
Association of American Publishers (AAP), 95
Association of Black Sociologists (ABS), 28, 69, 89
Atlantic Philanthropies, 67
Augusta State University, 69
Awards, ASA
  -Distinguished Career Award for the Practice of Sociology, 12, 25
  -Distinguished Scholarly Publication Award, 91
  -Dissertation Award, 12, 98
  -ASA Award for Excellence in the Reporting of Social Issues, 93
  -Jessie Bernard Award, 51
  -Award for Public Understanding of Sociology, 51
  -Dubois-Johnson-Frazier Award, 51
  -Career Of Distinguished Scholarship Award, 12
Awards, ASA Policy on, 12, 51–52, 92–93

B

Basil Blackwell, 20, 60–61
Behavioral and Social Science Research Coordinating Committee (NIH) (BSSR-CC), 92
Biographical Directory of Members, 20
Boyd Printing Company, 8, 19, 60, 62
Brajuha case, 10–11, 49, 75
Budgets and finances (see also investment policy), 1, 5–6, 40–41, 46, 92
Building Fund (House Fund) (ASA), 40, 46
Business Meeting (see also Annual Meeting), 12, 32, 48–50, 53, 64, 91
Bylaws (see also Governance), 4, 9–10, 12–13, 47–48, 52–54, 56, 58, 90, 93

C

California Proposition 54, 86, 88
Canadian Sociological and Anthropological Association, 79
Carnegie Academy for the Scholarship of Teaching and Learning (CASTL), 66
Carnegie Endowment for the Advancement of Teaching, 23
Census (see U.S. Bureau of the Census)
Centennial (ASA), 41, 85–86, 91, 97, 99–104

Center for Advanced Study (Stanford), 18
Certification Program, 2, 13, 15, 24–26, 51, 56–57
Certified Clinical Sociologist (CCS), 57
Chairlink, 43, 66, 98
China, 2, 32, 81
Chronicle of Higher Education, 11, 73
City and Community, 36, 61, 95
Classification by Race, Ethnicity, Color and National Origin (CRECNO), (*see* California Proposition 54)
Coalition for the Advancement of Health through Behavioral and Social Science Research (CAHT-BSSR), 92
Coalition for Health Funding, 92
Coalition for National Science Funding (CNSF), 73, 92, 96
Coalition of Associations for Foreign Language and International Studies (CAFLIS), 25
COFRAT (*see* Committee on Freedom of Research and Teaching)
Collaborations (with other organizations, coalitions), 2, 16–17, 22–24, 29–31, 66, 72–73, 76, 78–80, 87, 89, 92, 95–98, 101
College and University Professional Association for Human Resources (CUPA-HR), 73
Commission on Professions in Science and Technology (CPST), 72–73, 96
Commission on Sociology and Society, 18
Committees, ASA, Blue Ribbon, 18
Committees, ASA, for the Advancement of the Profession, 30
Committees, ASA, on:
 -ASA/AAAs Relations, 53
 -ASA's Organizational Ties, 17
 -Archives, 53
 -Awards (was Committee on Awards Policy), 12, 48, 52–53, 93
 -Certification (later Committee on Certification and Licensure), 26, 57
 -Classification, 4
 -Committees (COC), 47–48, 53–54
 -Employment, 2, 53
 -Executive Office and Budget (EOB), 5–7, 9, 35, 37, 40–41, 45–46, 55–56, 58, 90, 92
 -Federal Standards for the Employment of Sociologists, 25
 -Freedom of Research and Teaching (COFRAT), 13–14, 36, 51, 53, 57–58
 -Graduate Education, 68
 -Hate Bias on Campus, 53
 -International Sociology (formerly Committee on World Sociology), 31–32, 53, 80
 -Membership, 4, 53
 -Minority Fellowship Program, 27–28
 -National Statistics, 53
 -Nominations (CON), 47–48, 53–54
 -Problems of the Discipline (POD), 29
 -Professional Ethics (COPE), 10, 47, 57, 75, 90
 -Professional Opportunities in Applied Sociology, 24
 -Program, 1, 9, 33, 83–84
 -Public Information, 26–27
 -Publications (COP), 10, 19–21, 48, 54, 59–64, 95,100
 -Regulation of Research, 18, 75
 -Research on the Profession, 3
 -Sections (COS), 13, 48, 51, 53, 56, 93
 -Sociological Practice, 49, 53
 -Sociologists in Government and International Agencies, 53
 -Sociology in Elementary and Secondary Schools, 23, 53, 67
 -Status of Gay, Lesbian, Bisexual, and Transgender Persons in Sociology (CSGLBT), 54, 94
 -Status of Persons with Disabilities in Sociology (PWD), 3, 54, 94
 -Status of Racial and Ethnic Minorities in Sociology (CSREMS), 3, 54, 72, 94
 -Status of Women in Sociology (CSWS), 3, 54, 72, 94
 -Teaching, 53, 67
Committees, ASA: restructuring, 47–48, 51–54, 58
Community Action Research Initiative (CARI), 71, 99
Community and Urban Sociology, Section on (CUSS), 61, 95
Computer systems (*see* Information Technology)
Computer Strategies, Inc., 43
Congressional briefings and seminars, 16, 37, 70–71, 74, 76–77, 88, 96, 99
Congressional Fellowship Program, 15, 25, 59, 71, 99
Congressional testimonies, 36, 74–76
Consortium of Social Science Associations (COSSA), 2, 16–17, 27, 30, 73, 75–76, 87–89, 92
Constitution and Bylaws (ASA) (*see* governance)
Contemporary Sociology (*CS*), 19–20, 44, 60, 63, 77
Contexts, 36, 61, 95
Contract with America, 37, 74
Cornerhouse Dissertation Grants, 27–28
Cornerhouse Fund (*see also* Spivack Program),

18–19, 28, 70
Council for Advancement and Support of Education (CASE), 46
Council for Undergraduate Research (CUR), 66
Council of Professional Associations for Federal Statistics (COPAFS), 2, 16, 92
Crisis in the Occupation of Sociology, 2
Cumulative Index, 20

D

Data Brief Series, 72
Decade of Behavior, 76, 92, 96
Departmental Resources Group (DRG), 65, 98
Departmental Services Program, 23
Development Campaign, 41
Dimensional Fund Advisors (DFA), 92
Directions in Applied Sociology, Workshop on, 24
Directory of Members, 3, 8, 20
Diversity, 2–3, 36, 54, 68, 83
Dues, ASA (restructuring), 3–4, 36, 51, 58–59
Dues, decoupling journals from dues, 51, 58–59
Duke University, 2

E

Eastern Europe, 2, 31–32, 79
Eastern Sociological Association, 28
Editor-designate, 21
Educational Testing Service, 67
Edwin Mellen Press, 11
Egypt, 81, 99
El Salvador, 2, 32
Election system (ASA), 9, 48, 53, 93
Electronic Networking, Advisory Group on, 44
Electronic publishing (*see* Information Technology)
Emeritus membership, 4, 9, 38, 47, 58–59
Employment Bulletin (*EB*), 19, 44, 62–63
Environment and Technology, Section on, 76
Ethics, ASA Code of (*see also* Committee on Professional Ethics), 9–11, 36, 44, 47–48, 75, 90
Eurekalert, 77
Executive Office, organization of, 6–8, 41–43, 94–95
Exxon Valdez Case, 49

F

Family, Section on, 90
Faulkner v. National Geographic Society, 86, 89–90
Federal classifications of jobs (sociologists), 25
Fiduciary Trust International, Inc., 40, 92
Ford Foundation, 27–28, 37, 68–69, 76, 100

Fund for the Advancement of the Discipline (FAD), 15, 29, 50, 78, 80–81, 94–6, 99
Fund for the Improvement of Postsecondary Education (FIPSE), 22, 67
Future Organizational Trends, ASA Ad Hoc Committee on, 13–14

G

General Social Survey (GSS), 74
Gender in the Early Stages of the Sociological Career (2000), 73
Gifts to ASA, 12, 51, 92–93
Global War on Terror, 86
Governance, ASA (*see also* Bylaws), 1, 9–10, 47–48, 93
Government Network Project, 65
Grinnell College, 69
Grutter v. Bollinger, 86, 89
Guide to Graduate Departments, 62, 72
Guidelines for Employment of Part-Time Faculty in Departments of Sociology, 14
Guidelines for Initial Appointments in Sociology, 14
Guidelines for the ASA Publications Portfolio, 36, 59–60

H

High School Affiliates Program, 66, 98
History of Sociology, Section on, 100
History of the American Sociological Association (1981), *vii, xv*, 60
Historically Black Colleges and Universities (HBCUs), 68
Homepage, ASA (asanet.org), 36–37, 43–44, 58–59, 62–63, 72–73, 80, 84, 86, 94–98, 100–101
Honors Program (ASA), 29, 83, 94, 98
H.R. 1271 ("The Family Privacy Protection Act of 1995"), 44, 73–74, 77
H.R. 2202 ("The Immigration in the National Interest Act"), 58
Husch Case, 11
Human rights, 2, 12, 32–33, 78, 80–81, 99
Human subjects of research, 10, 15, 18, 73, 75

I

Impact Assessment Inc, (IAI), 49
Inclusivity (see diversity)
Independent Scholar, 2
Indiana University, 67
Information Technology (IT), 8, 33, 36, 41, 43–46,

62–63, 84, 97
Ingenta, 95
Institute for Global Conflict and Cooperation, 32
Institutional Review Boards (IRB), 86
Integrating Data Analysis (IDA) project, 66, 98
Inter-university Consortium for Political and Social Research (ICPSR), 69
International activities, 30–33, 78–81, 99–101
International Institute of Sociology (IIS), 31, 80
International Research & Exchanges Board (IREX), 31–32
International Social Survey (ISS), 80
International Sociological Association (ISA), 31, 78–80, 99–101
Internship Handbook, 25
Issue Series in Social Research and Social Policy, 71
Investment policy (socially responsible investments), 5, 33, 40–41, 87, 92

J

James Madison University, 66
JL Systems (see NOAH), 43, 97
Jossey-Bass, 20, 24
Journal Builder software, 95
Journal of Health and Social Behavior (JHSB), 19–20, 44, 60, 77
Journal Storage system (JSTOR), 44, 62–63, 90, 95

K

K-12 education and sociology, 23, 67

L

Law and Society Association, 89
Legal counsel (ASA), 11, 14, 47–48, 90–91
Lesbian, Gay, Bisexual, and Transgender (LGBT) Sociologists, Caucus, 90
Lewis A. Coser Award, 92–93
Liberal Learning and the Sociology Major (1990), 24, 67
Liberal Learning and the Sociology Major Updated (2004), 67
Library of Congress, vii, 81
Lilly Foundation, 22, 67

M

MacArthur Foundation, 37, 99
Mass Media Fellowship (AAAS/ASA), 71, 77
Mattei Dogan Foundation Prize, 100
Maurice Falk Medical Fund, 28
Mellon Foundation, 44
Member Forum, 46
Member resolutions, 9, 12–13, 47, 86–87, 90–92
Membership, trends, 3–5, 37–39
Mental Health, Section on, 55
Mid-South Sociological Association, 28
Mid-West Sociological Society, 28
Minorities at Three Stages in the Sociology Pipeline (2001), 73
Minority Affairs Program (MAP), 36, 43, 65–66, 68–70, 94, 97–98
Minority Fellowship Program (MFP), 2, 15, 18, 27–29, 37, 42–43, 68–69, 98–99
Minority Opportunities Through School Transformation (MOST), 28, 42, 60, 66, 68–70, 77
Minority Opportunity Summer Training (MOST I), 15, 27–28, 42, 69
Minority participation in ASA, 3–5, 13, 39
Mission Statement of the Association, 35–36, 103–4
MOST (*see* Minority Opportunities Through School Transformation)

N

Nation at Risk, 23
National Academy of Sciences (NAS), 74, 88–89
National Association of State Universities and Land Grant Colleges (NASULGC), 46
National Center for Education Statistics (NCES), 73
National Consortium on Violence Research (NCOVR), 76
National Council on Social Studies (NCSS), 23, 66
National Endowment for the Humanities (NEH), 2, 76
National Humanities Alliance (NHA), 2, 16, 73, 76, 92
National Institute of Child Health and Human Development (NICHD), 74–75
National Institute of Education (NIE), 2
National Institute of Mental Health (NIMH), 2, 6, 16, 27–29, 55, 68–69, 75, 98–99
National Institute on Aging (NIA), 16
National Institutes of Health (NIH), 37, 74–75, 88, 92, 97

National Human Research Protections Advisory Committee (NHRPAC), 75
National Opinion Research Center (NORC), 80
National Science Foundation (NSF), 6, 16, 30–31, 37, 42–43, 66, 73–74, 78–80, 92, 95–96, 98–99
National Television Violence Study, 76,
New Doctorates in Sociology: Professions Inside and Outside the Academy (2000), 73
New Yorker Magazine, 100
Newswise (wire services), 77
NOAH (membership database), 38, 43, 45, 63, 72, 95
North Carolina State University, 67
North-South Foundation, 37

O

Oberlin College, 22
Office of Behavioral and Social Science Research (OBSSR), 37, 75, 77
Office of Foreign Assets Control (OFAC) (U.S. Treasury Dept.), 97
Office of Science and Technology Policy (OSTP), 76, 92
Ombudsperson, 7
Operations and Meeting Services Department, 94
Oppenheimer & Co., 40

P

PCDOCs (document manager), 43
Peer review process, challenges to, 37, 74–75, 88, 97
Pennsylvania State University, *vii*, 69, 82
Pew Charitable Trusts, 67
PhD Tracking survey, 72–73, 95
Pitzer College, 69
Plagiarism, 11
Plural Histories of Sociology, 100
Policy statements, 9–12, 49–51, 83
Population Association of American (PAA), 8
Population, Section on Sociology of, 75
Postdoctoral fellows, 39, 43, 68–69, 72
Preparing Future Faculty (PFF), 67, 98
Presidential Series, 19–20
President's Commission on Excellence in Education, 23
Problems of the Discipline (POD), 29–30
Professional Development Program (PDP), 2, 15, 24–26, 65

Programs (ASA):
   see Program by specific name:
   -Academic and Professional Affairs Program (APAP)
   -Certification Program
   -Minority Affairs Program (MAP)
   -Minority Fellowship Program (MFP)
   -Professional Development Program (PDP)
   -Public Affairs Program
   -Public Information Program
   -Research Program on the Discipline and the Profession
   -Sydney S. Spivack Program in Applied Social Research and Social Policy
   -Teaching Services Program (TSP)
Project 2061, 23
Promoting Diversity and Excellence in Higher Education through Department Change, 70
Public Affairs Program, 36, 42, 65, 73–77, 94, 96–97
Public Information Program, 2, 15, 24, 26–27, 36, 42, 65, 73, 77, 94, 96–97
Public sociology, 86, 94
Publication and Membership Department, 94–5
Publication Guidelines (*see Guidelines for the ASA Publications Portfolio*)
Publications Program, 2, 13, 15–16, 19–22, 35–36, 41, 44, 59–65, 85, 90, 94–95, 97, 100

R

Race, ASA Statement on, 87–88
Race, White House Initiative on Race, 76
Racial and Ethnic Minorities, Section on, 64
Reagan Administration, 2, 16
Realities of Affirmative Action in Employment, 60, 71, 77
Research and Development Department, 95–96
Research Brief Series, 72–73
Research on the Profession, 15–18
Research Program on the Discipline and the Profession, 36, 38, 42, 65, 72–73
Rose Monograph Series, 19, 60–61
Rose Series in Sociology, 60–61
Russell Sage Foundation, 61, 79

S

Sage Publications, Inc., 20, 22
Salisbury State College, 29
Scarce, (Rik) case, 49, 75

Science policy issues (*see also* policy statements), 73–75, 82, 85–89, 96–97
Sections, ASA, 1, 8–9, 12–14, 21–22, 30–31, 36, 44–45, 48, 50–51, 53–56, 60–61, 78, 85, 92–93, 104
Sexualities, Section on, 90
Sloan Foundation, 73
Small Grants Program (*see* Fund for the Advancement of the Discipline)
Smithsonian, 31, 99
Social and Economic Sciences (NSF Division) (SES), 74
Social Causes of Violence: Crafting a Science Agenda, 60
Social Forces, 20
Social Psychology Quarterly (*SPQ*), 19, 60
Social Science Data Analysis Network (SSDAN) (*see* Integrating Data Analysis project)
Social Science Research Council (SSRC), 17, 62, 81
Society for the Study of Social Problems, 89
Sociological Associations, Regional and State, 4, 22, 28, 38, 72, 86, 91
Sociological Methodology (*SM*), 19–20, 60, 95
Sociological practice, 2, 10, 24–26
Sociological Practice Association (SPA), 57
Sociological Practice Review (*SPR*), 19–20, 60–61
Sociological Theory (*ST*), 19–20, 60, 95
Sociologists and Political Scientists Without Borders, 90
Sociologists for Women in Society (SWS), 28, 53, 69, 89
Sociologists in Business, 26
Sociology of Education (*SOE*), 19–20, 55, 60, 63
Sociology of Education, Section on, 55
Sorokin Lectures (Sorokin Fund), 91–92
Soros Foundation, 37
South Africa, 5, 33, 41
Southwestern Sociological Association, 28
Southwestern University, 69
Soviet-U.S. (and former Soviet Union) exchanges, relations, 32, 79, 86, 100
Spectrum Systems, 43
Spencer Foundation, 55
Spivack Dissertation Awards, 18, 28
Spivack Program in Applied Social Research and Social Policy, 18–19, 36, 42, 50, 60, 65, 70–71, 73, 76–77, 81, 88, 94, 97, 99
Spivack, Sydney S., 18, 70
Statement on Race, ASA, 87
Status Committees (*see* Committees, Status Committees)

Strategic Plan of 1992, 35–37, 41, 65, 68, 73, 77
Students (*see also* MFP, Honors Program), 1, 3–4, 10, 22, 32–33, 37–39, 58, 83, 86, 89–90, 98, 103
Student Forum, 94, 98

T

Task Force on Campus Hate Crimes and Bias-Related Incidents, 67
Task Force on Current Knowledge on Hate/Bias Acts on College and University Campuses, 67
Task Force on Journal Diversity, 65
Task Force on the Advanced Placement (AP) Course in Sociology, 66, 98
Task Force on the International Focus of American Sociology (TFIFAS), 78–79, 99
Task Force on the Scholarly Dimensions of the Professional Work of Sociologists, 67
Task Group on Graduate Education (TAGGE), 24, 67–68
Teaching Enhancement Fund (Teaching Endowment Fund), 29, 99
Teaching *Newsletter*, 20, 22
Teaching Resources Center (TRC), 22, 65, 98
Teaching Resources Group (TRG) (*see also* Departmental Resources Group), 22–23, 65
Teaching Services Program (TSP), 2, 15, 22–24, 65
Teaching Sociology (*TS*), 19–20, 22, 44, 60, 100
Teaching workshops, 22–23
Terrorism, Terrorist attacks of September 11, 2001, 37, 73, 75–76, 85–86, 96, 99
Texas A&M University, 67, 69
The American Sociologist (*TAS*), 3, 20, 100
Theory, Section on, 92–93
Tracker software, 45
Transaction Publishers, 20

U

Unification Church v. Molko/Leal, 11
University of California-Berkeley, 28, 69, 100
University of California Press, 61
University of California-Santa Barbara, 69
University of California-Santa Cruz, 14
University of Central Florida, 29
University of Delaware, 28, 69
University of Michigan, 28, 69. 89. 98
University of Nebraska-Lincoln, 67, 69
University of Puerto Rico-Mayagüez, 69
University of Rochester, 14
University of Texas-El Paso, 69
University of Wisconsin-Madison, 28, 69

U.S. Bureau of the Census, 73–74, 96
U.S. Department of Education, 55
U.S. Department of Health and Human Services (DHHS), 18, 37, 74–75
U.S. Department of Homeland Security, 97
U.S. Department of Housing and Urban Development (HUD), 25
U.S. Department of Justice, 76, 86
U.S. Institute of Peace, 32
U.S. Public Health Service, 25

W

W. K. Kellogg Foundation, 37, 76
Washington University, 2, 14
Website, ASA (*see also* ASA homepage)
William Paterson University, 69
Wingspread Conference, 23
Women, participation in ASA governance, 39